Ursula Robson - 1952

Everyman, I will go with thee, and be thy guide,
In thy most need to go by thy side.

EVERYMAN'S LIBRARY

Founded 1906 by J. M. Dent (d. 1926)
Edited by Ernest Rhys (d. 1946)

No. 921

POETRY & THE DRAMA

THE GOLDEN BOOK OF
MODERN ENGLISH POETRY
SELECTED BY THOMAS CALD-
WELL WITH ADDITIONAL SELEC-
TIONS BY PHILIP HENDERSON

THE GOLDEN BOOK
OF MODERN ENGLISH POETRY

THOMAS CALDWELL

LONDON: J. M. DENT & SONS LTD.
NEW YORK: E. P. DUTTON & CO. INC.

J. M. DENT & SONS LTD.
Aldine House · Bedford St. · London

Made in Great Britain
by
The Temple Press · Letchworth · Herts.
First published 1922
First published in this edition 1935
Last reprinted 1948

INTRODUCTORY NOTE

THE scope and purpose of this anthology is defined in the late Mr. Caldwell's preface. In selection and general arrangement the bulk of the book is essentially his. All I have done is to make room for the work of several poets who have grown in reputation since Mr. Caldwell made his original selection, giving a fuller representation to writers such as Gerard Manley Hopkins, D. H. Lawrence, and Wilfred Owen. I have also revised to some extent the last sixty-four pages in order to include such important names as Roy Campbell and T. S. Eliot, who is shown in both his earlier and later mood, and to give at least a taste of the poetry that is being written by some of the younger men at the present time.

The development of recent poetry since the serenely imitative classicism of Robert Bridges and the more domestic Muse of the Georgians, would take more space and greater facilities than were at my disposal to illustrate. It is plain, however, that there is a gulf set between nearly all poetry written before and after the First World War, with all its attendant upheavals and profound spiritual crises. Before that cataclysm the majority of English poets felt themselves inhabitants of a secure world and heirs of a stable tradition. To-day everything is changed. The profound difference between the poetry of the years immediately preceeding the war and the best of our time can be seen by comparing the cloistral poetry of Rupert Brooke with that of Stephen Spender, who belongs essentially to the 1930's; while the change of attitude to the war itself is apparent in the transition from the early idealistic self-immolation of a Rupert Brooke or a Julian Grenfell, through all the indignation and pity and weary disillusionment of Wilfred Owen, to the final harsh bitterness of Siegfried Sassoon. The poets who followed were, for a time, only too eager to forget, though now the menace, far more overwhelming than before, once again looms upon us.

The greater part of the poetry in this book belongs, then, to the romantic tradition of the later nineteenth century. But at least something of the attitude of the modern poet to his art can be gathered from the last few pages, where it will be seen that the imagery of the modern world has quite naturally replaced the 'classical' tradition of the past by a more courageous grappling with contemporary problems. If one were asked to say in a few words what were the chief characteristics of the best poetry being written to-day, one might answer that, in the first place, it is more direct and realistic and far more acutely aware of its social environment than was the poetry of the last century: it is, perhaps, more classical in the real sense. Secondly, it is no longer traditional, in so far as it is not content to perpetuate a conventional technique suited to the tempo of another age, although, of course, mixed influences may be seen at work inherited from such diverse sources as the early English poets, the symphonic style of Gerard Manley Hopkins, the grave splendour of Wilfred Owen, and the colloquial speech of T. S. Eliot, who is himself clearly indebted to both Browning and the French Symbolists.

So that while sweeping generalizations are to be avoided as far as possible, one can say that, like the age we live in, poetry to-day is above all eagerly experimental, self-conscious and dissatisfied and often extremely complex. It is to be regretted, however, that no example of the work of W. H. Auden could be included, since he is a writer who is already exerting a decisive influence upon the future of poetry in this country. For if poetry is to be a living force in the world to-day, and not merely an escape into a world of dreams, it must deal in the terms of the present, rather than lull its readers into the contemplation of remote golden ages or seek repose in the flight to metaphysical abstraction.

PHILIP HENDERSON

1935.

EDITOR'S PREFACE
TO THE FIRST EDITION

THE half-century, 1870–1920, is one of those definite periods which lend themselves to review within the limits of an anthology.

This anthology is intended to serve as some guide to what is best and most notable in the poetry written during the course of the period mentioned; and it finds its justification in the fact that no similar collection professes to survey modern English poetry in equal detail.

The principal aim of the anthology is to give poems representative of the finest work of modern poets; but an attempt has also been made to show that the most significant poetry of our time is either classical or romantic in character, and not—as some critics would have it—of the realistic school.

The scope of the anthology is defined in its title. The present and the immediate past together constitute the modern age; and the anthology, in reviewing the poetry of the five decades in question, gives what is, in the fullest sense of the term, modern in spirit.

No profession is made of including poets, who, although continuing to write after 1870, were known to the public before that date. All the poets represented here published their first volume of verse subsequent to 1870. This fact separates the elder among them from the true Victorians.

There is reason for regarding the year 1870 as an important turning-point in relation to English poetry. The poets who belong wholly to the Victorian age had by then, with some few exceptions, produced the work upon which their reputations in the main rest; whilst their successors, the younger men, afterwards to become the doyens of our own day, were putting forth their first efforts in verse.

And the half-century which followed 1870 is one of decided interest and importance; one that has seen the appearance of many poets of distinguished merit; one that is conspicuous for the excellence, variety, and high technical skill of the poetry which it has contributed to the common stock of English verse. These are qualities which, to say no more, render it comparable with any similar period in the history of our literature not crowned by names of unquestionable pre-eminence.

The order of arrangement of the anthology is according to the birth dates of the poets, so far as these could be ascertained. Several departures from this principle have, however, been made to permit of more effective grouping of certain poems. The result assists, none the less, to illustrate the changes in style and manner peculiar to the poetry written in the course of what has been markedly a period of transition and experiment.

Copyright difficulties must be held responsible for the omission of a few poems which might have been included. But it is claimed that the name of every poet of real and accepted distinction, who has appeared between the years 1870 to 1920, is to be found in these pages; and that the anthology is representative of what is finest in that body of poetry from which its contents have been chosen.

1922.   THOMAS CALDWELL

ACKNOWLEDGMENTS

For permission to include copyright poems in this collection, acknowledgments are due to:

Mr. Richard Aldington and The Egoist Press, Ltd., for one poem.

Mr. Martin Armstrong and Mr. Martin Secker for *The Buzzards*.

The Hon. Maurice Baring and Mr. Martin Secker for *In Memoriam, A. H.*

Mr. Laurence Binyon and Messrs. Elkin Mathews, Ltd., for three poems. For permission to print *For the Fallen* thanks are also accorded to *The Times*.

Mr. Basil Blackwell for poems by the Rev. A. S. Cripps and Miss Fredegond Shove.

Mr. F. C. Boden and Messrs. J. M. Dent & Sons, Ltd., for two poems from *Pit-Head Poems*.

The Poetry Bookshop for poems by Mr. Robert Graves, Miss Charlotte Mew, and Mr. Harold Monro.

Mr. Gordon Bottomley and Messrs. Constable & Co., Ltd., for *Atlantis*.

Mrs. Bourdillon for a poem by the late Mr. F. W. Bourdillon.

Mr. Cloudesley Brereton and the Editor of the *Pall Mall Gazette and Globe* for a poem.

Mr. Horatio F. Brown, literary executor of the Author, and Messrs. Kegan Paul, Trench, Trübner & Co., Ltd., for sonnets by the late Mr. J. A. Symonds. Thanks are also expressed to Mr. John Murray in respect of *To the Genius of Eternal Slumber*.

Messrs. Chatto & Windus for poems by Mr. Robert Nichols and the late Mr. Robert Louis Stevenson.

Mr. G. K. Chesterton and Messrs. J. M. Dent & Sons, Ltd., for *The Donkey* and *The Praise of Dust*. The other poems by Mr. Chesterton appear by permission of the Author and Messrs. Burns, Oates & Washbourne, Ltd.

The Clarendon Press and Messrs. Heinemann for the late Mr. Robert Bridges's *The Shakespeare Ode*. The other poems by Mr. Bridges appear by permission of Mr. John Murray.

Mr. Padraic Colum and Messrs. Maunsel & Roberts, Ltd., for two poems.

Messrs. Constable & Co., Ltd., for a poem by the late Mrs. Shorter (Dora Sigerson Shorter) from *The Sad Years*.

Messrs. Constable & Co., Ltd., for seven poems from *Poems with Fables in Prose* by the late Mr. Herbert Trench.

Mrs. Cornford and The Poetry Bookshop for *Pre-existence*.

Lord Crewe for two poems. Thanks are also due to Mr. John Murray for permission to print *Seven Years*.

Mrs. Cust for the late Mr. Henry Cust's *Non Nobis*.

Mr. Charles Dalmon and Mr. Grant Richards for a poem.

Mr. W. H. Davies and Mr. Jonathan Cape for *Truly Great* (from *Nature Poems*), *The Kingfisher* (from *Farewell to Poesy*), *The Moon* (from *The Bird of Paradise*), *Lovely Dames* (from *Forty New Poems*), and *Leisure* (from *Songs of Joy*). Acknowledgments are also made to Messrs. Methuen & Co., Ltd., in respect of the poem from *The Bird of Paradise*.

Mr. Walter de la Mare and Messrs. Constable & Co., Ltd., for four poems.

Messrs. J. M. Dent & Sons, Ltd., for *Rioupérous* and *To a Poet* by the late Mr. J. E. Flecker.

Lord Desborough for the late Hon. Julian Grenfell's *Into Battle* (Captain the late Hon. Julian Grenfell, D.S.O., Royal Dragoons, was wounded at Ypres, 13th May, and died at Boulogne, 26th May, 1915.)

Mr. P. J. Dobell for an excerpt from *The City of Dreadful Night* by the late Mr. James Thomson (B. V.).

The Executors of the Author and The Oxford University Press for poems by the late Mr. Austin Dobson.

Lord Alfred Douglas and Mr. Martin Secker for sonnets.

Mr. John Drinkwater and Messrs. Sidgwick & Jackson, Ltd., for three poems.

Messrs. Duckworth & Co. for poems by Mr. Hilaire Belloc.

Madame Duclaux (Miss A. M. F. Robinson) and Mr. T. Fisher Unwin for a poem.

Lord Dunsany and *The Times* for *A Dirge of Victory*.

Mrs. Flecker and Mr. Martin Secker for *The Old Ships* and *Gates of Damascus* by the late Mr. J. E. Flecker.

Mr. Norman R. Gale for four poems.

Mr. W. W. Gibson and Messrs. Macmillan for *Flannan Isle*.

Miss Eva Gore-Booth for two poems.

Mr. Gerald Gould for *The Earth Child*. The Sonnet by Mr. Gould appears by permission of the Author and Messrs. W. Collins Sons & Co., Ltd.

Messrs. Heinemann for a poem by the late Mr. Edmund Gosse.

Messrs. Heinemann for poems by Mr. Siegfried Sassoon.

Mrs. Hinkson and Messrs. Kegan Paul, Trench, Trübner & Co. Ltd., for *The Doves*.

Miss Hopkins for a poem by Gerard Manley Hopkins.

Mr. A. E. Housman for four poems.

Mr. Laurence Housman and Messrs. Sidgwick & Jackson, Ltd., for a poem.

Mr. F. Madox Hueffer and Mr. Martin Secker for two poems.

Mr. Aldous Huxley and the Editor of the *Spectator* for *The Cicadas*.

Mr. Douglas Hyde for one of his poems from the Irish.

Mrs. Jacob and Mr. John Murray for a poem.

Mr. Coulson Kernahan, representing the executors of the Author, and The Walter Scott Publishing Co., Ltd., for a poem by the late Mr. P. B. Marston.

Mr. Rudyard Kipling, Messrs. Methuen & Co., Ltd., and Messrs. Hodder & Stoughton, Ltd., for *Sussex*, *The Song of Diego Valdez*, and *The Flowers*. For permission to include *A Dedication* (first published under the title of *My New-cut Ashlar*), and *Cities and Thrones and Powers*, thanks are rendered to Mr. Kipling, Messrs. Macmillan & Co., Ltd., and Messrs. Hodder & Stoughton, Ltd.

Messrs. John Lane for poems by Mr. Lascelles Abercrombie, the late Dean Beeching, the late Mr. John Davidson, the late Mr. Ernest Dowson, the late Rev. E. C. Lefroy, the late Mr. Stephen Phillips, and Mrs. Woods.

Messrs. John Lane for three poems by the late Mr. A. C. Benson.

Messrs. John Lane, and Messrs. Hodder & Stoughton, Ltd., for three poems by the late Sir William Watson.

Mr. Shane Leslie and Messrs. Burns, Oates & Washbourne, Ltd., for a poem.

Miss E. Lister, executrix of the late Mr. A. H. Bullen, for a poem by Mr. W. Bliss Carman.

Messrs. Longmans, Green & Co., for three poems by the late Mr. Andrew Lang.

Miss Rose Macaulay and Messrs. Constable & Co., Ltd., for a poem.

Messrs. Macmillan & Co., Ltd., for poems by the late Mr. W. S. Blunt, the late Mr. T. E. Brown, the late Mr. W. E. Henley, Mr. Ralph Hodgson, Mr. S. R. Lysaght, and the late Mr. G. W. Russell (A. E.).

Messrs. Macmillan & Co., Ltd., for poems by the late Mr. Thomas Hardy and an excerpt from *The Dynasts*.

Mr. Edward Marsh, literary executor of the Author, and Messrs. Sidgwick & Jackson, Ltd., for poems by the late Mr. Rupert Brooke.

Mr. John Masefield (Poet Laureate) and Messrs. Heinemann for poems and sonnets. The excerpt from *The Everlasting Mercy* is included by permission of Mr. Masefield and Messrs. Sidgwick & Jackson, Ltd.

Messrs. Elkin Mathews, Ltd., for poems by Mr. Gordon Bottomley (*To Ironfounders*), the late Mr. Lionel Johnson, and Miss May Probyn.

The Trustees of the Author and Messrs. Constable & Co., Ltd., for the late Mr. George Meredith's *Hymn to Colour*.

Mr. Wilfrid Meynell and Messrs. Burns, Oates & Washbourne, Ltd., for poems by the late Mrs. Meynell and the late Mr. Francis Thompson. Special thanks are offered to Mr. Meynell for permitting this very full selection of Mr. Thompson's poems to be included.

Mr. T. Sturge Moore and Messrs. Duckworth & Co., for *The Gazelles*. Mr. Sturge Moore is also thanked for the poems by 'Michael Field,' of whom he is the executor.

Mr. John Murray for poems by the late Canon R. W. Dixon and Miss W. M. Letts.

Mr. J. Middleton Murry and Mr. R. Cobden-Sanderson for a poem.

Sir Henry Newbolt and Mr. John Murray for poems. Sir Henry Newbolt is also thanked for the poems by the late Miss Mary Coleridge, of whom he is the executor.

Mr. Alfred Noyes and Messrs. W. Blackwood & Sons for four poems.

Miss Moira O'Neill and Messrs. W. Blackwood & Sons for two poems from *Songs of the Glens of Antrim*.

Mrs. Owen for two poems by her son, the late Lieut. Wilfred Owen.

Professor J. S. Phillimore and Messrs. Maclehose, Jackson & Co. for a poem.

Mr. Ezra Pound for three poems.

Mr. O. Mostyn Pritchard, representing the executors of the Author, for poems by the late Mr. John Payne.

The Proprietors of *Punch*, Messrs. Hodder & Stoughton, Ltd., and Mr. William Briggs (of Toronto) for the late Colonel John McCrae's *In Flanders Fields*.

Sir Arthur Quiller-Couch and Messrs. Methuen & Co., Ltd., for a poem.

Mr. Ernest Rhys and Messrs. J. M. Dent & Sons, Ltd., for a poem.

Mr. Grant Richards for Mr. T. Sturge Moore's *The Panther*, and the late Mr. John Davidson's *A Runnable Stag*.

Major Charles G. D. Roberts for a poem.

Mrs. Rolleston for a poem by the late Mr. T. W. Rolleston.

Lady Margaret Sackville and Messrs. Constable & Co., Ltd., for a poem.

Miss Victoria Sackville-West and Messrs. John Lane, the Bodley Head, Ltd., for *Sailing Ships* from *Orchards and Vineyards*.

Mr. George Santayana and Messrs. Constable & Co., Ltd., for a poem.

The Walter Scott Publishing Co., Ltd., for sonnets by the last Mr. E. Lee-Hamilton.

Messrs. Selwyn & Blount, Ltd., for poems by Mr. John Freeman and the late Mr. Edward Thomas.

Mrs. Sharp for a poem by the late Mr. William Sharp ('Fiona Macleod').

Messrs. Sidgwick & Jackson, Ltd., for poems by Mr. Edmund Blunden and Mr. W. J. Turner.

Sir John Squire and Messrs. Hodder & Stoughton, Ltd., for three poems.

Mr. James Stephens and Messrs. Macmillan & Co., Ltd., for two poems.

Mr. Arthur Symons and Messrs. Heinemann for four poems.

Miss Evelyn Underhill and Messrs. J. M. Dent & Sons, Ltd., for a poem.

Mr. T. Fisher Unwin for a poem by the late Mr. Richard Middleton.

Mrs. Watts-Dunton for sonnets and an excerpt from *Christmas at the Mermaid* by the late Mr. T. Watts-Dunton.

Mrs. Welby-Everard, literary executrix of the Author, for an excerpt from the late Mr. Maurice Hewlett's *The Song of the Plow.*

Mr. Humbert Wolfe for two poems.

The Literary Executors of the Author and Messrs. Methuen & Co., Ltd., for *The Harlot's House* from *Poems by Oscar Wilde.*

Mr. W. B. Yeats and Mr. T. Fisher Unwin for the first four of the poems by Mr. Yeats which are included. The other poems by Mr. Yeats appear by permission of the Author and Messrs. Macmillan & Co., Ltd.

Mr. Francis Brett Young and Messrs. W. Collins, Sons & Co., Ltd., for a poem.

ADDITIONAL ACKNOWLEDGMENTS
(1935 EDITION)

Mr. Henderson is deeply grateful to the following for their kind permission to reprint copyright material:

Mr. Roy Campbell for his poem, *Tristan da Cunha.*

Messrs. Chatto & Windus, Ltd., for a poem by Wilfred Owen.

Messrs. J. M. Dent & Sons, Ltd., for poems by Frank Kendon, Herbert Palmer, and Richard Church.

Messrs. Faber & Faber, Ltd., for poems by Stephen Spender, Herbert Read, and T. S. Eliot.

Mrs. Frieda Lawrence for *Sicilian Cyclamens* by D. H. Lawrence.

Mr. C. Day Lewis and The Hogarth Press for two poems.

Mr. Hugh Macdiarmid and Messrs. Victor Gollancz, Ltd., for *Stony Limits.*

CONTENTS

[1] Pen-name used jointly by:
  Katherine Harris Bradley, 1846–1914.
  Edith Emma Cooper, 1862–1913.

THE GOLDEN BOOK
F MODERN ENGLISH POETRY

ROBERT BRIDGES

ODE ON THE TERCENTENARY
COMMEMORATION OF SHAKESPEARE, 1916

KIND dove-wing'd Peace, for whose green olive-crown
The noblest kings would give their diadems,
   Mother, who hast ruled our home so long,
    How suddenly art thou fled!
   Leaving our cities astir with war;
   And yet on the fair fields deserted
   Lingerest, wherever the gaudy seasons
    Deck with excessive splendour
    The sorrow-stricken year,
Where cornlands bask and high elms rustle gently,
And still the unweeting birds sing on by brae and bourn.

The trumpet blareth and calleth the true to be stern:
Be then thy soft reposeful music dumb;
   Yet shall thy lovers awhile give ear
    —An' tho' full-arm'd they come—
To the praise of England's gentlest son;
   Whom, when she bore the Muses lov'd
   Above the best of eldest honour
    —Yea, save one without peer—
    And by great Homer set,
Not to impugn his undisputed throne,
The myriad-hearted by the mighty-hearted one.

For God of His gifts pour'd on him a full measure,
And gave him to know Nature and the ways of men:
    And he dower'd with inexhaustible treasure
        A world conquering speech,
    Which surg'd as a river high-descended
    That, gathering tributaries of many lands,
    Rolls through the plain a bounteous flood,
        Picturing towers and temples
        And ruin of bygone times,
And floateth the ships deep-laden with merchandise
Out to the windy seas to traffic in foreign climes.

Thee, SHAKESPEARE, to-day we honour; and evermore
Since England bore thee, the master of human song,
    Thy folk are we, children of thee.
        Who, knitting in one her realm
    And strengthening with pride her sea-borne clans,
    Scorn'st in the grave the bruize of death.
    All thy later-laurel'd choir
        Laud thee in thy world-shrine:
        London's laughter is thine;
One with thee is our temper in melancholy or might,
And in thy book Great Britain's rule readeth her right.

Her chains are chains of Freedom, and her bright arms
Honour, Justice and Truth and Love to man.
    Though first from a pirate ancestry
        She took her home on the wave,
    Her gentler spirit arose disdainful,
    And, smiting the fetters of slavery,
    Made the high seaways safe and free,
        In wisdom bidding aloud
        To world-wide brotherhood,
Till her flag was hail'd as the ensign of Liberty,
And the boom of her guns went round the earth in salvoe
    of peace.

And thou, when Nature bow'd her mastering hand
To borrow an ecstacy of man's art from thee,
 Thou, her poet, secure as she
  Of the shows of eternity,
 Didst never fear thy work should fall
 To fashion's craze nor pedant's folly
 Nor devastator, whose arrogant arms
  Murder and maim mankind;
  Who, when in scorn of grace
He hath batter'd and burn'd some loveliest dearest shrine,
Laugheth in ire and boasteth aloud his brazen god.

 . . . . . .

I saw the Angel of Earth from strife aloof
Mounting the heavenly stair with Time on high,
 Growing ever younger in the brightening air
  Of the everlasting dawn:
 It was not terror in his eyes nor wonder,
 That glance of the intimate exaltation
 Which lieth as Power under all Being,
  And broodeth in Thought above—
  As a bird wingeth over the ocean,
Whether indolently the heavy water sleepeth
Or is dash'd in a million waves, chafing or lightly laughing.

I hear his voice in the music of lamentation,
In echoing chant and cadenced litany,
 In country song and pastoral piping
  And silvery dances of mirth:
 And oft, as the eyes of a lion in the brake,
 His presence hath startled me . . .
 In austere shapes of beauty lurking,
  Beautiful for Beauty's sake;
  As a lonely blade of life
Ariseth to flower, whenever the unseen Will
Stirreth with kindling aim the dark fecundity of Being.

Man knoweth but as in a dream of his own desire
The thing that is good for man, and he dreameth well:
    But the lot of the gentle heart is hard
      That is cast in an epoch of life
When evil is knotted and demons fight,
Who know not, they, that the lowest lot
Is treachery, hate and trust in sin
      And perseverance in ill,
      Doom'd to oblivious Hell,
To pass with the shames unspoken of men away,
Wash'd out with their tombs by the grey unpitying te:
    of Heaven.

But ye, dear Youth, who lightly in the day of fury
Put on England's glory as a common coat,
    And in your stature of masking grace
      Stood forth warriors complete,
No praise o'ershadoweth yours to-day,
Walking out of the home of love
To match the deeds of all the dead.—
      Alas! alas! fair Peace,
      These were thy blossoming roses.
Look on thy shame, fair Peace, thy tearful shame!
Turn to thine isle, fair Peace; return thou and guard
    well!

I LOVE ALL BEAUTEOUS THINGS

    I LOVE all beauteous things,
      I seek and adore them;
    God hath no better praise,
    And man in his hasty days
      Is honoured for them.

    I too will something make
      And joy in the making;
      Altho' to-morrow it seem
    Like the empty words of a dream
      Remembered on waking.

THE VOICE OF NATURE

TAND on the cliff and watch the veiled sun paling
A silver field afar in the mournful sea,
e scourge of the surf, and plaintive gulls sailing
At ease on the gale that smites the shuddering lea:
  Whose smile severe and chaste
June never hath stirred to vanity, nor age defaced.
lofty thought strive, O spirit, for ever:
courage and strength pursue thine own endeavour.

! if it were only for thee, thou restless ocean
Of waves that follow and roar, the sweep of the tides;
er't only for thee, impetuous wind, whose motion
Precipitate all o'errides, and turns, nor abides:
  For you sad birds and fair,
Or only for thee, bleak cliff, erect in the air;
en well could I read wisdom in every feature,
well should I understand the voice of Nature.

t far away, I think, in the Thames valley,
The silent river glides by flowery banks:
ıd birds sing sweetly in branches that arch an alley
Of cloistered trees, moss-grown in their ancient ranks:
  Where if a light air stray,
'Tis laden with hum of bees and scent of may.
ve and peace be thine, O spirit, for ever:
rve thy sweet desire: despise endeavour.

ıd if it were only for thee, entrancèd river,
That scarce dost rock the lily on her airy stem,
: stir a wave to murmur, or a rush to quiver;
Wer't but for the woods, and summer asleep in them:
  For you my bowers green,
My hedges of rose and woodbine, with walks between,
en well could I read wisdom in every feature,
well should I understand the voice of Nature.

DELIGHT AND THY DELIGHT

My delight and thy delight
Walking, like two angels white,
In the gardens of the night:

My desire and thy desire
Twining to a tongue of fire,
Leaping live, and laughing higher;
Thro' the everlasting strife
In the mystery of life.

Love, from whom the world begun,
Hath the secret of the sun.

Love can tell, and love alone,
Whence the million stars were strewn,
Why each atom knows its own,
How, in spite of woe and death,
Gay is life, and sweet is breath:

This he taught us, this we knew,
Happy in his science true,
Hand in hand as we stood
'Neath the shadows of the wood,
Heart to heart as we lay
In the dawning of the day.

NIGHTINGALES

BEAUTIFUL must be the mountains whence ye come,
And bright in the fruitful valleys the streams, wherefrom
Ye learn your song:
Where are those starry woods? O might I wander there,
Among the flowers, which in that heavenly air
Bloom the year long!

Nay, barren are those mountains and spent the streams:
Our song is the voice of desire, that haunts our dreams,
    A throe of the heart,
Those pining visions dim, forbidden hopes profound,
No dying cadence nor long sigh can sound,
    For all our art.

Alone, aloud in the raptured ear of men
We pour our dark nocturnal secret; and then,
    As night is withdrawn
From these sweet-springing meads and bursting boughs of
    May,
Dream, while the innumerable choir of day
    Welcome the dawn.

ON A DEAD CHILD

PERFECT little body, without fault or stain on thee,
  With promise of strength and manhood full and fair!
    Though cold and stark and bare,
The bloom and the charm of life doth awhile remain on
    thee.

Thy mother's treasure wert thou;—alas! no longer
  To visit her heart with wondrous joy; to be
    Thy father's pride;—ah, he
Must gather his faith together, and his strength make
    stronger.

To me, as I move thee now in the last duty,
  Dost thou with a turn or gesture anon respond;
    Startling my fancy fond
With a chance attitude of the head, a freak of beauty.

Thy hand clasps, as 'twas wont, my finger, and holds it:
  But the grasp is the grasp of Death, heartbreaking and
    stiff;
    Yet feels to my hand as if
'Twas still thy will, thy pleasure and trust that enfolds it.

So I lay there, thy sunken eyelids closing,—
  Go lie there in thy coffin, thy last little bed!—
    Propping thy wise, sad head,
Thy firm, pale hands across thy chest disposing.

So quiet! doth the change content thee?—Death, whith
    hath he taken thee?
  To a world, do I think, that rights the disaster of this?
    The vision of which I miss,
Who weep for the body, and wish but to warm thee a
    awaken thee?

Ah! little at best can all our hopes avail us
  To lift this sorrow, or cheer us, when in the dark,
    Unwilling, alone we embark,
And the things we have seen and have known and ha
    heard of, fail us.

A PASSER-BY

Whither, O splendid ship, thy white sails crowding,
  Leaning across the bosom of the urgent West,
That fearest nor sea rising, nor sky clouding,
  Whither away, fair rover, and what thy quest?
  Ah! soon, when Winter has all our vales opprest,
When skies are cold and misty, and hail is hurling,
  Wilt thóu glíde on the blue Pacific, or rest
In a summer haven asleep, thy white sails furling.

I there before thee, in the country that well thou knowe
  Already arrived am inhaling the odorous air:
I watch thee enter unerringly where thou goest,
  And anchor queen of the strange shipping there,
  Thy sails for awnings spread, thy masts bare;
Nor is aught from the foaming reef to the snow-cappe
    grandest
  Peak, that is over the feathery palms more fair
Than thou, so upright, so stately, and still thou standest.

And yet, O splendid ship, unhailed and nameless,
 I know not if, aiming a fancy, I rightly divine
That thou hast a purpose joyful, a courage blameless,
 Thy port assured in a happier land than mine.
 But for all I have given thee, beauty enough is thine,
As thou, aslant with trim tackle and shrouding,
 From the proud nostril curve of a prow's line
In the offing scatterest foam, thy white sails crowding.

AWAKE, MY HEART, TO BE LOVED

Awake, my heart, to be loved, awake, awake!
The darkness silvers away, the morn doth break,
It leaps in the sky: unrisen lustres slake
The o'ertaken moon. Awake, O heart, awake!

She too that loveth awaketh and hopes for thee;
Her eyes already have sped the shades that flee,
Already they watch the path thy feet shall take:
Awake, O heart, to be loved, awake, awake!

And if thou tarry from her,—if this could be,—
She cometh herself, O heart, to be loved, to thee;
For thee would unashamèd herself forsake:
Awake to be loved, my heart, awake, awake!

Awake, the land is scattered with light, and see,
Uncanopied sleep is flying from field and tree:
And blossoming boughs of April in laughter shake;
Awake, O heart, to be loved, awake, awake!

Lo, all things wake and tarry and look for thee:
She looketh and saith, 'O sun, now bring him to me.
Come more adored, O adored, for his coming's sake,
And awake my heart to be loved: awake, awake!'

B 921

LONDON SNOW

When men were all asleep the snow came flying,
In large white flakes falling on the city brown,
Stealthily and perpetually settling and loosely lying,
   Hushing the latest traffic of the drowsy town;
Deadening, muffling, stifling its murmurs failing;
Lazily and incessantly floating down and down:
   Silently sifting and veiling road, roof and railing;
Hiding difference, making unevenness even,
Into angles and crevices softly drifting and sailing.
   All night it fell, and when full inches seven
It lay in the depth of its uncompacted lightness,
The clouds blew off from a high and frosty heaven;
   And all woke earlier for the unaccustomed brightness
Of the winter dawning, the strange unheavenly glare:
The eye marvelled—marvelled at the dazzling whiteness;
   The ear hearkened to the stillness of the solemn air;
No sound of wheel rumbling nor of foot falling,
And the busy morning cries came thin and spare.
   Then boys I heard, as they went to school, calling,
They gathered up the crystal manna to freeze
Their tongues with tasting, their hands with snow-balling;
   Or rioted in a drift, plunging up to the knees;
Or peering up from under the white-mossed wonder,
'O look at the trees!' they cried, 'O look at the trees!'
   With lessened load a few carts creak and blunder,
Following along the white deserted way,
A country company long dispersed asunder:
   When now already the sun, in pale display
Standing by Paul's high dome, spread forth below
His sparkling beams, and awoke the stir of the day.
   For now doors open, and war is waged with the
      snow;
And trains of sombre men, past tale of number,
Tread long brown paths, as toward their toil they go:
   But even for them awhile no cares encumber

Their minds diverted; the daily word is unspoken,
The daily thoughts of labour and sorrow slumber
At the sight of the beauty that greets them, for the charm
    they have broken.

SONNETS FROM *THE GROWTH OF LOVE*

VIII

For beauty being the best of all we know
Sums up the unsearchable and secret aims
Of nature, and on joys whose earthly names
Were never told can form and sense bestow;
And man hath sped his instinct to outgo
The step of science; and against her shames
Imagination stakes out heavenly claims,
Building a tower above the head of woe.

    Nor is there fairer work for beauty found
Than that she win in nature her release
From all the woes that in the world abound:
Nay, with his sorrow may his love increase,
If from man's greater need beauty redound,
And claim his tears for homage of his peace.

XVIII

Where San Miniato's convent from the sun
At forenoon overlooks the city of flowers
I sat, and gazing on her domes and towers
Call'd up her famous children one by one;
And three who all the rest had far outdone,
Mild Giotto first, who stole the morning hours,
I saw, and god-like Buonarroti's powers,
And Dante, gravest poet, her much-wrong'd son.

Is all this glory, I said, another's praise?
Are these heroic triumphs things of old,
And do I dead upon the living gaze?
Or rather doth the mind, that can behold
The wondrous beauty of the works and days,
Create the image that her thoughts enfold?

XXXV

All earthly beauty hath one cause and proof,
To lead the pilgrim soul to beauty above:
Yet lieth the greater bliss so far aloof,
That few there be are wean'd from earthly love.
  Joy's ladder it is, reaching from home to home,
The best of all the work that all was good;
Whereof 'twas writ the angels aye upclomb,
Down sped, and at the top the Lord God stood.

But I my time abuse, my eyes by day
Center'd on thee, by night my heart on fire—
Letting my number'd moments run away—
Nor e'en 'twixt night and day to heaven aspire:
  So true it is that what the eye seeth not
But slow is loved, and loved is soon forgot.

GEORGE MEREDITH

HYMN TO COLOUR

WITH Life and Death I walked when Love appeared,
And made them on each side a shadow seem.
Through wooded vales the land of dawn we neared,
Where down smooth rapids whirls the helmless dream
To fall on daylight; and night puts away
    Her darker veil for grey.

In that grey veil green grassblades brushed we by;
We came where woods breathed sharp, and overhead
Rocks raised clear horns on a transforming sky:
Around, save for those shapes, with him who led
And linked them, desert varied by no sign
      Of other life than mine.

By this the dark-winged planet, raying wide,
From the mild pearl-glow to the rose upborne,
Drew in his fires, less faint than far descried,
Pure-fronted on a stronger wave of morn:
And those two shapes the splendour interweaved,
      Hung web-like, sank and heaved.

Love took my hand when hidden stood the sun
To fling his robe on shoulder-heights of snow.
Then said: There lie they, Life and Death in one.
Whichever is, the other is: but know,
It is thy craving self that thou dost see,
      Not in them seeing me.

Shall man into the mystery of breath
From his quick beating pulse a pathway spy?
Or learn the secret of the shrouded death,
By lifting up the lid of a white eye?
Cleave thou thy way with fathering desire
      Of fire to reach to fire.

Look now where Colour, the soul's bridegroom, makes
The house of heaven splendid for the bride.
To him as leaps a fountain she awakes,
In knotting arms, yet boundless: him beside,
She holds the flower to heaven, and by his power
      Brings heaven to the flower.

He gives her homeliness in desert air,
And sovereignty in spaciousness; he leads
Through widening chambers of surprise to where
Throbs rapture near an end that aye recedes,
Because his touch is infinite and lends
      A yonder to all ends.

Death begs of Life his blush; Life Death persuades
To keep long day with his caresses graced.
He is the heart of light, the wing of shades,
The crown of beauty: never soul embraced
Of him can harbour unfaith; soul of him
      Possessed walks never dim.

Love eyed his rosy memories: he sang:
O bloom of dawn, breathed up from the gold sheaf
Held springing beneath Orient! that dost hang
The space of dewdrops running over leaf;
Thy fleetingness is bigger in the ghost
      Than Time with all his host!

Of thee to say behold, has said adieu:
But Love remembers how the sky was green,
And how the grasses glimmered lightest blue;
How saint-like grey took fervour; how the screen
Of cloud grew violet; how thy moment came
      Between a blush and flame.

Love saw the emissary eglantine
Break wave round thy white feet above the gloom;
Lay finger on thy star; thy raiment line
With cherub wing and limb; wed thy soft bloom,
Gold-quivering like sunrays in thistle-down,
      Earth under rolling brown.

They do not look through love to look on thee,
Grave heavenliness! nor know they joy of sight,
Who deem the wave of rapt desire must be
Its wrecking and last issue of delight.
Dead seasons quicken in one petal-spot
      Of colour unforgot.

This way have men come out of brutishness
To spell the letters of the sky and read
A reflex upon earth else meaningless.
With thee, O fount of the Untimed! to lead;
Drink they of thee, thee eyeing, they unaged
      Shall on through brave wars waged.

More gardens will they win than any lost;
The vile plucked out of them, the unlovely slain.
Not forfeiting the beast with which they are crossed,
To stature of the Gods will they attain.
They shall uplift their Earth to meet her Lord,
      Themselves the attuning chord!

The song had ceased; my vision with the song.
Then of those Shadows, which one made descent
Beside me I knew not: but Life ere long
Came on me in the public ways and bent
Eyes deeper than of old: Death met I too,
      And saw the dawn glow through.

THOMAS EDWARD BROWN

———

WHITE FOXGLOVE

WHITE foxglove, by an angle in the wall,
Secluded, tall,
No vulgar bees
Consult you, wondering
If such a dainty thing
Can give them ease.
Yet what was that? Sudden a breeze
From the far moorland sighed,
And you replied,
Quiv'ring a moment with a thrill
Sweet, but ineffable.

Was it a kiss that sought you from the bowers
Of happier flowers,
And did not heed
Accessible loveliness,
And with a quaint distress
Hinted the need,
And paused and trembled for its deed,

And so you trembled, too,
No roseate hue
Revealing how the alarmèd sense
Blushed quick—intense?

Ah me!
Such kisses are for roses in the prime,
For braid of lime,
For full-blown blooms,
For ardent breaths outpoured
Obvious, or treasure stored
In honied rooms
Of rare delight, in which the looms
Of nature still conspire
To sate desire.
Not such are you beside the wall,
Cloistered and virginal.

'Twas your wild purple sisters there that passed
Unseen, and cast
The spell.   They hold
The vantage of the heights,
And in you they have rights,
And they are bold:
They know not ever to be cold
Or coy, but they would play
With you alway.
Wherefore their little sprites a-wing
Make onslaught from the ling.

So spake I to the foxglove in my mood,
But was not understood.
Rather she shrank, and in a tenfold whiteness
Condemned what must have seemed to her my lightness.

THEODORE WATTS-DUNTON

WASSAIL CHORUS

CHRISTMAS AT THE MERMAID

CHORUS

CHRISTMAS knows a merry, merry place,
Where he goes with fondest face,
Brightest eye, brightest hair:
Tell the Mermaid where is that one place:
Where?

RALEIGH

'Tis by Devon's glorious halls,
Whence, dear Ben, I come again:
Bright with golden roofs and walls—
El Dorado's rare domain—
Seem those halls when sunlight launches
Shafts of gold through leafless branches,
Where the winter's feathery mantle blanches
Field and farm and lane.

CHORUS

Christmas knows a merry, merry place,
Where he goes with fondest face,
Brightest eye, brightest hair:
Tell the Mermaid where is that one place:
Where?

DRAYTON

'Tis where Avon's wood-sprites weave
Through the boughs a lace of rime,
While the bells of Christmas Eve
Fling for Will the Stratford-chime
O'er the river-flags emboss'd
Rich with flowery runes of frost—
O'er the meads where snowy tufts are toss'd—
Strains of olden time.

CHORUS

Christmas knows a merry, merry place,
    Where he goes with fondest face,
        Brightest eye, brightest hair:
Tell the Mermaid where is that one place:
        Where?

SHAKESPEARE'S FRIEND

'Tis, methinks, on any ground
    Where our Shakespeare's feet are set.
There smiles Christmas, holly-crown'd
    With his blithest coronet:
Friendship's face he loveth well:
'Tis a countenance whose spell
Sheds a balm o'er every mead and dell
    Where we used to fret.

CHORUS

Christmas is a merry, merry place,
    Where he goes with fondest face,
        Brightest eye, brightest hair:
Tell the Mermaid where is that one place:
        Where?

HEYWOOD

More than all the pictures, Ben,
    Winter weaves by wood or stream,
Christmas loves our London, when
    Rise thy clouds of wassail-steam—
Clouds like these, that, curling, take
Forms of faces gone, and wake
Many a lay from lips we loved, and make
    London like a dream.

CHORUS

Christmas knows a merry, merry place,
    Where he goes with fondest face,
        Brightest eye, brightest hair:
Tell the Mermaid where is that one place:
        Where?

BEN JONSON

Love's old songs shall never die,
　　Yet the new shall suffer proof;
Love's old drink of Yule brew I,
　　Wassail for new love's behoof:
Drink the drink I brew, and sing
Till the berried branches swing,
Till our song make all the Mermaid ring—
　　Yea from rush to roof.

FINALE

Christmas loves this merry, merry place:—
　　Christmas saith with fondest face,
　　Brightest eye, brightest hair:
'Ben! the drink tastes rare of sack and mace:
　　Rare!'

SONNETS

I

When hope lies dead—ah, when 'tis death to live,
　　And wrongs remembered make the heart still bleed,
　　Better are Sleep's kind lies for Life's blind need
Than truth, if lies a little peace can give.
A little peace! 'tis thy prerogative,
　　O Sleep! to lend it; thine to quell or feed
　　This love that starves—this starving soul's long greed,
And bid Regret, the queen of hell, forgive.
Yon moon that mocks me thro' the uncurtained glass
　　Recalls that other night, that other moon,—
　　Two English lovers on a grey lagoon,—
The voices from the lantern'd gondolas,
　　The kiss, the breath, the flashing eyes, and, soon,
The throbbing stillness: all the heaven that was.

II

Natura Maligna

The Lady of the Hills with crimes untold
Followed my feet with azure eyes of prey;
By glacier-brink she stood—by cataract-spray—
When mists were dire, or avalanche-echoes rolled.
At night she glimmered in the death-wind cold,
And if a footprint shone at break of day,
My flesh would quail, but straight my soul would say:
"'Tis hers whose hand God's mightier hand doth hold."
I trod her snow-bridge, for the moon was bright,
Her icicle-arch across the sheer crevasse,
When lo, she stood! . . . God bade her let me pass,
Then felled the bridge! . . . Oh, there in sallow light,
There down the chasm, I saw her, cruel, white,
And all my wondrous days as in a glass.

RICHARD WATSON DIXON

———

THE FEATHERS OF THE WILLOW

The feathers of the willow
Are half of them grown yellow
  Above the swelling stream;
And ragged are the bushes,
And rusty now the rushes,
  And wild the clouded gleam.

The thistle now is older,
His stalk begins to moulder,
  His head is white as snow;
The branches all are barer,
The linnet's song is rarer,
  The robin pipeth now.

JAMES THOMSON
(B. V.)

———

FROM *THE CITY OF DREADFUL NIGHT*

LARGE glooms were gathered in the mighty fane,
   With tinted moongleams slanting here and there;
And all was hush: no swelling organ-strain,
   No chant, no voice or murmuring of prayer;
No priests came forth, no tinkling censers fumed,
And the high altar space was unillumed.

Around the pillars and against the walls
   Leaned men and shadows; others seemed to brood
Bent or recumbent in secluded stalls.
   Perchance they were not a great multitude
Save in that city of so lonely streets
Where one may count up every face he meets.

All patiently awaited the event
   Without a stir or sound, as if no less
Self-occupied, doomstricken, while attent.
   And then we heard a voice of solemn stress
From the dark pulpit, and our gaze there met
Two eyes which burned as never eyes burned yet:

Two steadfast and intolerable eyes
   Burning beneath a broad and rugged brow;
The head behind it of enormous size,
   And as black fir-groves in a large wind bow,
Our rooted congregation, gloom-arrayed,
By that great sad voice deep and full were swayed:—

O melancholy Brothers, dark, dark, dark!
O battling in black floods without an ark!
   O spectral wanderers of unholy Night!

My soul hath bled for you these sunless years,
With bitter blood-drops running down like tears:
   Oh, dark, dark, dark, withdrawn from joy and light !

My heart is sick with anguish for your bale;
Your woe hath been my anguish; yea, I quail
   And perish in your perishing unblest.
And I have searched the heights and depths, the scope
Of all our universe, with desperate hope
   To find some solace for your wild unrest.

And now at last authentic word I bring,
Witnessed by every dead and living thing;
   Good tidings of great joy for you, for all;
There is no God; no Fiend with names divine
Made us and tortures us; if we must pine,
   It is to satiate no Being's gall.

It was the dark delusion of a dream,
That living Person conscious and supreme,
   Whom we must curse for cursing us with life;
Whom we must curse because the life He gave
Could not be buried in the quiet grave,
   Could not be killed by poison or by knife.

This little life is all we must endure,
The grave's most holy peace is ever sure,
   We fall asleep and never wake again;
Nothing is of us but the mouldering flesh,
Whose elements dissolve and merge afresh
   In earth, air, water, plants, and other men.

We finish thus; and all our wretched race
Shall finish with its cycle, and give place
   To other beings, with their own time-doom
Infinite æons ere our kind began;
Infinite æons after the last man
   Has joined the mammoth in earth's tomb and womb.

We bow down to the universal laws,
Which never had for man a special clause
   Of cruelty or kindness, love or hate:
If toads and vultures are obscene to sight,
If tigers burn with beauty and with might,
   Is it by favour or by wrath of fate?

All substance lives and struggles evermore
Through countless shapes continually at war,
   By countless interactions interknit:
If one is born a certain day on earth,
All times and forces tended to that birth,
   Not all the world could change or hinder it.

I find no hint throughout the Universe
Of good or ill, or blessing or of curse;
   I find alone Necessity Supreme;
With infinite Mystery, abysmal, dark,
Unlighted ever by the faintest spark
   For us the flitting shadows of a dream.

O Brothers of sad lives! they are so brief;
A few short years must bring us all relief:
   Can we not bear these years of labouring breath?
But if you would not this poor life fulfil,
Lo, you are free to end it when you will,
   Without the fear of waking after death.—

The organ-like vibrations of his voice
   Thrilled through the vaulted aisles and died away;
The yearning of the tones which bade rejoice
   Was sad and tender as a requiem lay:
Our shadowy congregation rested still
As brooding on that 'End it when you will.'

THOMAS HARDY

IN TIME OF 'THE BREAKING OF NATIONS'
1915

I

Only a man harrowing clods
  In a slow silent walk
With an old horse that stumbles and nods
  Half asleep as they stalk.

II

Only thin smoke without flame
  From the heaps of couch-grass;
Yet this will go onward the same
  Though Dynasties pass.

III

Yonder a maid and her wight
  Come whispering by:
War's annals will cloud into night
  Ere their story die.

WHEN I SET OUT FOR LYONNESSE

When I set out for Lyonnesse,
  A hundred miles away,
  The rime was on the spray,
And starlight lit my lonesomeness
When I set out for Lyonnesse
  A hundred miles away.

What would bechance at Lyonnesse
  While I should sojourn there
  No prophet durst declare,
Nor did the wisest wizard guess
What would bechance at Lyonnesse
  While I should sojourn there.

When I came back from Lyonnesse
    With magic in my eyes,
    All marked with mute surmise
My radiance rare and fathomless,
When I came back from Lyonnesse
    With magic in my eyes.

GREAT THINGS

SWEET cyder is a great thing,
    A great thing to me,
Spinning down to Weymouth town
    By Ridgway thirstily,
And maid and mistress summoning
    Who tend the hostelry:
O cyder is a great thing,
    A great thing to me!

The dance it is a great thing,
    A great thing to me,
With candles lit and partners fit
    For night-long revelry;
And going home when day-dawning
    Peeps pale upon the lea:
O dancing is a great thing,
    A great thing to me!

Love is, yea, a great thing,
    A great thing to me,
When, having drawn across the lawn
    In darkness silently,
A figure flits like one a-wing
    Out from the nearest tree:
O love is, yes, a great thing,
    A great thing to me!

Will these be always great things,
    Great things to me? . . .
Let it befall that One will call,
    'Soul, I have need of thee';
What then?   Joy-jaunts, impassioned flings,
    Love, and its ecstasy,
Will always have been great things,
    Great things to me!

THE END OF THE EPISODE

INDULGE no more may we
In this sweet-bitter pastime:
The love-light shines the last time
    Between you, Sweet, and me.

There shall remain no trace
Of what so closely tied us,
And blank as ere love eyed us
    Will be our meeting-place.

The flowers and the thymy air,
Will they now miss our coming?
The dumbles thin their humming
    To find we haunt not there?

Though fervent was our vow,
Though ruddily ran our pleasure,
Bliss has fulfilled its measure,
    And sees its sentence now.

Ache deep; but make no moans:
Smile out; but stilly suffer:
The paths of love are rougher
    Than thoroughfares of stones.

AFTERWARDS ✓

WHEN the Present has latched its postern behind my
    tremulous stay,
  And the May month flaps its glad green leaves like wings,
Delicate-filmed as new-spun silk, will the neighbours say,
  'He was a man who used to notice such things'?

If it be in the dusk when, like an eyelid's soundless blink,
  The dewfall-hawk comes crossing the shades to alight
Upon the wind-warped upland thorn, a gazer may think,
  'To him this must have been a familiar sight.'

If I pass during some nocturnal blackness, mothy and warm,
  When the hedgehog travels furtively over the lawn,
One may say, 'He strove that such innocent creatures should
    come to no harm.
  But he could do little for them; and now he is gone.'

If, when hearing that I have been stilled at last, they stand at
    the door,
  Watching the full-starred heavens that winter sees,
Will this thought rise on those who will meet my face no more,
  'He was one who had an eye for such mysteries' ?

And will any say when my bell of quittance is heard in the
    gloom,
  And a crossing breeze cuts a pause in its outrollings,
Till they rise again, as they were a new bell's boom,
  'He hears it not now, but used to notice such things' ?

FROM *THE DYNASTS*

Semichorus I of the Years (aerial music)

Last as first the question rings
Of the Will's long travailings;
  Why the All-mover,
  Why the All-prover
Ever urges on and measures out the chordless chime of Things.[1]

Semichorus II

Heaving dumbly
As we deem
Moulding numbly
As in dream,
Apprehending not how fare the sentient subjects of Its scheme.

Semichorus I of the Pities

Nay;—shall not Its blindness break?
Yea, must not Its heart awake,
  Promptly tending
  To Its mending
In a genial germing purpose, and for loving-kindness' sak?

Semichorus II

Shall It never
Curb or cure
Aught whatever
Those endure
Whom It quickens, let them darkle to extinction swift and sure.

Chorus

But—a stirring thrills the air
Like to sounds of joyance there
  That the rages
  Of the ages
Shall be cancelled, and deliverance offered from the darts that were
Consciousness the Will informing, till It fashions all things fair

[1] Hor., *Epis.*, i. 12.

JOHN ADDINGTON SYMONDS

SONNETS

I

NEVER, oh never more shall I behold
    A sunrise on the glacier:—stars of morn
    Paling in primrose round the crystal horn;
    Soft curves of crimson mellowing into gold
O'er sapphire chasm, and silvery snow-field cold,
    Fire that o'er-floods the horizon; beacons borne
    From wind-worn peak to storm-swept peak forlorn:
    Clear hallelujahs through heaven's arches rolled.

Never, oh never more these feet shall feel
    The firm elastic tissue of upland turf,
    Or the crisp edge of the high rocks; or cling
Where the embattled cliffs beneath them reel
    Through cloud-wreaths eddying like the Atlantic surf,
    Far, far above the wheeling eagle's wing.

II

A CRUCIFIX IN THE ETSCH THAL

BLUE mists lie curled along the sullen stream;
Clouds furl the pine-clad highlands whence we came;
Stage after stage, interminably tame,
Stretch the gaunt mountain-flanks without one gleam.
All things are frozen in a dull dead dream;
It is a twilight land without a name;
Each half-awakened hamlet seems the same
Home of grey want and misery supreme.

Heart-breaking is the world-old human strife
With niggard nature traced adown this vale
In records fugitive as human life.
Ah Christ! the land is Thine!   Those tortured eyes,
That thorn-crowned brow, those mute lips, thin and pale,
Appeal from man's pain to the impiteous skies.

III

To the Genius of Eternal Slumber

SLEEP, that art named eternal!   Is there then
  No chance of waking in thy noiseless realm?
  Come there no fretful dreams to overwhelm
  The feverish spirits of o'erlaboured men?
Shall conscience sleep where thou art; and shall pain
  Lie folded with tired arms around her head;
  And memory be stretched upon a bed
  Of ease, whence she shall never rise again?
O Sleep, that art eternal!   Say, shall love
  Breathe like an infant slumbering at thy breast?
  Shall hope there cease to throb; and shall the smart
Of things impossible at length find rest?
  Thou answerest not.   The poppy-head above
  Thy calm brows sleep.   How cold, how still thou art!

WILFRID SCAWEN BLUNT

ST. VALENTINE'S DAY

TO-DAY, all day, I rode upon the down,
With hounds and horsemen, a brave company.
On this side in its glory lay the sea,
On that side Sussex weald, a sea of brown.
The wind was light, and brightly the sun shone,
And still we galloped on from gorse to gorse:
And once, when checked, a thrush sang, and my horse
Pricked his quick ears as to a sound unknown.
  I knew the Spring was come.   I knew it even
Better than all by this, that through my chase
In bush and stone and hill and sea and heaven
I seemed to see and follow still your face.
Your face my quarry was.   For it I rode,
My horse a thing of wings, myself a god.

THE OLD SQUIRE

I LIKE the hunting of the hare
   Better than that of the fox;
I like the joyous morning air,
   And the crowing of the cocks.

I like the calm of the early fields,
   The ducks asleep by the lake,
The quiet hour which Nature yields,
   Before mankind is awake.

I like the pheasants and feeding things
   Of the unsuspicious morn;
I like the flap of the wood-pigeon's wings
   As she rises from the corn.

I like the blackbird's shriek, and his rush
   From the turnips as I pass by,
And the partridge hiding her head in a bush,
   For her young ones cannot fly.

I like these things, and I like to ride
   When all the world is in bed,
To the top of the hill where the sky grows wide,
   And where the sun grows red.

The beagles at my horse heels trot
   In silence after me;
There's Ruby, Roger, Diamond, Dot,
   Old Slut and Margery,—

A score of names well used, and dear,
   The names my childhood knew;
The horn, with which I rouse their cheer,
   Is the horn my father blew.

I like the hunting of the hare
    Better than that of the fox;
The new world still is all less fair
    Than the old world it mocks.

I covet not a wider range
    Than these dear manors give;
I take my pleasure without change,
    And as I lived I live.

I leave my neighbours to their thought;
    My choice it is, and pride
On my own lands to find my sport,
    In my own fields to ride.

The hare herself no better loves
    The field where she was bred,
Than I the habit of these groves,
    My own inherited.

I know my quarries every one,
    The meuse where she sits low;
The road she chose to-day was run
    A hundred years ago.

The lags, the gills, the forest ways,
    The hedgerows one and all,
These are the kingdoms of my chase,
    And bounded by my wall;

Nor has the world a better thing,
    Though one should search it round,
Than thus to live one's own sole king,
    Upon one's own sole ground.

I like the hunting of the hare;
    It brings me, day by day,
The memory of old days as fair,
    With dead men past away.

To these, as homeward still I ply,
    And pass the churchyard gate
Where all are laid as I must lie,
    I stop and raise my hat.

I like the hunting of the hare;
    New sports I hold in scorn.
I like to be as my fathers were,
    In the days ere I was born.

ON THE SHORTNESS OF TIME

IF I could live without the thought of Death,
Forgetful of Time's waste, the soul's decay,
I would not ask for other joy than breath
With light and sound of birds and the sun's ray.
I could sit on untroubled day by day
Watching the grass grow, and the wild flowers range
From blue to yellow and from red to grey
In natural sequence as the seasons change.
I could afford to wait, but for the hurt
Of this dull tick of time which chides my ear.
But now I dare not sit with loins ungirt
And staff unlifted, for Death stands too near.
I must be up and doing—ay, each minute.
The grave gives time for rest when we are in it.

AUSTIN DOBSON

A GARDEN SONG

HERE, in this sequestered close,
    Bloom the hyacinth and rose;
Here beside the modest stock
    Flaunts the flaring hollyhock;
Here, without a pang, one sees
    Ranks, conditions, and degrees.

All the seasons run their race
In this quiet resting-place;
Peach, and apricot, and fig
Here will ripen, and grow big;
Here is store and overplus,—
More had not Alcinoüs!

Here, in alleys cool and green,
Far ahead the thrush is seen;
Here along the southern wall
Keeps the bee his festival;
All is quiet else—afar
Sounds of toil and turmoil are.

Here be shadows large and long;
Here be spaces meet for song;
Grant, O garden-god, that I,
Now that none profane is nigh,—
Now that mood and moment please,—
Find the fair Pierides!

THE LADIES OF ST. JAMES'S

A Proper New Ballad of the Country and the Town

Phyllida amo ante alias.—VIRGIL

THE ladies of St. James's
    Go swinging to the play;
Their footmen run before them,
    With a 'Stand by! Clear the way!'
But Phyllida, my Phyllida!
    She takes her buckled shoon,
When we go out a-courting
    Beneath the harvest moon.

The ladies of St. James's
  Wear satin on their backs;
They sit all night at *Ombre*,
  With candles all of wax:
But Phyllida, my Phyllida!
  She dons her russet gown,
And runs to gather May dew
  Before the world is down.

The ladies of St. James's!
  They are so fine and fair,
You 'd think a box of essences
  Was broken in the air:
But Phyllida, my Phyllida!
  The breath of heath and furze,
When breezes blow at morning,
  Is not so fresh as hers.

The ladies of St. James's!
  They 're painted to the eyes,
Their white it stays for ever,
  Their red it never dies:
But Phyllida, my Phyllida!
  Her colour comes and goes;
It trembles to a lily,—
  It wavers to a rose.

The ladies of St. James's!
  You scarce can understand
The half of all their speeches,
  Their phrases are so grand:
But Phyllida, my Phyllida!
  Her shy and simple words
Are clear as after rain-drops
  The music of the birds.

The ladies of St. James's!
    They have their fits and freaks;
They smile on you—for seconds;
    They frown on you—for weeks:
But Phyllida, my Phyllida!
    Come either storm or shine,
From Shrove-tide unto Shrove-tide,
    Is always true—and mine.

My Phyllida! my Phyllida!
    I care not though they heap
The hearts of all St. James's,
    And give me all to keep;
I care not whose the beauties
    Of all the world may be,
For Phyllida—for Phyllida
    Is all the world to me.

ON A FAN THAT BELONGED TO THE
MARQUISE DE POMPADOUR

CHICKEN-SKIN, delicate, white,
    Painted by Carlo Vanloo,
Loves in a riot of light,
    Roses and vaporous blue;
    Hark to the dainty *frou-frou!*
Picture above if you can,
    Eyes that could melt as the dew,—
This was the Pompadour's fan!

See how they rise at the sight,
    Thronging the *Œil de Bœuf* through,
Courtiers as butterflies bright,
    Beauties that Fragonard drew,
    Talon-rouge, falbala, queue,
Cardinal, Duke,—to a man,
    Eager to sigh or to sue,—
This was the Pompadour's fan!

Ah! but things more than polite
  Hung on this toy, *voyez-vous!*
Matters of state and of might,
  Things that great ministers do;
  Things that, maybe, overthrew
Those in whose brains they began;
  Here was the sign and the cue,—
This was the Pompadour's fan!

Envoy

Where are the secrets it knew?
  Weavings of plot and of plan?
  —But where is the Pompadour, too?
This was the Pompadour's *Fan!*

A FANCY FROM FONTENELLE

'*De mémoires de Roses on n'a point vu mourir le Jardinier.*'

The Rose in the garden slipped her bud,
And she laughed in the pride of her youthful blood,
As she thought of the Gardener standing by—
'He is old,—so old! And he soon must die!'

The full Rose waxed in the warm June air,
And she spread and spread till her heart lay bare;
And she laughed once more as she heard his tread—
'He is older now! He will soon be dead!'

But the breeze of the morning blew, and found
That the leaves of the blown Rose strewed the ground;
And he came at noon, that Gardener old,
And he raked them gently under the mould.

And I wove the thing to a random rhyme,
For the Rose is Beauty, the Gardener, Time.

JOHN PAYNE

RONDEL

From Charles d'Orléans

THE year has cast its wede away
  Of rain, of tempest and of cold,
  And put on broidery of gold
Of sunbeams bright and clear and gay.
There is no bird or beast to-day
  But sings and shouts in field and fold,
'The year has cast its wede away
  Of rain, of tempest and of cold.'

The silver fret-work of the May
  Is over brook and spring enscrolled,
A blazon lovely to behold.
Each thing has put on new array:
The year has cast its wede away
  Of rain, of tempest and of cold.

ROCOCO

STRAIGHT and swift the swallows fly
To the sojourn of the sun;
All the golden year is done,
All the flower-time flitted by;
Thro' the boughs the witch-winds sigh;
But heart's summer is begun;
Life and love at last are one;
Love-lights glitter in the sky.

Summer days were soon outrun
With the setting of the sun;
Love's delight is never done.
Let the turn-coat roses die;
We are lovers, Love and I;
In Love's lips my roses lie.

SAMUEL WADDINGTON

MORNING

Now o'er the topmost pine,
  The distant pine-clad peak,
  There dawns a golden streak
Of light, an orient line:—
Phœbus, the light is thine,
  Thine is the glory,—seek
  Each dale and dewy creek,
And in full splendour shine!

Thy steeds now chafe and fret
  To scour the dusky plain:
  Speed forth with flashing rein,
Speed o'er the land,—and yet,
  Ah! linger in this lane,
Kissing each violet.

BEATA BEATRIX

'Ella ha perduta la sua Beatrice:
  E le parole ch' uom di lei può dire
Hanno virtù di far piangere altrui.'

            Vita Nuova.

AND was it thine, the light whose radiance shed
  Love's halo round the gloom of Dante's brow?
  Was thine the hand that touched his hand, and thou
The spirit to his inmost spirit wed?
O gentle, O most pure, what shall be said
  In praise of thee to whom Love's minstrels bow?
  O heart that held his heart, for ever now
Thou with his glory shalt be garlanded.

Lo, 'mid the twilight of the waning years,
  Firenze claims once more our love, our tears:
  But thou, triumphant on the throne of song,—
By Mary seated in the realm above,—
    O give us of that gift than death more strong,
    The loving spirit that won Dante's love.

ARTHUR O'SHAUGHNESSY

ODE

WE are the music makers,
    And we are the dreamers of dreams,
Wandering by lone sea-breakers,
    And sitting by desolate streams;—
World-losers and world-forsakers,
    On whom the pale moon gleams:
Yet we are the movers and shakers
    Of the world for ever, it seems.

With wonderful deathless ditties
We build up the world's great cities,
    And out of a fabulous story
    We fashion an empire's glory:
One man with a dream, at pleasure,
    Shall go forth and conquer a crown;
And three with a new song's measure
    Can trample a kingdom down.

We, in the ages lying
    In the buried past of the earth,
Built Nineveh with our sighing,
    And Babel itself in our mirth;
And o'erthrew them with prophesying
    To the old of the new world's worth;
For each age is a dream that is dying,
    Or one that is coming to birth.

SONG OF PALMS

MIGHTY, luminous, and calm
   Is the country of the palm,
Crowned with sunset and sunrise,
   Under blue unbroken skies,
Waving from green zone to zone,
Over wonders of its own;
Trackless, untraversed, unknown,
   Changeless through the centuries.

Who can say what thing it bears?
   Blazing bird and blooming flower,
Dwelling there for years and years,
   Hold the enchanted secret theirs:
Life and death and dream have made
Mysteries in many a shade,
Hollow haunt and hidden bower
Closed alike to sun and shower.

Who is ruler of each race
Living in each boundless place,
   Growing, flowering, and flying,
   Glowing, revelling, and dying?
Wave-like, palm by palm is stirred,
And the bird sings to the bird,
And the day sings one rich word,
   And the great night comes replying.

Long red reaches of the cane,
Yellow winding water-lane,
   Verdant isle and amber river,
Lisp and murmur back again,
   And ripe under-worlds deliver
Rapturous souls of perfume, hurled
   Up to where green oceans quiver
In the wide leaves' restless world.

Like a giant led astray
Seemeth each effulgent day,
    Wandering amazed and lonely
Up and down each forest way,
Lured by bird and charmed by bloom,
Lulled to sleep by great perfume,
    Knowing, marvelling and only
Bearing some rich dream away.

Many thousand years have been,
And the sun alone hath seen,
    Like a high and radiant ocean,
    All the fair palm world in motion;
But the crimson bird hath fed
With its mate of equal red,
    And the flower in soft explosion
With the flower hath been wed.

And its long luxuriant thought
Lofty palm to palm hath taught,
    While a single vast liana
All one brotherhood hath wrought,
    Crossing forest and savannah,
Binding fern and coco-tree,
    Fig-tree, buttress-tree, banana,
Dwarf cane and tall marití.

And no sun hath reached the rock
Shaken by the water shock,
    Where with flame-like plumage flutter
Golden birds in glaring flock,
    Bright against the darkness utter,
Lighting up the solitude,
    Where dim cascades roar and mutter
Through the river's foaming feud.

And beyond the trees are scant,
　And a hidden lake is lying
Under wide-leaved water-plant,
　Blossom with white blossom vying.
Who shall say what thing is heard,
Who shall say what liquid word,
Caught by the bentivi bird,
　Over lake and blossom flying?

All around and overhead,
Spells of splendid change are shed;
　Who shall tell enchanted stories
Of the forests that are dead?
Lo! the soul shall grow immense,
Looking on strange hues intense,
　Gazing at the flaunted glories
　Of the hundred-coloured lories.

SONG

I MADE another garden, yea,
　For my new Love:
I left the dead rose where it lay
　And set the new above.
Why did my summer not begin?
　Why did my heart not haste?
My old Love came and walked therein,
　And laid the garden waste.

She entered with her weary smile,
　Just as of old;
She looked around a little while
　And shivered at the cold:
Her passing touch was death to all,
　Her passing look a blight;
She made the white-rose petals fall,
　And turn'd the red rose white.

Her pale robe clinging to the grass
    Seemed like a snake
That bit the grass and ground, alas!
    And a sad trail did make.
She went up slowly to the gate,
    And then, just as of yore,
She turn'd back at the last to wait
    And say farewell once more.

GERARD MANLEY HOPKINS

———

THE LEADEN ECHO AND THE GOLDEN ECHO
(*Maidens' song from 'St. Winefred's Well'*)

THE LEADEN ECHO

How to kéep—is there ány any, is there none such, nowhere
    known some, bow or brooch or braid or brace, láce,
    latch or catch or key to keep

Back beauty, keep it, beauty, beauty, beauty, . . . from
    vanishing away?

Ó is there no frowning of these wrinkles, rankèd wrinkles deep,
Dówn? no waving off of these most mournful messengers,
    still messengers, sad and stealing messengers of grey?
No there 's none, there 's none, O no there 's none,
Nor can you long be, what you now are, called fair,
Do what you may do, what, do what you may,
And wisdom is early to despair:
Be beginning; since, no, nothing can be done
To keep at bay
Age and age's evils, hoar hair,
Ruck and wrinkle, drooping, dying, death's worst, winding
    sheets, tombs and worms and tumbling to decay;
So be beginning, be beginning to despair.

O there's none; no no no there's none:
Be beginning to despair, to despair,
Despair, despair, despair, despair.

THE GOLDEN ECHO

    Spare!
There ís one, yes I have one (Hush there!);
Only not within seeing of the sun,
Not within the singeing of the strong sun,
Tall sun's tingeing, or treacherous the tainting of the earth's air,
Somewhere elsewhere this is ah well where! one,
Óne. Yes I can tell such a key, I do know such a place,
Where whatever's prized and passes of us, everything that's
    fresh and fast flying of us, seems to us sweet of us and
    swiftly away with, done away with, undone,
Undone, done with, soon done with, and yet dearly and
    dangerously sweet
Of us, the wimpled-water-dimpled, not-by-morning-matchèd
    face,
The flower of beauty, fleece of beauty, too too apt to, ah!
    to fleet,
Never fleets móre, fastened with the tenderest truth
To its own best being and its loveliness of youth: it is an
    everlastingness of, O it is an all youth!
Come then, your ways and airs and looks, locks, maiden gear,
    gallantry and gaiety and grace,
Winning ways, airs innocent, maiden manners, sweet looks,
    loose locks, long locks, lovelocks, gaygear, going gallant,
    girlgrace—
Resign them, sign them, seal them, send them, motion them
    with breath,
And with sighs soaring, soaring síghs deliver
Them; beauty-in-the-ghost, deliver it, early now, long before
    death
Give beauty back, beauty, beauty, beauty, back to God,
    beauty's self and beauty's giver.

See; not a hair is, not an eyelash, not the least lash lost; every
　　　hair
Is, hair of the head, numbered.
Nay, what we had lighthanded left in surly the mere mould
Will have waked and have waxed and have walked with the
　　　wind what while we slept,
This side, that side hurling a heavyheaded hundredfold
Whatwhile we, while we slumbered.
O then, weary then whý should we tread? O why are we
　　　so haggard at the heart, so care-coiled, care-killed, so
　　　fagged, so fashed, so cogged, so cumbered,
When the thing we freely fórfeit is kept with fonder a care,
Fonder a care kept than we could have kept it, kept
Far with fonder a care (and we, we should have lost it) finer,
　　　fonder
A care kept.—Where kept? Do but tell us where kept,
　　　where.—
Yonder.—What high as that! We follow, now we follow.
　　　—Yonder, yes, yonder, yonder,
Yonder.

THE STARLIGHT NIGHT

LOOK at the stars! look, look up at the skies!
　　O look at all the fire-folk sitting in the air!
　　The bright boroughs, the quivering citadels there!
The dim woods quick with diamond wells; the elf-eyes!
The grey lawns cold where quaking gold-dew lies!
　　Wind-beat white-beam! airy abeles all on flare!
　　Flake-doves sent floating out at a farmyard scare!—
Ah well! it is a purchase and a prize.

Buy then! Bid then!—What?—Prayer, patience, alms,
　　vows.—
Look, look! a May-mess, like on orchard boughs;

Look! March-bloom, like on meal'd-with-yellow sallows.—
These are indeed the barn: withindoors house
The shocks.   This piece-bright paling hides the Spouse
   Christ, and the mother of Christ and all His hallows.

ANDREW LANG

THE ODYSSEY

As one that for a weary space has lain
   Lulled by the song of Circe and her wine
   In gardens near the pale of Proserpine,
Where that Aeaean isle forgets the main,
And only the low lutes of love complain,
   And only shadows of wan lovers pine—
   As such an one were glad to know the brine
Salt on his lips, and the large air again,—
So gladly, from the songs of modern speech
   Men turn, and see the stars, and feel the free
      Shrill wind beyond the close of heavy flowers,
      And through the music of the languid hours
They hear like Ocean on the western beach
   The surge and thunder of the Odyssey.

BALLADE OF HIS CHOICE OF A SEPULCHRE

HERE I would come when weariest;
         Here the breast
Of the Windburg's tufted over
Deep with bracken; here his crest
         Takes the west,
Where the wide-winged hawk doth hover.

Silent here are lark and plover;
         In the cover
Deep below the cushat best
Loves his mate and croons above her
         O'er their nest,
Where the wide-winged hawk doth hover!

Bring me here life's tired out guest,
　　To the blest
Bed that waits the weary rover,
Here should failure be confessed;
　　　　Ends my quest
Where the wide-winged hawk doth hover!

ENVOY

Friend, or stranger kind, or lover,
Ah, fulfil a last behest,
　　　Let me rest
Where the wide-winged hawk doth hover!

ALMAE MATRES

(ST. ANDREWS, 1862—OXFORD, 1865)

St. Andrews by the Northern Sea
A haunted town it is to me!
A little city, worn and gray,
　　The gray North Ocean girds it round,
And o'er the rocks, and up the bay,
　　The long sea-rollers surge and sound.
And still the thin and biting spray
　　Drives down the melancholy street,
And still endure, and still decay,
　　Towers that the salt winds vainly beat.
Ghost-like and shadowy they stand
Clear mirror'd in the wet sea-sand.

O, ruin'd chapel, long ago
　　We loiter'd idly where the tall
Fresh-budded mountain-ashes blow
　　Within thy desecrated wall:

The tough roots broke the tomb below,
  The April birds sang clamorous,
We did not dream, we could not know
  How soon the Fates would sunder us!

O, broken minster, looking forth
  Beyond the bay, above the town,
O, winter of the kindly North,
  O, college of the scarlet gown,
And shining sands beside the sea,
  And stretch of links beyond the sand,
Once more I watch you, and to me
  It is as if I touch'd his hand!
And therefore art thou yet more dear,
  O, little city, gray and sere,
Though shrunken from thine ancient pride,
  And lonely by thy lonely sea,
Than these fair halls on Isis' side,
  Where Youth an hour came back to me.

A land of waters green and clear,
  Of willows and of poplars tall,
And in the spring-time of the year,
  The white may breaking over all,
And Pleasure quick to come at call;
  And summer rides by marsh and wold,
And Autumn with her crimson pall
  About the towers of Magdalen roll'd:
And strange enchantments from the past,
  And memories of the friends of old,
And strong Tradition, binding fast
  The flying terms with bands of gold,—
All these hath Oxford: all are dear,
  But dearer far the little town,
The drifting surf, the wintry year,
  The college of the scarlet gown:
St. Andrews by the Northern Sea,
That is a haunted town to me!

* C 921

EUGENE LEE-HAMILTON

SUNKEN GOLD

In dim green depths rot ingot-laden ships,
　　While gold doubloons that from the drowned hand fell
　　Lie nestled in the Ocean's flower bell
With Love's gemmed rings once kissed by now dead lips.
　　And round some wrought-gold cup the sea-grass whips
　　And hides lost pearls, near pearls still in their shell,
　　Where seaweed forests fill each ocean dell,
And seek dim sunlight with their countless tips.

So lie the wasted gifts, the long-lost hopes,
　　Beneath the now hushed surface of myself,
In lovelier depths than where the diver gropes
　　They lie deep, deep; but I at times behold
　　In doubtful glimpses, on some reefy shelf,
　　The gleam of irrecoverable gold.

SEA-SHELL MURMURS

The hollow sea-shell that for years hath stood
　　On dusty shelves, when held against the ear
　　Proclaims its stormy parent; and we hear
The faint far murmur of the breaking flood.

We hear the sea. The sea? It is the blood
　　In our own veins, impetuous and near,
　　And pulses keeping pace with hope and fear
And with our feelings' every shifting mood.

Lo, in my heart I hear, as in a shell,
　　The murmur of a world beyond the grave,
Distinct, distinct, though faint and far it be.

Thou fool; this echo is a cheat as well,—
　　The hum of earthly instincts; and we crave
A world unreal as the shell-heard sea.

WINE OF OMAR KHAYYÁM

HE rode the flame-winged dragon-steed of Thought
 Through Space and Darkness, seeking Heaven and Hell;
 And searched the furthest stars where souls might dwell
To find God's justice: and in vain he sought.

Then, looking on the dusk-eyed girl who brought
 His dream-filled wine beside his garden-well,
 He said: 'Her kiss; the wine-jug's drowsy spell;
Bulbul; the roses; death; . . . all else is nought:

So drink till that.'—What, drink, because the abyss
 Of Nothing waits? because there is for man
But one swift hour of consciousness and light?

No,—just because we have no life but this,
 Turn it to use; be noble while you can;
Search, help, create; then pass into the night.

D. M. DOLBEN

———

A SONG

THE world is young to-day:
 Forget the gods are old,
 Forget the years of gold
When all the months were May.

A little flower of love
 Is ours, without a root,
 Without the end of fruit,
Yet—take the scent thereof.

There may be hope above,
 There may be rest beneath;
 We see them not, but Death
Is palpable—and Love.

EDMUND GOSSE

LYING IN THE GRASS

Between two golden tufts of summer grass,
I see the world through hot air as through glass,
And by my face sweet lights and colours pass.

Before me, dark against the fading sky,
I watch three mowers mowing, as I lie:
With brawny arms they sweep in harmony.

Brown English faces by the sun burnt red,
Rich glowing colour on bare throat and head,
My heart would leap to watch them, were I dead!

And in my strong young living as I lie,
I seem to move with them in harmony,—
A fourth is mowing, and that fourth am I.

The music of the scythes that glide and leap,
The young men whistling as their great arms sweep,
And all the perfume and sweet sense of sleep,

The weary butterflies that droop their wings,
The dreamy nightingale that hardly sings,
And all the lassitude of happy things,

Is mingling with the warm and pulsing blood
That gushes through my veins a languid flood,
And feeds my spirit as the sap a bud.

Behind the mowers, on the amber air,
A dark-green beech-wood rises, still and fair,
A white path winding up it like a stair.

And see that girl, with pitcher on her head,
And clean white apron on her gown of red,—
Her even-song of love is but half-said:

She waits the youngest mower. Now he goes:
Her cheeks are redder than a wild blush-rose:
They climb up where the deepest shadows close.

But though they pass, and vanish, I am there;
I watch his rough hands meet beneath her hair,
Their broken speech sounds sweet to me like prayer.

Ah! now the rosy children come to play,
And romp and struggle with the new-mown hay;
Their clear high voices sound from far away.

They know so little why the world is sad,
They dig themselves warm graves and yet are glad;
Their muffled screams and laughter make me mad!

I long to go and play among them there;
Unseen, like wind, to take them by the hair,
And gently make their rosy cheeks more fair.

The happy children! full of frank surprise,
And sudden whims and innocent ecstasies;
What godhead sparkles from their liquid eyes!

No wonder round those urns of mingled clays
That Tuscan potters fashioned in old days,
And coloured like the torrid earth ablaze,

We find the little gods and loves portrayed,
Through ancient forests wandering undismayed,
And fluting hymns of pleasure unafraid.

They knew, as I do now, what keen delight,
A strong man feels to watch the tender flight
Of little children playing in his sight;

What pure sweet pleasure, and what sacred love,
Comes drifting down upon us from above,
In watching how their limbs and features move.

I do not hunger for a well-stored mind,
I only wish to live my life, and find
My heart in unison with all mankind.

My life is like the single dewy star
That trembles on the horizon's primrose-bar,—
A microcosm where all things living are.

And if, among the noiseless grasses, Death
Should come behind and take away my breath,
I should not rise as one who sorroweth;

For I should pass, but all the world would be
Full of desire and young delight and glee,
And why should men be sad through loss of me?

The light is flying; in the silver-blue
The young moon shines from her bright window through:
The mowers all are gone, and I go too.

WILLIAM ERNEST HENLEY

INVICTUS

Out of the night that covers me,
    Black as the pit from pole to pole,
I thank whatever gods may be
    For my unconquerable soul.

In the fell clutch of circumstance
    I have not winced nor cried aloud;
Under the bludgeonings of chance
    My head is bloody, but unbow'd.

Beyond this place of wrath and tears
    Looms but the Horror of the Shade,
And yet the menace of the years
    Finds and shall find me unafraid.

It matters not how strait the gate,
    How charged with punishments the scroll,
I am the master of my fate:
    I am the captain of my soul.

MARGARITAE SORORI

A LATE lark twitters from the quiet skies;
And from the west,
Where the sun, his day's work ended,
Lingers as in content,
There falls on the old, gray city
An influence luminous and serene,
A shining peace.

The smoke ascends
In a rosy-and-golden haze.   The spires
Shine and are changed.   In the valley
Shadows rise.   The lark sings on.   The sun,
Closing his benediction,
Sinks, and the darkening air
Thrills with a sense of the triumphing night—
Night with her train of stars
And her great gift of sleep.

So be my passing!
My task accomplish'd and the long day done,
My wages taken, and in my heart
Some late lark singing,
Let me be gather'd to the quiet west,
The sundown splendid and serene,
Death.

ROBERT LOUIS STEVENSON

THE VAGABOND

(TO AN AIR OF SCHUBERT)

GIVE to me the life I love,
  Let the lave go by me,
Give the jolly heaven above
  And the byway nigh me.
Bed in the bush with stars to see,
  Bread I dip in the river—
There 's the life for a man like me,
  There 's the life for ever.

Let the blow fall soon or late,
  Let what will be o'er me;
Give the face of earth around
  And the road before me.
Wealth I seek not, hope nor love,
  Nor a friend to know me;
All I seek, the heaven above
  And the road below me.

Or let autumn fall on me
  Where afield I linger,
Silencing the bird on tree,
  Biting the blue finger.
White as meal the frosty field—
  Warm the fireside haven—
Not to autumn will I yield,
  Not to winter even!

Let the blow fall soon or late.
  Let what will be o'er me;
Give the face of earth around
  And the road before me.

Wealth I ask not, hope nor love,
  Nor a friend to know me;
All I ask, the heaven above
  And the road below me.

THE ROADSIDE FIRE

I WILL make you brooches and toys for your delight
Of bird-song at morning and star-shine at night.
I will make a palace fit for you and me,
Of green days in forests and blue days at sea.

I will make my kitchen, and you shall keep your room,
Where white flows the river and bright blows the broom,
And you shall wash your linen and keep your body white
In rainfall at morning and dewfall at night.

And this shall be for music when no one else is near,
The fine song for singing, the rare song to hear!
That only I remember, that only you admire,
Of the broad road that stretches and the roadside fire.

BLOWS THE WIND TO-DAY

BLOWS the wind to-day, and the sun and the rain are flying,
  Blows the wind on the moors to-day and now,
Where about the graves of the martyrs the whaups are
    crying,
  My heart remembers how!

Grey recumbent tombs of the dead in desert places,
  Standing stones on the vacant wine-red moor,
Hills of sheep, and the homes of the silent vanished races,
  And winds austere and pure:

Be it granted to me to behold you again in dying,
  Hills of home! and to hear again the call;
Hear about the graves of the martyrs the peewees crying,
  And hear no more at all.

IN THE HIGHLANDS

IN the highlands, in the country places,
  Where the old plain men have rosy faces,
    And the young fair maidens
      Quiet eyes;
Where essential silence cheers and blesses,
And for ever in the hill-recesses
    Her more lovely music
      Broods and dies.

O to mount again where erst I haunted;
  Where the old red hills are bird-enchanted,
    And the low green meadows
      Bright with sward;
And when even dies, the million-tinted,
And the night has come, and planets glinted,
    Lo! the valley hollow,
      Lamp-bestarred.

O to dream, O to awake and wander
  There, and with delight to take and render,
    Through the trance of silence,
      Quiet breath;
Lo! for there, among the flowers and grasses,
Only the mightier movement sounds and passes;
    Only winds and rivers,
      Life and death.

REQUIEM

UNDER the wide and starry sky,
Dig the grave and let me lie.
Glad did I live and gladly die,
  And I laid me down with a will.

This be the verse you grave for me:
Here he lies where he long'd to be ;
Home is the sailor, home from sea,
  And the hunter home from the hill.

PHILIP BOURKE MARSTON

THE ROSE AND THE WIND

Dawn

THE ROSE

When think you comes the Wind,
The Wind that kisses me and is so kind?
Lo, how the Lily sleeps! her sleep is light;
Would I were like the Lily, pale and white!
Will the Wind come?

THE BEECH

       Perchance for thee too soon.

THE ROSE

If not, how could I live until the noon?
What, think you, Beech-tree, makes the Wind delay?
Why comes he not at breaking of the day?

THE BEECH

Hush, child, and, like the Lily, go to sleep.

THE ROSE

You know I cannot.

THE BEECH

       Nay, then, do not weep.
       (*After a pause*)
Thy lover comes, be happy now, O Rose!
He softly through my bending branches goes.
Soon he shall come, and you shall feel his kiss.

THE ROSE

Already my flushed heart grows faint with bliss;
Love, I have longed for thee through all the night.

THE WIND

And I to kiss thy petals warm and bright.

THE ROSE

Laugh round me, Love, and kiss me; it is well.
Nay, have no fear; the Lily will not tell.

Morning

THE ROSE

'Twas dawn when first you came; and now the sun
Shines brightly, and the dews of dawn are done.
'Tis well you take me so in your embrace,
But lay me back again into my place,
For I am worn, perhaps with bliss extreme.

THE WIND

Nay, you must wake, Love, from this childish dream.

THE ROSE

'Tis thou, Love, seemest changed; thy laugh is loud,
And 'neath thy stormy kiss my head is bowed.
O Love, O Wind, a space wilt thou not spare?

THE WIND

Not while thy petals are so soft and fair!

THE ROSE

My buds are blind with leaves, they cannot see.
O Love, O Wind, wilt thou not pity me?

Evening

THE BEECH

O Wind! a word with you before you pass:
What did you to the Rose, that on the grass
Broken she lies, and pale, who loved you so?

THE WIND

Roses must live and love, and winds must blow.

ALICE MEYNELL

THE SHEPHERDESS

SHE walks—the lady of my delight—
  A shepherdess of sheep.
Her flock are thoughts.   She keeps them white;
  She guards them from the steep.
She feeds them on the fragrant height,
  And folds them in for sleep.

She roams maternal hills and bright,
  Dark valleys safe and deep.
Into that tender breast at night
  The chastest stars may peep.
She walks—the lady of my delight—
  A shepherdess of sheep.

She holds her little thoughts in sight,
  Though gay they run and leap.
She is so circumspect and right;
  She has her soul to keep.
She walks—the lady of my delight—
  A shepherdess of sheep.

CHRIST IN THE UNIVERSE

WITH this ambiguous earth
His dealings have been told us.   These abide:
The signal to a maid, the human birth,
The lesson, and the young Man crucified.

  But not a star of all
The innumerable host of stars has heard
How He administered this terrestrial ball.
Our race have kept their Lord's entrusted Word.

Of His earth-visiting feet
None knows the secret, cherished, perilous,
The terrible, shamefast, frightened, whispered, sweet,
Heart-shattering secret of His way with us.

No planet knows that this
Our wayside planet, carrying land and wave,
Love and life multiplied, and pain and bliss,
Bears, as chief treasure, one forsaken grave.

Nor, in our little day,
May His devices with the heavens be guessed;
His pilgrimage to thread the Milky Way,
Or His bestowals there be manifest.

But in the eternities
Doubtless we shall compare together, near
A million alien Gospels, in what guise
He trod the Pleiades, the Lyre, the Bear.

O, be prepared, my soul!
To read the inconceivable, to scan
The million forms of God those stars unroll
When, in our turn, we show to them a Man.

RENOUNCEMENT

I MUST not think of thee; and, tired yet strong,
   I shun the thought that lurks in all delight—
   The thought of thee—and in the blue Heaven's height,
And in the sweetest passage of a song.

Oh, just beyond the fairest thoughts that throng
   This breast, the thought of thee waits, hidden yet bright;
   But it must never, never come in sight;
I must stop short of thee the whole day long.

But when sleep comes to close each difficult day,
    When night gives pause to the long watch I keep,
    And all my bonds I needs must loose apart,

Must doff my will as raiment laid away,—
    With the first dream that comes with the first sleep
    I run, I run, I am gathered to thy heart.

IN EARLY SPRING

O Spring, I know thee! Seek for sweet surprise
    In the young children's eyes.
But I have learnt the years, and know the yet
    Leaf-folded violet.
Mine ear, awake to silence, can foretell
    The cuckoo's fitful bell.
I wander in a grey time that encloses
    June and the wild hedge-roses.
A year's procession of the flowers doth pass
    My feet, along the grass.
And all you wild birds silent yet, I know
    The notes that stir you so,
Your songs yet half devised in the dim dear
    Beginnings of the year.
In these young days you meditate your part;
    I have it all by heart.

I know the secrets of the seeds of flowers
    Hidden and warm with showers,
And how, in kindling Spring, the cuckoo shall
    Alter his interval.
But not a flower or song I ponder is
    My own, but memory's.
I shall be silent in those days desired
    Before a world inspired.
O all brown birds, compose your old song-phrases
    Earth, thy familiar daisies!

A poet mused upon the dusky height,
   Between two stars towards night,
His purpose in his heart. I watched, a space,
   The meaning of his face:
There was the secret, fled from earth and skies,
   Hid in his grey young eyes.
My heart and all the Summer wait his choice,
   And wonder for his voice.
Who shall foretell his songs, and who aspire
   But to divine his lyre?
Sweet earth, we know thy dimmest mysteries,
   But he is lord of his.

A LETTER FROM A GIRL TO HER OWN OLD AGE

LISTEN, and when thy hand this paper presses,
O time-worn woman, think of her who blesses
What thy thin fingers touch, with her caresses.

O mother, for the weight of years that break thee!
O daughter, for slow time must yet awake thee,
And from the changes of my heart must make thee.

O fainting traveller, morn is grey in heaven.
Dost thou remember how the clouds were driven?
And are they calm about the fall of even?

Pause near the ending of thy long migration,
For this one sudden hour of desolation
Appeals to one hour of thy meditation.

Suffer, O silent one, that I remind thee
Of the great hills that stormed the sky behind thee,
Of the wild winds of power that have resigned thee.

Know that the mournful plain where thou must wander
Is but a grey and silent world, but ponder
The misty mountains of the morning yonder.

Listen:—the mountain winds with rain were fretting,
And sudden gleams the mountain-tops besetting.
I cannot let thee fade to death, forgetting.

What part of this wild heart of mine I know not
Will follow with thee where the great winds blow not,
And where the young flowers of the mountain grow not.

Yet let my letter with thy lost thoughts in it
Tell what the way was when thou didst begin it,
And win with thee the goal when thou shalt win it.

Oh, in some hour of thine my thoughts shall guide thee.
Suddenly, though time, darkness, silence, hide thee,
This wind from thy lost country flits beside thee,—

Telling thee: all thy memories moved the maiden,
With thy regrets was morning over-shaden,
With sorrow, thou hast left, her life was laden.

But whither shall my thoughts turn to pursue thee?
Life changes, and the years and days renew thee.
Oh, Nature brings my straying heart unto thee.

Her winds will join us, with their constant kisses
Upon the evening as the morning tresses,
Her summers breathe the same unchanging blisses.

And we, so altered in our shifting phases,
Track one another 'mid the many mazes
By the eternal child-breath of the daisies.

I have not writ this letter of divining
To make a glory of thy silent pining,
A triumph of thy mute and strange declining.

Only one youth, and the bright life was shrouded.
Only one morning, and the day was clouded.
And one old age with all regrets is crowded.

Oh, hush, oh, hush ! Thy tears my words are steeping.
Oh, hush, hush, hush ! So full, the fount of weeping?
Poor eyes, so quickly moved, so near to sleeping?

Pardon the girl; such strange desires beset her.
Poor woman, lay aside the mournful letter
That breaks thy heart; the one who wrote, forget her.

The one who now thy faded features guesses,
With filial fingers thy grey hair caresses,
With morning tears, thy mournful twilight blesses.

AT NIGHT
To W. M.

Home, home from the horizon far and clear,
 Hither the soft wings sweep;
Flocks of the memories of the day draw near
 The dovecote doors of sleep.

Oh, which are they that come through sweetest light
 Of all these homing birds?
Which with the straightest and the swiftest flight?
 Your words to me, your words !

FRANCIS WILLIAM BOURDILLON

THE NIGHT HAS A THOUSAND EYES

The night has a thousand eyes,
 And the day but one;
Yet the light of the bright world dies
 With the dying sun.

The mind has a thousand eyes,
 And the heart but one;
Yet the light of a whole life dies
 When love is done.

EDWARD CRACROFT LEFROY

THE FLUTE OF DAPHNIS
(An Echo from Theocritus)

I am the flute of Daphnis.   On this wall
   He nail'd his tribute to the great god Pan,
What time he grew from boyhood, shapely, tall,
   And felt the first deep ardours of a man.
   Through adult veins more swift the song-tide ran,—
A vernal stream whose swollen torrents call
   For instant ease in utterance.   Then began
That course of triumph reverenced by all.

Him the gods loved, and more than other men
   Blessed with the flower of beauty, and endow'd
His soul of music with the strength of ten.
   Now on a festal day I see the crowd
Look fondly at my resting-place, and when
   I think whose lips have press'd me, I am proud.

WILLIAM SHARP
(*Fiona Macleod*)

SHULE, SHULE, SHULE, AGRAH! [1]

His face was glad as dawn to me,
His breath was sweet as dusk to me,
His eyes were burning flames to me,
   Shule, Shule, Shule, agrah!

The broad noon-day was night to me,
The full-moon night was dark to me,
The stars whirled and the poles span
The hour God took him far from me.

Perhaps he dreams in heaven now,
Perhaps he doth in worship bow,
A white flame round his foam-white brow,
   Shule, Shule, Shule, agrah!

[1] I do not give the correct spelling of the Gaelic.   The line signifies 'Move, move, move to me, my Heart's Love.'—*Author's Note.*

I laugh to think of him like this,
Who once found all his joy and bliss
Against my heart, against my kiss,
   Shule, Shule, Shule, agrah!

Star of my joy, art still the same
Now thou hast gotten a new name?
Pulse of my heart, my Blood, my Flame,
   Shule, Shule, Shule, agrah!

MARGARET LOUISA WOODS

GAUDEAMUS IGITUR

Come no more of grief and dying!
Sing the time too swiftly flying.
     Just an hour
     · Youth's in flower,
Give me roses to remember
In the shadow of December.

Fie on steeds with leaden paces!
Winds shall bear us on our races,
     Speed, O Speed,
     Wind, my steed,
Beat the lightning for your master,
Yet my fancy shall fly faster.

Give me music, give me rapture,
Youth that's fled can none recapture;
     Not with thought
     Wisdom's bought.
Out on pride and scorn and sadness!
Give me laughter, give me gladness.

Sweetest Earth, I love and love thee,
Seas about thee, skies above thee,
      Suns and storms,
      Hues and forms
Of the clouds with floating shadows
On thy mountains and thy meadows.

Earth, there 's none that can enslave thee,
Not thy lords it is that have thee;
      Not for gold
      Art thou sold,
But thy lovers at their pleasure
Take thy beauty and thy treasure.

While sweet fancies meet me singing,
While the April blood is springing
      In my breast,
      While a jest
And my youth thou yet must leave me,
Fortune, 'tis not thou canst grieve me.

When at length the grasses cover
Me, the world's unwearied lover,
      If regret
      Haunt me yet,
It shall be for joys untasted,
Nature lent and folly wasted.

Youth and jests and summer weather,
Goods that kings and clowns together
      Waste or use
      As they choose,
These, the best, we miss pursuing
Sullen shades that mock our wooing.

Feigning Age will not delay it—
When the reckoning comes we 'll pay it.
      Our own mirth
      Has been worth
All the forfeit light or heavy
Wintry Time and Fortune levy.

Feigning grief will not escape it,
What though ne'er so well you ape it—
　　Age and care
　　All must share,
All alike must pay hereafter,
Some for sighs and some for laughter.

Know, ye sons of Melancholy,
To be young and wise is folly.
　　'Tis the weak
　　Fear to wreak
On this clay of life their fancies,
Shaping battles, shaping dances.

While ye scorn our names unspoken,
Roses dead and garlands broken,
　　O ye wise,
　　We arise,
Out of failures, dreams, disasters,
We arise to be your masters.

MARCH THOUGHTS FROM ENGLAND

O THAT I were lying under the olives,
Lying alone among the anemones!
Shell-colour'd blossoms they bloom there and scarlet,
Far under stretches of silver woodland,
Flame in the delicate shade of the olives.

O that I were lying under the olives!
Grey grows the thyme on the shadowless headland,
The long low headland, where white in the sunshine
The rocks run seaward.　It seems suspended
Lone in an infinite gulf of azure.

There, were I lying under the olives,
Might I behold come following seaward,
Clear brown shapes in a world of sunshine,
A russet shepherd, his sheep too, russet.
Watch them wander the long grey headland
Out to the edge of the burning azure.

O that I were lying under the olives!
So should I see the far-off cities
Glittering low by the purple water,
Gleaming high on the purple mountain;
See where the road goes winding southward.
It passes the valleys of almond blossom,
Curves round the crag o'er the steep-hanging orchards,
Where almond and peach are aflush 'mid the olives—
Hardly the amethyst sea shines through them—
Over it cypress on solemn cypress
Lead to the lonely pilgrimage places.

O that I were dreaming under the olives!
Hearing alone on the sun-steeped headland
A crystalline wave, almost inaudible,
Steal round the shore; and thin, far off,
The shepherd's music.   So did it sound
In fields Sicilian: Theocritus heard it,
Moschus and Bion piped it at noontide.

O that I were listening under the olives!
So should I hear behind in the woodland
The peasants talking.   Either a woman,
A wrinkled grandame, stands in the sunshine,
Stirs the brown soil in an acre of violets—
Large odorous violets—and answers slowly
A child's swift babble; or else at noon
The labourers come.   They rest in the shadow,
Eating their dinner of herbs, and are merry.

Soft speech Provençal under the olives!
Like a queen's raiment from days long perish'd,

Breathing aromas of old unremember'd
Perfumes and shining in dust-cover'd places
With sudden hints of forgotten splendour—
So on the lips of the peasant his language,
His only now, the tongue of the peasant.

Would I were listening under the olives!
So should I see in an airy pageant
A proud chivalrous pomp sweep by me;
Hear in high courts the joyous ladies
Devising of Love in a world of lovers;
Hear the song of the Lion-hearted,
A deep-voiced song—and O! perchance,
Ghostly and strange and sweet to madness,
Rudel sing the Lady of Tripoli.

GOOD FRIDAY NIGHT

Now lies the Lord in a most quiet bed.
     Stillness profound
Steeps like a balm the wounded body wholly,
More still than the hushed night brooding around.
     The moon is overhead,
Sparkling and small, and somewhere a faint sound
Of water dropping in a cistern slowly.
Now lies the Lord in a most quiet bed.

Now rests the Lord in perfect loneliness.
One little grated window has the tomb,
     A patch of gloom
Impenetrable, where the moonbeams whiten
     And arabesque its wall
With leafy shadows, light as a caress.
The palms that brood above the garden brighten,
     But in that quiet room
Darkness prevails, deep darkness fills it all.
Now rests the Lord in perfect loneliness.

Now sleeps the Lord secure from human sorrow.
The sorrowing women sometimes fall asleep
   Wrapped in their hair,
Which while they slumber yet warm tears will steep,
Because their hearts mourn in them ceaselessly.
   Uprising, half aware,
They myrrh and spices and rich balms put by
For their own burials, gather hastily,
   Dreaming it is that morrow
When they the precious body may prepare.
Now sleeps the Lord secured from human sorrow.

Now sleeps the Lord unhurt by Love's betrayal.
   Peter sleeps not,
He lies yet on his face and has not stirred
Since the iron entered in his soul red-hot.
The disciples trembling mourn their disillusion,
   That He whose word
Could raise the dead, on whom God had conferred
Power, as they trusted, to redeem Israel,
Had been that bitter day put to confusion,
   Crucified and interred.
Now sleeps the Lord unhurt by Love's betrayal.

Now rests the Lord, crowned with ineffable peace.
Have they not peace to-night who feared Him, hated
   And hounded to His doom,
The red thirst of their vengeance being sated?
No, they still run about and bite the beard,
   Confer, nor cease
To tease the contemptuous Pilate, are afeared
Still of Him tortured, crushed, humiliated,
   Cold in a blood-stained tomb.
Now rests the Lord, crowned with ineffable peace.

Now lies the Lord serene, august, apart,
That mortal life His mother gave Him ended.
   No word save one
Of Mary more, but gently as a cloud

On her perdurable silence has descended.
   Hush! In her heart
Which first felt the faint life stir in her son,
   Perchance is apprehended
Even now new mystery, grief less loud
Clamours, the Resurrection has begun.
Now lies the Lord serene, august, apart.

THOMAS WILLIAM ROLLESTON

THE DEAD AT CLONMACNOIS

FROM THE IRISH OF ANGUS O'GILLAN

In a quiet water'd land, a land of roses,
 Stands Saint Kieran's city fair;
And the warriors of Erin in their famous generations
 Slumber there.

There beneath the dewy hillside sleep the noblest
 Of the clan of Conn,
Each below his stone with name in branching Ogham
 And the sacred knot thereon.

There they laid to rest the seven Kings of Tara,
 There the sons of Cairbra sleep—
Battle-banners of the Gael that in Kieran's plain of crosses
 Now their final hosting keep.

And in Clonmacnois they laid the men of Teffra,
 And right many a lord of Breagh;
Deep the sod above Clan Creide and Clan Conaill,
 Kind in hall and fierce in fray.

Many and many a son of Conn the Hundred-Fighter
 In the red earth lies at rest;
Many a blue eye of Clan Colman the turf covers,
 Many a swan-white breast.

OSCAR WILDE

THE HARLOT'S HOUSE

WE caught the tread of dancing feet,
We loitered down the moonlit street,
And stopped beneath the harlot's house.

Inside, above the din and fray,
We heard the loud musicians play
The 'Treues Liebes Herz' of Strauss.

Like strange mechanical grotesques,
Making fantastic arabesques,
The shadows raced across the blind.

We watched the ghostly dancers spin
To sound of horn and violin,
Like black leaves wheeling in the wind.

Like wire-pulled automatons,
Slim silhouetted skeletons
Went sidling through the slow quadrille.

They took each other by the hand,
And danced a stately saraband;
Their laughter echoed thin and shrill.

Sometimes a clockwork puppet pressed
A phantom lover to her breast,
Sometimes they seemed to try to sing.

Sometimes a horrible marionette
Came out, and smoked its cigarette
Upon the steps like a live thing.

Then, turning to my love, I said,
The dead are dancing with the dead,
The dust is whirling with the dust.

But she—she heard the violin,
She left my side and entered in:
Love passed into the house of lust.

Then suddenly the tune went false,
The dancers wearied of the waltz,
The shadows ceased to wheel and whirl.

And down the long and silent street,
The dawn, with silver-sandalled feet,
Crept like a frightened girl.

JOHN DAVIDSON

A CINQUE PORT

BELOW the down the stranded town,
  What may betide forlornly waits,
With memories of smoky skies,
  When Gallic navies crossed the straits;
When waves with fire and blood grew bright,
And cannon thundered through the night.

With swinging stride the rhythmic tide
  Bore to the harbour barque and sloop;
Across the bar the ship of war,
  In castled stern and lanterned poop,
Came up with conquests on her lee,
The stately mistress of the sea.

Where argosies have wooed the breeze,
  The simple sheep are feeding now;
And near and far across the bar
  The ploughman whistles at the plough;
Where once the long waves washed the shore,
Larks from their lowly lodgings soar.

Below the down the stranded town
 Hears far away the rollers beat;
About the wall the seabirds call;
 The salt wind murmurs through the street;
Forlorn the sea's forsaken bride
Awaits the end that shall betide.

ALL HALLOWS' EVE

BASIL MENZIES BRIAN PERCY

BRIAN. Tearfully sinks the pallid sun.

MENZIES. Bring in the lamps: Autumn is done.

PERCY. Nay, twilight silvers the flashing drops;
 And a whiter fall is behind.

BRIAN. And the wild east mouths the chimney-tops,
 The Pandean pipes of the wind.

MENZIES. The dripping ivy drapes the walls;
 The drenched red creepers flare;
And the draggled chestnut plumage falls
 In every park and square.

PERCY. Nay, golden garlands strew the way
 For the old triumph of decay.

BASIL. And I know, in a living land of spells—
 In an excellent land of rest,
Where a crimson fount of sunset wells
 Out of the darkling west—

That the poplar, the willow, the scented lime,
 Full-leaved in the shining air,
Tarry as if the enchanter time
 Had fixed them deathless there.

In arbours and noble palaces
   A gallant people live,
With every manner of happiness
   The amplest life can give.

PERCY. Where? where?   In Elfland?

MENZIES. No; oh no!
   In Elfland is no rest,
But rumour and stir and endless woe
   Of the unfulfilled behest—
The doleful yoke of the Elfin folk
   Since first the sun went west.

The cates they eat and the wine they drink,
   Savourless nothings are;
The hopes they cherish, the thoughts they think
   Are neither near nor far;
And well they know they cannot go
   Even to a desert star:

One planet is all their poor estate,
   Though a million systems roll;
They are dogged and worried, early and late,
   As the demons nag a soul,
By the moon and the sun, for they never can shun
   Time's tyrannous control.

The haughty delicate style they keep
   Only the blind can see;
On holynights in the forest deep,
   When they make high revelry
Under the moon, the dancing tune
   Is the wind in a cypress tree.

They burn the elfin midnight oil
   Over their tedious lore;
They spin the sand; and still they toil
   Though their inmost hearts are sore—
The doleful yoke of the restless folk
   For ever and ever more.

But could you capture the elfin queen
   Who once was Caesar's prize,
Daunt and gyve her with glances keen
   Of unimpassioned eyes,
And hear unstirred her magic word,
   And scorn her tears and sighs,

Lean would she seem at once, and old;
   Her rosy mouth decayed;
Her heavy tresses of living gold
   All withered in the braid;
In your very sight the dew and the light
   Of her eyes would parch and fade;

And she, the immortal phantom dame,
   Would vanish from your ken;
For the fate of the elves is nearly the same
   As the terrible fate of men:
To love; to rue: to be and pursue
   A flickering wisp of the fen.

We must play the game with a careless smile,
   Though there's nothing in the hand;
We must toil as if it were worth our while
   Spinning our ropes of sand;
And laugh and cry, and live and die
   At the waft of an unseen wand.

But the elves, besides the endless woe
   Of the unfulfilled behest,
Have only a phantom life, and so
   They neither can die nor rest—
Have no real being at all, and know
   That therefore they never can rest—
The doleful yoke of the deathless folk
   Since first the sun went west.

PERCY. Then where is the wonderful land of spells,
Where a crimson fount of sunset wells,
And the poplar, the willow, the scented lime
Tarry, full-leaved, till the winter-time,
Where endless happiness life can give,
And only heroic people live?

BASIL. We know, we know, we spinners of sand!
In the heart of the world is that gracious land;
And it never can fade while the sap returns,
While the sun gives light, and the red blood burns.

A LOAFER

I HANG about the streets all day,
　　At night I hang about;
I sleep a little when I may,
　　But rise betimes the morning's scout;
For through the year I always hear
　　Afar, aloft, a ghostly shout.

My clothes are worn to threads and loops;
　　My skin shows here and there;
About my face like seaweed droops
　　My tangled beard, my tangled hair;
From cavernous and shaggy brows
　　My stony eyes untroubled stare.

I move from eastern wretchedness
　　Through Fleet Street and the Strand;
And as the pleasant people press
　　I touch them softly with my hand,
Perhaps to know that still I go
　　Alive about a living land.

For, far in front the clouds are riven;
   I hear the ghostly cry,
As if a still voice fell from heaven
   To where sea-whelmed the drowned folks lie
In sepulchres no tempest stirs
And only eyeless things pass by.

In Piccadilly spirits pass:
   Oh, eyes and cheeks that glow!
Oh, strength and comeliness!   Alas,
   The lustrous health is earth I know
From shrinking eyes that recognise
   No brother in my rags and woe.

I know no handicraft, no art,
   But I have conquered fate;
For I have chosen the better part,
   And neither hope, nor fear, nor hate.
With placid breath on pain and death,
   My certain alms, alone I wait.

And daily, nightly comes the call,
   The pale unechoing note,
The faint 'Aha!' sent from the wall
   Of heaven, but from no ruddy throat
Of human breed or seraph's seed,
   A phantom voice that cries by rote.

LONDON

Athwart the sky a lowly sigh
   From west to east the sweet wind carried;
The sun stood still on Primrose Hill;
   His light in all the city tarried:
The clouds on viewless columns bloomed
Like smouldering lilies unconsumed.

'Oh, sweetheart, see ! how shadowy,
　　Of some occult magician's rearing,
Or swung in space of heaven's grace
　　Dissolving, dimly reappearing,
Afloat upon ethereal tides
St. Paul's above the city rides !'

A rumour broke through the thin smoke
　　Enwreathing abbey, tower, and palace,
The parks, the squares, the thoroughfares,
　　The million-peopled lanes and alleys,
An ever-muttering prisoned storm,
The heart of London beating warm.

A BALLAD OF HEAVEN

HE wrought at one great work for years;
　　The world passed by with lofty look:
Sometimes his eyes were dashed with tears;
　　Sometimes his lips with laughter shook.

His wife and child went clothed in rags,
　　And in a windy garret starved:
He trod his measures on the flags,
　　And high on heaven his music carved.

Wistful he grew but never feared;
　　For always on the midnight skies
His rich orchestral score appeared
　　In stars and zones and galaxies.

He thought to copy down his score:
　　The moonlight was his lamp: he said,
'Listen, my love'; but on the floor
　　His wife and child were lying dead.

Her hollow eyes were open wide;
  He deem'd she heard with special zest:
Her death's-head infant coldly eyed
  The desert of her shrunken breast.

'Listen, my love: my work is done;
  I tremble as I touch the page
To sign the sentence of the sun
  And crown the great eternal age.

'The slow adagio begins;
  The winding-sheets are ravelled out
That swathe the minds of men, the sins
  That wrap their rotting souls about.

'The dead are heralded along;
  With silver trumps and golden drums,
And flutes and oboes, keen and strong,
  My brave andante singing comes.

'Then like a python's sumptuous dress
  The frame of things is cast away,
And out of Time's obscure distress
  The thundering scherzo crashes Day.

'For three great orchestras I hope
  My mighty music shall be scored:
On three high hills they shall have scope
  With heaven's vault for a sounding-board.

'Sleep well, love; let your eyelids fall;
  Cover the child; good-night, and if . . .
What? Speak . . . the traitorous end of all!
  Both . . . cold and hungry . . . cold and stiff!

'But no, God means us well, I trust:
  Dear ones, be happy, hope is nigh:
We are too young to fall to dust,
  And too unsatisfied to die.'

He lifted up against his breast
   The woman's body stark and wan;
And to her withered bosom pressed
   The little skin-clad skeleton.

'You see you are alive,' he cried.
   He rocked them gently to and fro.
'No, no, my love, you have not died;
   Nor you, my little fellow; no.'

Long in his arms he strained his dead
   And crooned an antique lullaby;
Then laid them on the lowly bed,
   And broke down with a doleful cry.

'The love, the hope, the blood, the brain,
   Of her and me, the budding life,
And my great music—all in vain!
   My unscored work, my child, my wife!

'We drop into oblivion,
   And nourish some suburban sod:
My work, this woman, this my son,
   Are now no more: there is no God.

'The world's a dustbin; we are due,
   And death's cart waits: be life accurst!'
He stumbled down beside the two,
   And clasping them, his great heart burst.

Straightway he stood at heaven's gate,
   Abashed and trembling for his sin:
I trow he had not long to wait,
   For God came out and led him in.

And then there ran a radiant pair,
   Ruddy with haste and eager-eyed
To meet him first upon the stair—
   His wife and child beatified.

They clad him in a robe of light,
　And gave him heavenly food to eat;
Great seraphs praised him to the height,
　Archangels sat about his feet.

God, smiling, took him by the hand,
　And led him to the brink of heaven:
He saw where systems whirling stand,
　Where galaxies like snow are driven.

Dead silence reigned; a shudder ran
　Through space; Time furled his wearied wings;
A slow adagio then began
　Sweetly resolving troubled things.

The dead were heralded along:
　As if with drums and trumps of flame,
And flutes and oboes keen and strong,
　A brave andante singing came.

Then like a python's sumptuous dress
　The frame of things was cast away,
And out of Time's obscure distress
　The conquering scherzo thundered Day.

He doubted; but God said 'Even so;
　Nothing is lost that's wrought with tears:
The music that you made below
　Is now the music of the spheres.'

A RUNNABLE STAG

WHEN the pods went pop on the broom, green broom,
　And apples began to be golden-skinned,
We harboured a stag in the Priory coomb,
　And we feathered his trail up-wind, up-wind,
　We feathered his trail up-wind—

A stag of warrant, a stag, a stag,
A runnable stag, a kingly crop,
Brow, bay and tray and three on top,
A stag, a runnable stag.

Then the huntsman's horn rang yap, yap, yap,
And 'Forwards' we heard the harbourer shout;
But 'twas only a brocket that broke a gap
In the beechen underwood, driven out,
From the underwood antlered out
By warrant and might of the stag, the stag,
The runnable stag, whose lordly mind
Was bent on sleep, though beamed and tined
He stood, a runnable stag.

So we tufted the covert till afternoon
With Tinkerman's Pup and Bell-of-the-North;
And hunters were sulky and hounds out of tune
Before we tufted the right stag forth,
Before we tufted him forth,
The stag of warrant, the wily stag,
The runnable stag with his kingly crop,
Brow, bay and tray and three on top,
The royal and runnable stag.

It was Bell-of-the-North and Tinkerman's Pup
That stuck to the scent till the copse was drawn.
'Tally ho! tally ho!' and the hunt was up,
The tufters whipped and the pack laid on,
The resolute pack laid on,
And the stag of warrant away at last,
The runnable stag, the same, the same,
His hoofs on fire, his horns like flame,
A stag, a runnable stag.

'Let your gelding be: if you check or chide
He stumbles at once and you're out of the hunt;
For three hundred gentlemen, able to ride,
On hunters accustomed to bear the brunt,
Accustomed to bear the brunt,

Are after the runnable stag, the stag,
The runnable stag with his kingly crop,
Brow, bay and tray and three on top,
The right, the runnable stag.'

By perilous paths in coomb and dell,
The heather, the rocks, and the river-bed,
The pace grew hot, for the scent lay well,
And a runnable stag goes right ahead,
The quarry went right ahead—
Ahead, ahead, and fast and far;
His antlered crest, his cloven hoof,
Brow, bay and tray and three aloof,
The stag, the runnable stag.

For a matter of twenty miles and more
By the densest hedge and the highest wall,
Through herds of bullocks he baffled the lore
Of harbourer, huntsman, hounds and all,
Of harbourer, hounds and all—
The stag of warrant, the wily stag,
For twenty miles, and five and five,
He ran, and he never was caught alive,
This stag, this runnable stag.

When he turned at bay in the leafy gloom,
In the emerald gloom where the brook ran deep,
He heard in the distance the rollers boom,
And he saw in a vision of peaceful sleep,
In a wonderful vision of sleep,
A stag of warrant, a stag, a stag,
A runnable stag in a jewelled bed,
Under the sheltering ocean dead,
A stag, a runnable stag.

So a fateful hope lit up his eye,
And he opened his nostrils wide again,
And he tossed his branching antlers high
As he headed the hunt down the Charlock glen,
As he raced down the echoing glen

For five miles more, the stag, the stag,
For twenty miles, and five and five,
Not to be caught now, dead or alive,
The stag, the runnable stag.

Three hundred gentlemen, able to ride,
   Three hundred horses as gallant and free,
Beheld him escape on the evening tide,
   Far out till he sank in the Severn Sea,
   Till he sank in the depths of the sea—
      The stag, the buoyant stag, the stag
      That slept at last in a jewelled bed
      Under the sheltering ocean spread,
   The stag, the runnable stag.

AGNES MARY FRANCES DUCLAUX
(ROBINSON-DARMESTETER)

———

ETRUSCAN TOMBS

I

To think the face we love shall ever die,
   And be the indifferent earth, and know us not!
To think that one of us shall live to cry
   On one long buried in a distant spot!

O wise Etruscans, faded in the night
   Yourselves, with scarce a rose-leaf on your trace;
You kept the ashes of the dead in sight,
   And shaped the vase to seem the vanished face.

But, O my love, my life is such an urn
   That tender memories mould with constant touch,
Until the dust and earth of it they turn
   To your dear image that I love so much:

A sacred urn, filled with the sacred past,
That shall recall you while the clay shall last.

II

These cinerary urns with human head
  And human arms that dangle at their sides,
The earliest potters made them for their dead,
  To keep the mother's ashes or the bride's.

O rude attempt of some long-spent despair—
  With symbol and with emblem discontent—
To keep the dead alive and as they were,
  The actual features and the glance that went!

The anguish of your art was not in vain,
  For lo, upon these alien shelves removed
The sad immortal images remain,
  And show that once they lived and once you loved.

But, oh, when I am dead may none for me
Invoke so drear an immortality!

III

Beneath the branches of the olive yard
  Are roots where cyclamen and violet grow;
Beneath the roots the earth is deep and hard,
  And there a king was buried long ago.

The peasants digging deeply in the mould
  Cast up the autumn soil about the place,
And saw a gleam of unexpected gold,
  And underneath the earth a living face.

With sleeping lids and rosy lips he lay,
  Among the wreaths and gems that mark the king,
One moment; then a little dust and clay
  Fell shrivelled over wreath and urn and ring.

A carven slab recalls his name and deeds,
Writ in a language no man living reads.

IV

Here lies the tablet graven in the past,
　　Clear-charactered and firm and fresh of line.
See, not a word is gone; and yet how fast
　　The secret no man living may divine!

What did he choose for witness in the grave?
　　A record of his glory on the earth?
The wail of friends?　The paeans of the brave?
　　The sacred promise of the second birth?

The tombs of ancient Greeks in Sicily
　　Are sown with slender disks of graven gold
Filled with the praise of death: thrice happy he
　　Who sleeps the milk-soft sleep of dreams untold.

They sleep their patient sleep in altered lands,
The golden promise in their fleshless hands.

MAY PROBYN

CHRISTMAS CAROL

Lacking samite and sable,
　　Lacking silver and gold,
The Prince Jesus in the poor stable
　　Slept, and was three hours old.

As doves by the fair water,
　　Mary, not touch'd of sin,
Sat by Him,—the King's daughter,
　　All glorious within.

A lily without one stain, a
　　Star where no spot hath room,
Ave, gratia plena—
　　Virgo Virginum!

Clad not in pearl-sewn vesture,
  Clad not in cramoisie,
She hath hush'd, she hath cradled to rest, her
  God the first time on her knee.

Where is one to adore Him?
  The ox hath dumbly confess'd,
With the ass, meek kneeling before Him,
  Et homo factus est.

Not throned on ivory or cedar,
  Not crown'd with a Queen's crown,
At her breast it is Mary shall feed her
  Maker, from Heaven come down.

The trees in Paradise blossom
  Sudden, and its bells chime—
She giveth Him, held to her bosom,
  Her immaculate milk the first time.

The night with wings of angels
  Was alight, and its snow-pack'd ways
Sweet made (say the Evangels)
  With the noise of their virelays.

Quem vidistis, pastores?
  Why go ye feet unshod?
Wot ye within yon door is
  Mary, the Mother of God?

No smoke of spice is ascending
  There—no roses are piled—
But, choicer than all balms blending,
  There Mary hath kiss'd her child.

Dilectus meus mihi
  Et ego Illi—cold
Small cheek against her cheek, He
  Sleepeth, three hours old.

MICHAEL FIELD

SONG

I COULD wish to be dead!
Too quick with life were the tears I shed,
Too sweet for tears is the life I led;
And, ah, too lonesome my marriage bed!
    I could wish to be dead.

I could wish to be dead,
For just a word that rings in my head;
Too dear, too dear are the words he said,
They must never be remembered.
    I could wish to be dead.

I could wish to be dead,
The wish to be loved is all mis-read,
And to love, one learns when one is wed,
Is to suffer bitter shame; instead
    I could wish to be dead.

SHEPHERD APOLLO

CLIMB with me, Laomedon's white fleeces,
Up to the hill tops, up to Ida,
To unshaded dews and earliest dawning.
Young and lustrous, god and yet a servant,
As a star past rock and tree I climb.
Raise your heads erect, ye flocks, and listen
To the note I strike from off my lyre!
They have heard, they stand each head erected;
Thus they wait the Grazing-Tune that woos
Slowly to the ridges and the sky.

I have struck it: all submissive listen,
Till they feed in mystery, advancing,

Drawn to solemn paces by a spell;
Then to sharper strains one way they hurry,
Fleece by fleece around me, till I strike
Sweet, soft notes that lay them down to slumber,
I beside them, where the sun no more
Falls across us, but the chilling moonlight:
There we sleep, my flock and I together,
I, a god, though servant of a king.

ROBERT OFFLEY ASHBURTON CREW-MILNES, MARQUESS OF CREWE

SEVEN YEARS

To join the ages they have gone,
       Those seven years,—
Receding as the months roll on;
Yet very oft my fancy hears
Your voice,—'twas music to my ears
       Those seven years.

Scant the shadow and high the sun
       Those seven years;
Can hearts be one, then ours were one,
One for laughter and one for tears,
Knit together in hopes and fears,
       Those seven years.

How, perchance, do they seem to you,
       Those seven years,
Spirit-free in the wider blue?
When Time in Eternity disappears,
What if all you have learn'd but the more endears
       Those seven years?

A HARROW GRAVE IN FLANDERS

1915

HERE in the marshland, past the battered bridge,
One of a hundred graves untimely sown,
Here with his comrades of the hard-won ridge
    He rests, unknown.

His horoscope had seemed so plainly drawn—
    School triumphs, earned apace in work and play;
Friendships at will; then love's delightful dawn
    And mellowing day.

Home fostering hope; some service to the State;
    Benignant age; then the long tryst to keep
Where in the yew-tree shadow congregate
    His fathers sleep.

Was here the one thing needful to distil
    From life's alembic, through this holier fate,
The man's essential soul, the hero will?
    We ask, and wait.

WILLIAM WATSON

ODE IN MAY

LET me go forth, and share
The overflowing Sun
With one wise friend, or one
Better than wise, being fair,
Where the pewit wheels and dips
On heights of bracken and ling,
And Earth, unto her leaflet tips,
Tingles with the Spring.

What is so sweet and dear
As a prosperous morn in May,
The confident prime of the day,
And the dauntless youth of the year,
When nothing that asks for bliss,
Asking aright, is denied,
And half of the world a bridegroom is,
And half of the world a bride?

The Song of Mingling flows,
Grave, ceremonial, pure,
As once, from the lips that endure,
The cosmic descant rose,
When the temporal lord of life,
Going his golden way,
Had taken a wondrous maid to wife
That long had said him nay.

For of old the Sun, our sire,
Came wooing the mother of men,
Earth, that was virginal then,
Vestal fire to his fire.
Silent her bosom and coy,
But the strong god sued and pressed;
And born of their starry nuptial joy
Are all that drink of her breast.

And the triumph of him that begot,
And the travail of her that bore,
Behold, they are evermore
As warp and weft in our lot.
We are children of splendour and flame,
Of shuddering, also, and tears.
Magnificent out of the dust we came,
And abject from the Spheres.

O bright irresistible lord,
We are fruit of Earth's womb, each one,
And fruit of thy loins, O Sun,
Whence first was the seed outpoured.
To thee as our Father we bow,
Forbidden thy Father to see,
Who is older and greater than thou, as thou
Art greater and older than we.

Thou art but as a word of his speech,
Thou art but as a wave of his hand;
Thou art brief as a glitter of sand
'Twixt tide and tide on his beach;
Thou art less than a spark of his fire,
Or a moment's mood of his soul:
Thou art lost in the notes on the lips of his choir
That chant the chant of the Whole.

LACRIMAE MUSARUM
(6TH OCTOBER 1892: THE DEATH OF TENNYSON)

Low, like another's, lies the laurelled head:
The life that seemed a perfect song is o'er:
Carry the last great bard to his last bed.
Land that he loved, thy noblest voice is mute.
Land that he loved, that loved him! nevermore
Meadow of thine, smooth lawn or wild sea-shore,
Gardens of odorous bloom and tremulous fruit,
Or woodlands old, like Druid couches spread,
The master's feet shall tread.
Death's little rift hath rent the faultless lute:
The singer of undying songs is dead.

Lo, in this season pensive-hued and grave,
While fades and falls the doomed, reluctant leaf
From withered Earth's fantastic coronal,
With wandering sighs of forest and of wave

Mingles the murmur of a people's grief
For him whose leaf shall fade not, neither fall.
He hath fared forth, beyond these suns and showers.
For us, the autumn glow, the autumn flame,
And soon the winter silence shall be ours:
Him the eternal spring of fadeless fame
Crowns with no mortal flowers.

What needs his laurel our ephemeral tears,
To save from visitation of decay?
Not in this temporal light alone, that bay
Blooms, nor to perishable mundane ears
Sings he with lips of transitory clay.
Rapt though he be from us,
Virgil salutes him, and Theocritus;
Catullus, mightiest-brained Lucretius, each
Greets him, their brother, on the Stygian beach;
Proudly a gaunt right hand doth Dante reach;
Milton and Wordsworth bid him welcome home;
Keats, on his lips the eternal rose of youth,
Doth in the name of Beauty that is Truth
A kinsman's love beseech;
Coleridge, his locks aspersed with fairy foam,
Calm Spenser, Chaucer suave,
His equal friendship crave:
And godlike spirits hail him guest, in speech
Of Athens, Florence, Weimar, Stratford, Rome.

Nay, he returns to regions whence he came.
Him doth the spirit divine
Of universal loveliness reclaim.
All nature is his shrine.
Seek him henceforward in the wind and sea,
In earth's and air's emotion or repose,
In every star's august serenity,
And in the rapture of the flaming rose.

There seek him if ye would not seek in vain,
There, in the rhythm and music of the Whole;
Yea, and for ever in the human soul
Made stronger and more beauteous by his strain.

For lo! creation's self is one great choir,
And what is nature's order but the rhyme
Whereto in holiest unanimity
All things with all things move unfalteringly,
Infolded and communal from their prime?
Who shall expound the mystery of the lyre?
In far retreats of elemental mind
Obscurely comes and goes
The imperative breath of song, that as the wind
Is trackless, and oblivious whence it blows.
Demand of lilies wherefore they are white,
Extort her crimson secret from the rose,
But ask not of the Muse that she disclose
The meaning of the riddle of her might:
Somewhat of all things sealed and recondite,
Save the enigma of herself, she knows.
The master could not tell, with all his lore,
Wherefore he sang, or whence the mandate sped:
Ev'n as the linnet sings, so I, he said:
Ah, rather as the imperial nightingale,
That held in trance the ancient Attic shore,
And charms the ages with the notes that o'er
All woodland chants immortally prevail!
And now, from our vain plaudits greatly fled,
He with diviner silence dwells instead,
And on no earthly sea with transient roar,
Unto no earthly airs, he sets his sail,
But far beyond our vision and our hail
Is heard for ever and is seen no more.

No more, O never now,
Lord of the lofty and the tranquil brow,
Shall men behold those wizard locks where Time
Let fall no wintry rime.

Once, in his youth obscure,
The weaver of this verse, that shall endure
By splendour of its theme which cannot die,
Beheld thee eye to eye,
And touched through thee the hand
Of every hero of thy race divine,
Ev'n to the sire of all the laurelled line,
The sightless wanderer on the Ionian strand.
Yes, I beheld thee, and behold thee yet:
Thou hast forgotten, but can I forget?
Are not thy words all goldenly impressed
On memory's palimpsest?
I hear the utterance of thy sovereign tongue,
I tread the floor thy hallowing feet have trod;
I see the hands a nation's lyre that strung,
The eyes that looked through life and gazed on God.

The seasons change, the winds they shift and veer;
The grass of yesteryear
Is dead; the birds depart, the groves decay:
Empires dissolve and peoples disappear:
Song passes not away.
Captains and conquerors leave a little dust,
And kings a dubious legend of their reign;
The swords of Caesars, they are less than rust:
The poet doth remain.
Dead is Augustus, Maro is alive;
And thou, the Mantuan of this age and soil,
With Virgil shalt survive,
Enriching Time with no less honeyed spoil,
The yielded sweet of every Muse's hive;
Heeding no more the sound of idle praise
In that great calm our tumults cannot reach,—
Master who crown'st our immelodious days
With flower of perfect speech.

ODE ON THE DAY OF THE CORONATION OF KING EDWARD VII

I

SIRE, we have looked on many and mighty things
In these eight hundred summers of renown
Since the Gold Dragon of the Wessex Kings
On Hastings field went down;
And slowly in the ambience of this crown
Have many crowns been gathered, till, to-day,
How many peoples crown thee, who shall say?
Time, and the ocean, and some fostering star,
In high cabal have made us what we are,
Who stretch one hand to Huron's bearded pines,
And one on Kashmir's snowy shoulder lay,
And round the streaming of whose raiment shines
The iris of the Australasian spray.
For waters have connived at our designs,
And winds have plotted with us—and behold,
Kingdom in kingdom, sway in oversway,
Dominion fold in fold:
Like to that immemorial regal stone
Thy namesake from the northland reft away,
Symbols of sovereignty and spoil of fray,
And closed in England's throne.
So wide of girth this little cirque of gold,
So great are we, and old.
Proud from the ages are we come, O King;
Proudly, as fits a nation that hath now
So many dawns and sunsets on her brow,
This duteous heart we bring.

II

The kings thy far forerunners; he that came
And smote us into greatness; he whose fame,
In dark armipotence and ivied pride,
Towers above Conway's tide,

And where Carnarvon ponders on the sea;
He, that adventurous name,
Who left at Agincourt the knightly head
Of France and all its charging plumes o'erthrown,
But hath in Shakespeare's conquest merged his own;
And she, a queen, yet fashioned king-like, she
Before whose prows, before whose tempests, fled
Spain on the ruining night precipitately;
And that worn face, in camps and councils bred,
The guest who brought us law and liberty
Raised well-nigh from the dead;
Yea, she herself, in whose immediate stead
Thou standest, in the shadow of her soul;
All these, O King, from their seclusion dread,
And guarded palace of eternity,
Mix in thy pageant with phantasmal tread,
Hear the long waves of acclamation roll,
And with yet mightier silence marshal thee
To the awful throne thou hast inherited.

III

Lo, at the Earth's high feast, ere Autumn bring
His afterthoughts on greatness to her ear,
And with monitions of mortality
Perturb the revelling year,
Thou goest forth and art anointed King.
Nature disdains not braveries: why should we
The sombre foil to all her splendours be?
Let London rustle with rich apparelling,
And all the ways, with festal faces lined,
Casement and coign and fluttering balcony,
Wave welcome on the wind.
Now the loud land flames with imperial gear,
And life itself, so late in hues austere
And the cold reign of iron custom bound,
Puts off its gray subjection, and is here

One moment throned and crowned.
Now the long glories prance and triumph by:
And now the pomps have passed, and we depart
Each to the peace or strife of his own heart:
And now the day whose bosom was so high
Sinks billowing down: and twilight sorceries change
Into remote and strange
What is most known and nigh:
And changelessly the river sends his sigh
Down leagues of hope and fear, and pride and shame,
And life and death; dim-journeying passionless
To where broad estuary and beaconing ness
Look towards the outlands whence our fathers came.
And high on Druid mountains hath the sun
Flamed valediction, as the last lights died
Beyond that fatal wave, that from our side
Sunders the lovely and the lonely Bride
Whom we have wedded but have never won.

IV

And night falls on an isle whose vassal seas
Remember not her prone regalities,
So withered from belief, so far and faint,
In such abjection before Time they lie,
Kingdoms and thrones forgotten of the sky.
Deira with her sea-face to the morn,
And Cumbria sunset-gazing; moist Dyvnaint,
A realm of coombs and tors; old greatnesses
From Dee to Severn, where the bards were born
Whose songs are in the wind by Idris' chair,
Whose lips won battles; and seats of puissance where,
With long grope of his desultory hand,
The ocean, prying deep into the land,
By Morven and the legends of wild Lorn,
Repents him, lost about Lochiel: all these
Have been and 'stablisht on their dust we stand;
Thy England; with the northern sister fair,

That hath the heath-bells in her blowing hair;
And the dark mountain maid
That dreams for ever in the wizard shade,
Hymning her heroes there.

V

O doom of overlordships! to decay
First at the heart, the eye scarce dimmed at all;
Or perish of much cumber and array,
The burdening robe of Empire, and its pall;
Or, of voluptuous hours the wanton prey,
Die of the poisons that most sweetly slay;
Or, from insensate height,
With prodigies, with light
Of trailing angers on the monstrous night,
Magnificently fall.
Far off from her that bore us be such fate,
And vain against her gate
Its knocking.   But by chinks and crannies, Death,
Forbid the doorways, oft-times entereth.
Let her drink deep of discontent, and sow
Abroad the troubling knowledge.   Let her show
Whence glories come, and wherefore glories go,
And what indeed are glories, unto these
'Twixt labour and the rest that is not ease
Made blank and darksome; who have hardly heard
Sound of her loftiest names, or any word
Of all that hath in gold been said and sung,
Since him of April heart and morning tongue,
Her ageless singing-bird.
For now the day is unto them that know,
And not henceforth she stumbles on the prize;
And yonder march the nations full of eyes.
Already is doom a-spinning, if unstirred
In leisure of ancient pathways she lose touch
Of the hour, and overmuch

Recline upon achievement, and be slow
To take the world arriving, and forget
How perilous are the stature and port that so
Invite the arrows, how unslumbering are
The hates that watch and crawl.
Nor must she, like the others, yield up yet
The generous dreams!　But rather live to be
Saluted in the hearts of men as she
Of high and singular election, set
Benignant in the sea;
That greatly loving freedom loved to free,
And was herself the bridal and embrace
Of strength and conquering grace.

ERNEST RHYS

THE LEAF BURNERS

UNDER two oak trees
　　on top of the fell,
With an old hawthorn hedge
　　to hold off the wind,
I saw the leaf burners
　　brushing the leaves
With their long brooms
　　into the blaze.
Above them the sky
　　scurried along
Pale as a plate,
　　and peered thro' the oaks,
While the hurrying wind
　　harried the hedge.
But fast as they swept
　　feeding the leaves
Into the flame
　　that flickered and fumed,

The wind, the tree-shaker,
  shaking the boughs,
Whirled others down
  withered and wan—
Summer's small folk,
  faded and fain
To give up their life;
  earth unto earth,
Ashes to ashes,
  life unto death.

Far on the fell
  where the road ran,
I heard the men march,
  in the mouth of the wind:
And the leaf burners heard
  and leaned down their heads,
Brow upon broom
  and let the leaves lie,
And counted their kin
  that crossed over sea,
And left wife and wean
  to fight in the war.

Forth over fell
  I fared on my way;
Yet often looked back,
  when the wind blew,
To see the flames coil
  like a curl of bright hair
Round the face of a child—
  a flower of fire,
Beneath the long boughs
  where lush and alive,
The leaves flourished long,
  loving the sun.

Much I thought then
   of men that went forth,
Or dropt like the leaves,
   to die and to live;
While the leaf burners
   with their long brooms
Drew them together
   on the day of their death.
I wondered at that,
   walking the fell—
Feeling the wind
   that wafted the leaves
And set their souls
   free of the smoke,
Free of the dead,
   speeding the flame
To spire on the air—
   a spark that should spring
In me, man of men;
   last of the leaves.

ALFRED EDWARD HOUSMAN

THE WEST

BEYOND the moor and mountain crest
—Comrade, look not on the west—
The sun is down and drinks away
From air and land the lees of day.

The long cloud and the single pine
Sentinel the ending line,
And out beyond it, clear and wan,
Reach the gulfs of evening on.

The son of woman turns his brow
West from forty counties now,
And, as the edge of heaven he eyes,
Thinks eternal thoughts, and sighs.

Oh wide 's the world, to rest or roam,
With change abroad and cheer at home,
Fights and furloughs, talk and tale,
Company and beef and ale.

But if I front the evening sky
Silent on the west look I,
And my comrade, stride for stride,
Paces silent at my side.

Comrade, look not on the west:
'Twill have the heart out of your breast;
'Twill take your thoughts and sink them far,
Leagues beyond the sunset bar.

Oh lad, I fear that yon 's the sea
Where they fished for you and me,
And there, from whence we both were ta'en,
You and I shall drown again.

Send not on your soul before
To dive from that beguiling shore,
And let not yet the swimmer leave
His clothes upon the sands of eve.

Too fast to yonder strand forlorn
We journey, to the sunken bourn,
To flush the fading tinges eyed
By other lads at eventide.

Wide is the world, to rest or roam,
And early 'tis for turning home:
Plant your heel on earth and stand,
And let 's forget our native land.

When you and I are spilt on air
Long we shall be strangers there;
Friends of flesh and bone are best:
Comrade, look not on the west.

THE FIRST OF MAY

THE orchards half the way
   From home to Ludlow fair
Flowered on the first of May
   In Mays when I was there;
And seen from stile or turning
   The plume of smoke would show
Where fires were burning
   That went out long ago.

The plum broke forth in green,
   The pear stood high and snowed,
My friends and I between
   Would take the Ludlow road;
Dressed to the nines and drinking
   And light in heart and limb,
And each chap thinking
   The fair was held for him.

Between the trees in flower
   New friends at fairtime tread
The way where Ludlow tower
   Stands planted on the dead.
Our thoughts, a long while after,
   They think, our words they say;
Theirs now 's the laughter,
   The fair, the first of May.

Ay, yonder lads are yet
   The fools that we were then;
For oh, the sons we get
   Are still the sons of men.

The sumless tale of sorrow
    Is all unrolled in vain:
May comes to-morrow
    And Ludlow fair again.

THE CULPRIT

THE night my father got me
    His mind was not on me;
He did not plague his fancy
    To muse if I should be
    The son you see.

The day my mother bore me
    She was a fool and glad,
For all the pain I cost her,
    That she had borne the lad
    That borne she had.

My mother and my father
    Out of the light they lie;
The warrant would not find them,
    And here 'tis only I
    Shall hang so high.

Oh let not man remember
    The soul that God forgot,
But fetch the county kerchief
    And noose me in the knot,
    And I will rot.

For so the game is ended
    That should not have begun.
My father and my mother
They had a likely son,
    And I have none.

FANCY'S KNELL

WHEN lads were home from labour
  At Abdon under Clee,
A man would call his neighbour
  And both would send for me.
And where the light in lances
  Across the mead was laid,
There to the dances
  I fetched my flute and played.

Ours were idle pleasures,
  Yet oh, content we were,
The young to wind the measures,
  The old to heed the air;
And I to lift with playing
  From tree and tower and steep
The light delaying,
  And flute the sun to sleep.

The youth toward his fancy
  Would turn his brow of tan,
And Tom would pair with Nancy
  And Dick step off with Fan;
The girl would lift her glances
  To his, and both be mute:
Well went the dances
  At evening to the flute.

Wenlock Edge was umbered,
  And bright was Abdon Burf,
And warm between them slumbered
  The smooth green miles of turf;
Until from grass and clover
  The upshot beam would fade,
And England over
  Advanced the lofty shade.

The lofty shade advances,
　　I fetch my flute and play:
Come, lads, and learn the dances
　　And praise the tune to-day.
To-morrow, more 's the pity,
　　Away we both must hie,
To air the ditty,
　　And to earth I.

FRANCIS THOMPSON

DAISY

WHERE the thistle lifts a purple crown
　　Six foot out of the turf,
And the harebell shakes on the windy hill—
　　O the breath of the distant surf!—

The hills look over on the South,
　　And southward dreams the sea;
And, with the sea-breeze hand in hand
　　Came innocence and she.

Where 'mid the gorse the raspberry
　　Red for the gatherer springs,
Two children did we stray and talk
　　Wise, idle, childish things.

She listened with big-lipped surprise,
　　Breast-deep mid flower and spine:
Her skin was like a grape, whose veins
　　Run snow instead of wine.

She knew not those sweet words she spake,
　　Nor knew her own sweet way;
But there 's never a bird, so sweet a song
　　Thronged in whose throat that day!

Oh, there were flowers in Storrington
  On the turf and on the spray;
But the sweetest flower on Sussex hills
  Was the Daisy-flower that day!

Her beauty smoothed earth's furrowed face
  She gave me tokens three:—
A look, a word of her winsome mouth,
  And a wild raspberry.

A berry red, a guileless look,
  A still word,—strings of sand!
And yet they made my wild, wild heart
  Fly down to her little hand.

For standing artless as the air,
  And candid as the skies,
She took the berries with her hand,
  And the love with her sweet eyes.

The fairest things have fleetest end,
  Their scent survives their close:
But the rose's scent is bitterness
  To him that loved the rose.

She looked a little wistfully
  Then went her sunshine way:—
The sea's eye had a mist on it,
  And the leaves fell from the day.

She went her unremembering way,
  She went and left in me
The pang of all the partings gone,
  And partings yet to be.

She left me marvelling why my soul
  Was sad that she was glad;
At all the sadness in the sweet,
  The sweetness in the sad.

Still, still I seemed to see her, still
  Look up with soft replies,
And take the berries with her hand,
  And the love with her lovely eyes.

Nothing begins, and nothing ends,
  That is not paid with moan;
For we are born in other's pain,
  And perish in our own.

THE FAIR INCONSTANT

Dost thou still hope thou shalt be fair,
  When no more fair to me?
Or those that by thee taken were
  Hold their captivity?
Is this thy confidence?   No, no;
Trust it not; it can not be so.

But thou too late, too late shalt find
  'Twas I that made thee fair;
Thy beauties never from thy mind
  But from my loving were;
And those delights that did thee stole
Confessed the vicinage of my soul.

The rosy reflex of my heart
  Did thy pale cheek attire;
And what I was, not what thou art,
  Did gazers-on admire.
Go, and too late thou shalt confess
I looked thee into loveliness!

THE MISTRESS OF VISION

SECRET was the garden;
Set i' the pathless awe
Where no star its breath can draw.
Life, that is its warden,
Sits behind the fosse of death.   Mine eyes saw not, and
     I saw.

It was a mazeful wonder;
Thrice three times it was enwalled
With an emerald—
Sealèd so asunder.
All its birds in middle air hung a-dream, their music thralled.

The Lady of fair weeping,
At the garden's core,
Sang a song of sweet and sore
And the after-sleeping;
In the land of Luthany, and the tracts of Elenore.

With sweet-pangèd singing
Sang she through a dream-night's day;
That the bowers might stay,
Birds bate their winging,
Nor the wall of emerald float in wreathèd haze away.

The lily kept its gleaming,
In her tears (divine conservers !)
Washèd with sad art;
And the flowers of dreaming
Palèd not their fervours,
· For her blood flowed through their nervures;
And the roses were most red, for she dipt them in her heart.

There was never moon,
Save the white sufficing woman:
Light most heavenly-human—

Like the unseen form of sound,
Sensed invisibly in tune,—
With a sun-derivèd stole
Did inaureole
All her lovely body round;
Lovelily her lucid body with that light was interstrewn.

The sun which lit that garden wholly,
Low and vibrant visible,
Tempered glory woke;
And it seemèd solely
Like a silver thurible
Solemnly swung, slowly,
Fuming clouds of golden fire, for a cloud of incense-smoke.

But woe 's me, and woe 's me,
For the secrets of her eyes!
In my visions fearfully
They are ever shown to be
As fringèd pools, whereof each lies
Pallid-dark beneath the skies
Of a night that is
But one blear necropolis.
And her eyes a little tremble, in the wind of her own sighs.

Many changes rise on
Their phantasmal mysteries.
They grow to an horizon
Where earth and heaven meet;
And like a wing that dies on
The vague twilight-verges,
Many a sinking dream doth fleet
Lessening down their secrecies.
And, as dusk with day converges,
Their orbs are troublously
Over-gloomed and over-glowed with hope and fear of
        things to be.

There is a peak on Himalay,
And on the peak undeluged snow,
And on the snow not eagles stray;
There if your strong feet could go,—
Looking over tow'rd Cathay
From the never-deluged snow—
Farthest ken might not survey
Where the peoples underground dwell whom antique fables
    know.

East, ah, east of Himalay,
Dwell the nations underground;
Hiding from the shock of Day,
For the sun's uprising-sound:
Dare not issue from the ground
At the tumults of the Day,
So fearfully the sun doth sound
Clanging up beyond Cathay;
For the great earthquaking sunrise rolling up beyond Cathay.

Lend me, O lend me
The terrors of that sound,
That its music may attend me,
Wrap my chant in thunders round;
While I tell the ancient secrets in that Lady's singing found.

On Ararat there grew a vine,
When Asia from her bathing rose,
Our first sailor made a twine
Thereof for his prefiguring brows.
Canst divine
Where, upon our dusty earth, of that vine a cluster grows?

On Golgotha there grew a thorn
Round the long-prefigured Brows.
Mourn, O mourn!
For the vine have we the spine? Is this all the Heaven
    allows?

On Calvary was shook a spear;
Press the point into thy heart—
Joy and fear!
All the spines upon the thorn into curling tendrils start.

O dismay!
I, a wingless mortal, sporting
With the tresses of the sun?
I, that dare my hand to lay
On the thunder in its snorting?
Ere begun,
Falls my singed song down the sky, even the old Icarian
way.

From the fall precipitant
These dim snatches of her chant
Only have remainèd mine;—
That from spear and thorn alone
May be grown
For the front of saint or singer any divinizing twine.

Her song said that no springing
Paradise but evermore
Hangeth on a singing
That has chords of weeping,
And that sings the after-sleeping
To souls which wake too sore.
'But woe the singer, woe!' she said; 'beyond the dead his
singing-lore,
All its art of sweet and sore
He learns, in Elenore!'

Where is the land of Luthany,
Where is the tract of Elenore?
I am bound therefor.

'Pierce thy heart to find the key;
With thee take
Only what none else would keep;
Learn to dream when thou dost wake,

Learn to wake when thou dost sleep.
Learn to water joy with tears,
Learn from fears to vanquish fears;
To hope, for thou dar'st not despair,
Exult, for that thou dar'st not grieve;
Plough thou the rock until it bear;
Know, for thou else couldst not believe;
Lose, that the lost thou may'st receive;
Die, for none other way canst live.
When earth and heaven lay down their veil,
And that apocalypse turns thee pale;
When thy seeing blindeth thee
To what thy fellow-mortals see;
When their sight to thee is sightless;
Their living, death; their light, most lightless;
Search no more—
Pass the gates of Luthany, tread the region Elenore.'

Where is the land of Luthany,
And where the region Elenore?
I do faint therefor.

'When to the new eyes of thee
All things by immortal power,
Near or far,
Hiddenly
To each other linkèd are,
That thou canst not stir a flower
Without troubling of a star;
When thy song is shield and mirror
To the fair snake-curlèd Pain,
Where thou dar'st affront her terror
That on her thou may'st attain
Perséan conquest; seek no more,
O seek no more !
Pass the gates of Luthany, tread the region Elenore.'

So sang she, so wept she,
Through a dream-night's day;
And with her magic singing kept she—
Mystical in music—
That garden of enchanting
In visionary May;
Swayless for my spirit's haunting,
Thrice-threefold walled with emerald from our mortal
    mornings grey.

And as a necromancer
Raises from the rose-ash
The ghost of the rose;
My heart so made answer
To her voice's silver plash,—
Stirred in reddening flash,
And from out its mortal ruins the purpureal phantom blows.

Her tears made dulcet fretting,
Her voice had no word,
More than thunder or the bird.
Yet, unforgetting,
The ravished soul her meanings knew. Mine ears heard
    not, and I heard.

When she shall unwind
All those wiles she wound about me,
Tears shall break from out me,
That I cannot find
Music in the holy poets to my wistful want, I doubt me!

THE HOUND OF HEAVEN

I FLED Him, down the nights and down the days;
    I fled Him, down the arches of the years;
I fled Him, down the labyrinthine ways
    Of my own mind; and in the mist of tears
I hid from Him, and under running laughter.

Up vistaed hopes I sped;
And shot, precipitated,
Adown Titanic glooms of chasmèd fears,
From those strong Feet that followed, followed after.
But with unhurrying chase,
And unperturbèd pace,
Deliberate speed, majestic instancy,
They beat—and a Voice beat
More instant than the Feet—
'All things betray thee, who betrayest Me.'

I pleaded, outlaw-wise,
By many a hearted casement, curtained red,
Trellised with intertwining charities;
(For, though I knew His love Who followèd,
Yet was I sore adread
Lest, having Him, I must have naught beside).
But, if one little casement parted wide,
The gust of His approach would clash it to.
Fear wist not to evade, as Love wist to pursue.
Across the margent of the world I fled,
And troubled the gold gateways of the stars,
Smiting for shelter on their clangèd bars;
Fretted to dulcet jars
And silvern chatter the pale ports o' the moon.
I said to Dawn: Be sudden—to Eve: Be soon;
With thy young skiey blossoms heap me over
From this tremendous Lover—
Float thy vague veil about me, lest He see!
I tempted all His servitors, but to find
My own betrayal in their constancy,
In faith to Him their fickleness to me,
Their traitorous trueness, and their loyal deceit.
To all swift things for swiftness did I sue;
Clung to the whistling mane of every wind.
But whether they swept, smoothly fleet,
The long savannahs of the blue;

Or whether, Thunder-driven,
They clanged his chariot 'thwart a heaven,
Plashy with flying lightnings round the spurn o' their
      feet:—
Fear wist not to evade as Love wist to pursue.
    Still with unhurrying chase,
    And unperturbèd pace,
  Deliberate speed, majestic instancy,
      Came on the following Feet,
      And a Voice above their beat—
'Naught shelters thee, who wilt not shelter Me.'

I sought no more that after which I strayed
    In face of man or maid;
But still within the little children's eyes
    Seems something, something that replies,
They at least are for me, surely for me!
I turned me to them very wistfully;
But just as their young eyes grew sudden fair
    With dawning answers there,
Their angel plucked them from me by the hair.
'Come then, ye other children, Nature's—share
With me' (said I) 'your delicate fellowship;
    Let me greet you lip to lip,
    Let me twine with you caresses,
      Wantoning
    With our Lady-Mother's vagrant tresses,
      Banqueting
    With her in her wind-walled palace,
    Underneath her azured daïs,
    Quaffing, as your taintless way is,
      From a chalice
Lucent-weeping out of the dayspring.'
      So it was done:
I in their delicate fellowship was one—
Drew the bolt of Nature's secrecies.
    I knew all the swift importings
    On the wilful face of skies;

I knew how the clouds arise
Spumèd of the wild sea-snortings;
　　All that 's born or dies
Rose and drooped with; made them shapers
Of mine own moods, or wailful or divine;
　　With them joyed and was bereaven.
　　I was heavy with the even,
　　When she lit her glimmering tapers
　　Round the day's dead sanctities.
　　I laughed in the morning's eyes.
I triumphed and I saddened with all weather,
　　Heaven and I wept together,
And its sweet tears were salt with mortal mine;
Against the red throb of its sunset-heart
　　I laid my own to beat,
　　And share commingling heat;
But not by that, by that, was eased my human smart.
In vain my tears were wet on Heaven's grey cheek.
For ah! we know not what each other says,
　　These things and I; in sound I speak—
Their sound is but their stir, they speak by silences.
Nature, poor stepdame, cannot slake my drouth;
　　Let her, if she would owe me,
Drop yon blue bosom-veil of sky, and show me
　　The breasts o' her tenderness:
Never did any milk of hers once bless
　　　My thirsting mouth.
　　　Nigh and nigh draws the chase,
　　　With unperturbèd pace,
　　Deliberate speed, majestic instancy;
　　　And past those noisèd Feet
　　　A voice comes yet more fleet—
　　'Lo! naught contents thee, who content'st not
　　　Me.'

Naked I wait Thy love's uplifted stroke!
My harness piece by piece Thou hast hewn from me,

And smitten me to my knee;
I am defenceless utterly.
I slept, methinks, and woke,
And, slowly gazing, find me stripped in sleep.
In the rash lustihead of my young powers,
I shook the pillaring hours
And pulled my life upon me; grimed with smears,
I stand amid the dust o' the mounded years—
My mangled youth lies dead beneath the heap.
My days have crackled and gone up in smoke,
Have puffed and burst as sun-starts on a stream.
Yea, faileth now even dream
The dreamer, and the lute the lutanist;
Even the linked fantasies, in whose blossomy twist
I swung the earth a trinket at my wrist,
Are yielding; cords of all too weak account
For earth with heavy griefs so overplussed.
Ah! is Thy love indeed
A weed, albeit an amaranthine weed,
Suffering no flowers except its own to mount?
Ah! must—
Designer infinite!—
Ah! must Thou char the wood ere Thou canst limn with it?
My freshness spent its wavering shower i' the dust;
And now my heart is as a broken fount,
Wherein tear-drippings stagnate, spilt down ever
From the dank thoughts that shiver
Upon the sighful branches of my mind.
Such is; what is to be?
The pulp so bitter, how shall taste the rind?
I dimly guess what Time in mists confounds;
Yet ever and anon a trumpet sounds
From the hid battlements of Eternity;
Those shaken mists a space unsettle, then
Round the half-glimpsèd turrets slowly wash again.
But not ere him who summoneth
I first have seen, enwound
With glooming robes purpureal, cypress-crowned;

His name I know, and what his trumpet saith.
Whether man's heart or life it be which yields
    Thee harvest, must Thy harvest fields
    Be dunged with rotten death?

    Now of that long pursuit
    Comes on at hand the bruit;
  That Voice is round me like a bursting sea;
    'And is thy earth so marred,
    Shattered in shard on shard?
Lo, all things fly thee, for thou fliest Me!
    Strange, piteous, futile thing!
Wherefore should any set thee love apart?
Seeing none but I makes much of naught' (He said),
'And human love needs human meriting:
    How hast thou merited—
Of all man's clotted clay the dingiest clot?
    Alack, thou knowest not
How little worthy of any love thou art!
Whom wilt thou find to love ignoble thee,
    Save Me, save only Me?
All which I took from thee I did but take,
    Not for thy harms,
But just that thou might'st seek it in My arms.
    All which thy child's mistake
Fancies as lost, I have stored for thee at home:
    Rise, clasp My hand, and come!'

    Halts by me that footfall:
    Is my gloom, after all,
Shade of His hand, outstretched caressingly?
    'Ah, fondest, blindest, weakest,
    I am He Whom thou seekest!
Thou dravest love from thee, who dravest Me.'

IN NO STRANGE LAND

THE KINGDOM OF GOD IS WITHIN YOU

O WORLD invisible, we view thee,
　O world intangible, we touch thee,
O world unknowable, we know thee,
　Inapprehensible, we clutch thee!

Does the fish soar to find the ocean,
　The eagle plunge to find the air—
That we ask of the stars in motion
　If they have rumour of thee there?

Not where the wheeling systems darken,
　And our benumbed conceiving soars!—
The drift of pinions, would we hearken,
　Beats at our own clay-shuttered doors.

The angels keep their ancient places;—
　Turn but a stone, and start a wing!
'Tis ye, 'tis your estrangèd faces,
　That miss the many-splendoured thing.

But (when so sad thou canst not sadder)
　Cry;—and upon thy so sore loss
Shall shine the traffic of Jacob's ladder
　Pitched betwixt Heaven and Charing Cross.

Yea, in the night, my Soul, my daughter,
　Cry,—clinging Heaven by the hems;
And lo, Christ walking on the water
　Not of Gennesareth, but Thames!

FROM *AN ANTHEM OF EARTH*

In nescientness, in nescientness,
Mother, we put these fleshly lendings on
Thou yield'st to thy poor children; took thy gift
Of life, which must, in all the after days,
Be craved again with tears,—
With fresh and still-petitionary tears.
Being once bound thine almsmen for that gift,
We are bound to beggary, nor our own can call
The journal dole of customary life,
But after suit obsequious for 't to thee.
Indeed this flesh, O Mother,
A beggar's gown, a client's badging,
We find, which from thy hands we simply took,
Naught dreaming of the after penury,
In nescientness.

In a little thought, in a little thought,
We stand and eye thee in a grave dismay,
With sad and doubtful questioning, when first
Thou speak'st to us as men: like sons who hear
Newly their mother's history, unthought
Before, and say—'She is not as we dreamed:
Ah me! we are beguiled!' What art thou, then,
That art not our conceiving? Art thou not
Too old for thy young children? Or perchance,
Keep'st thou a youth perpetual-burnishable
Beyond thy sons decrepit? It is long
Since Time was first a fledgeling;
Yet thou may'st be but as a pendant bulla
Against his stripling bosom swung. Alack!
For that we seem indeed
To have slipped the world's great leaping-time, and come
Upon thy pinched and dozing days: these weeds,
These corporal leavings, thou not cast'st us new,

Fresh from thy craftship, like the lilies' coats,
But foist'st us off
With hasty tarnished piecings negligent,
Snippets and waste
From old ancestral wearings,
That have seen sorrier usage; remainder-flesh
After our fathers' surfeits; nay with chinks,
Some of us, that, if speech may have free leave,
Our souls go out at elbows.   We are sad
With more than our sires' heaviness, and with
More than their weakness weak; we shall not be
Mighty with all their mightiness, nor shall not
Rejoice with all their joy.   Ay, Mother! Mother!
What is this Man, thy darling kissed and cuffed,
Thou lustingly engender'st,
To sweat, and make his brag, and rot,
Crowned with all honour and all shamefulness?
From nightly towers
He dogs the secret footsteps of the heavens,
Sifts in his hands the stars, weighs them as gold-dust,
And yet is he successive unto nothing
But patrimony of a little mould,
And entail of four planks.   Thou hast made his mouth
Avid of all dominion and all mightiness,
All sorrow, all delight, all topless grandeurs,
All beauty, and all starry majesties,
And dim transtellar things;—even that it may,
Filled in the ending with a puff of dust,
Confess—'It is enough.'   The world left empty
What that poor mouthful crams.   His heart is builded
For pride, for potency, infinity,
All heights, all deeps, and all immensities,
Arrased with purple like the house of kings,
To stall the grey-rat, and the carrion-worm
Statelily lodge.   Mother of mysteries!
Sayer of dark sayings in a thousand tongues,
Who bringest forth no saying yet so dark
As we ourselves, thy darkest!   We the young,

In a little thought, in a little thought,
At last confront thee, and ourselves in thee,
And wake disgarmented of glory: as one
On a mount standing, and against him stands,
On the mount adverse, crowned with westering rays,
The golden sun, and they two brotherly
Gaze each on each;
He faring down
To the dull vale, his Godhead peels from him
Till he can scarcely spurn the pebble—
For nothingness of new-found mortality—
That mutinies against his gallèd foot.
Littly he sets him to the daily way,
With all around the valleys growing grave,
And known things changed and strange; but he holds on
Though all the land of light be widowèd,
In a little thought.

    .   .   .   .

In a little dust, in a little dust,
Earth, thou reclaim'st us, who do all our lives
Find of thee but Egyptian villeinage.
Thou dost this body, this enhavocked realm,
Subject to ancient and ancestral shadows;
Descended passions sway it; it is distraught
With ghostly usurpation, dinned and fretted
With the still-tyrannous dead; a haunted tenement,
Peopled from barrows and outworn ossuaries.
Thou giv'st us life not half so willingly
As thou undost thy giving; thou that teem'st
The stealthy terror of the sinuous pard,
The lion maned with curlèd puissance,
The serpent, and all fair strong beasts of ravin,
Thyself most fair and potent beast of ravin;
And thy great eaters thou, the greatest, eat'st.
Thou hast devoured mammoth and mastodon,
And many a floating bank of fangs,
The scaly scourges of thy primal brine,
And the tower-crested plesiosaure.

Thou fill'st thy mouth with nations, gorgest slow
On purple aeons of kings; man's hulking towers
Are carcase for thee, and to modern sun
Disglutt'st their splintered bones.
Rabble of Pharaohs and Arsacidae
Keep their cold house within thee; thou hast sucked down
How many Ninevehs and Hecatompyloi
And perished cities whose great phantasmata
O'erbrow the silent citizens of Dis:—
Hast not thy fill?
Tarry awhile, lean Earth, for thou shalt drink,
Even till thy dull throat sicken,
The draught thou grow'st most fat on; hear'st thou not
The world's knives bickering in their sheaths? O patience!
Much offal of a foul world comes thy way,
And man's superfluous cloud shall soon be laid
In a little blood.

In a little peace, in a little peace,
Thou dost rebate thy rigid purposes
Of imposed being, and relenting, mend'st
Too much, with naught. The westering Phoebus' horse
Paws i' the lucent dust as when he shocked
The East with rising; O how may I trace
In this decline that morning when we did
Sport 'twixt the claws of newly-whelped existence,
Which had not yet learned rending? we did then
Divinely stand, not knowing yet against us
Sentence had passed of life, nor commutation
Petitioning into death. What 's he that of
The Free State argues? Tellus, bid him stoop,
Even where the low *hic jacet* answers him;
Thus low, O Man! there 's freedom's seignory,
Tellus' most reverend sole free commonweal,
And model deeply-policied: there none
Stands on precedence, nor ambitiously
Woos the impartial worm, whose favours kiss

With liberal largesse all; there each is free
To be e'en what he must, which here did strive
So much to be he could not; there all do
Their uses just, with no flown questioning.
To be took by the hand of equal earth
They doff her livery, slip to the worm,
Which lacqueys them, their suits of maintenance,
And, that soiled workaday apparel cast,
Put on condition: Death's ungentle buffet
Alone makes ceremonial manumission;
So are the heavenly statutes set, and those
Uranian tables of the primal Law.
In a little peace, in a little peace,
Like fierce beasts that a common thirst makes brothers,
We draw together to one hid dark lake;
In a little peace, in a little peace,
We drain with all our burthens of dishonour
Into the cleansing sands o' the thirsty grave
The fiery pomps, brave exhalations,
And all the glistering shows o' the seeming world,
Which the sight aches at, we unwinking see
Through the smoked glass of Death; Death, wherewith
      fined
The muddy wine of life; that earth doth purge
Of her plethora of man; Death, that doth flush
The cumbered gutters of humanity;
Nothing, of nothing king, with front uncrowned,
Whose hand holds crownets; playmate swart o' the strong
Tenebrous moon that flux and refluence draws
Of the high-tided man; skull-housèd asp
That stings the heel of kings; true Fount of Youth,
Where he that dips is deathless; being's drone-pipe;
Whose nostril turns to blight the shrivelled stars,
And thicks the lusty breathing of the sun;
Pontifical Death, that doth the crevasse bridge
To the steep and trifid God; one mortal birth
That broker is of immortality.
Under this dreadful brother uterine,

This kinsman feared, Tellus, behold me come,
Thy son stern-nursed; who mortal-motherlike,
To turn thy weanlings' mouth averse, embitter'st
Thine over-childed breast.   Now, mortal-sonlike,
I thou hast suckled, Mother, I at last
Shall sustenant be to thee.   Here I untrammel,
Here I pluck loose the body's cerementing,
And break the tomb of life; here I shake off
The bur o' the world, man's congregation shun,
And to the antique order of the dead
I take the tongueless vows: my cell is set
Here in thy bosom; my little trouble is ended
In a little peace.

HENRY CHARLES BEECHING

THE TREE OF LIFE

A RECOGNITION IN FOUR SEASONS

ARGUMENT

A prophet, desiring to recover for men the fruit of the Tree of
Life, seems to find Paradise by certain traditional signs of beauty in
nature.   He is further persuaded by observing the beauty and innocence
of children.   By and by he comes upon the Tree of Knowledge, whose
fruit, now old, he discerns to be evil; but from which, to his desire,
new is brought forth, which is good.   At each recognition one of
the Guardian Angels of the Tree of Life is withdrawn, until there is
left only the Angel of Death, in the light of whose sword he perceives it.
The Angels' songs are not heard by the prophet.

I. SPRING

Prophet

O TREE of Life, blissful tree,
Old as the world, still springing green,
Planted, watered by God; whose fruit
Hath year by year fallen about the root,
    And century by century;
Grant me that I thy glory unseen
    At last attain to see!

Chorus of Angels

The flame of our eyes still hideth
The fatal tree:
Which God in charge confideth
That none may see,
Till 'gainst our light advances
A purer ray,
And melts with fervid glances
Our swords of day.

Prophet

Considerate
lilia agri
quomodo
crescunt.

This garden I consider: If not the wise
Repute it Paradise,
The wise may err and ancient fame be lost;
As Ophir on the swart Arabian coast,—
Whence she, of Saba queen,
In silk raiment and gold,
Bearing spices manifold,
Not unlike this lily's purer sheen,
Came a weary way to salute Solomon,
Fainting to see, and fainted having seen
Such wisdom dazzled from his throne,—
    Now Ophir lies unknown;
Yet stumbling haply on gold, a man shall say
    Who feeds his flocks by the well,
    'Lo Ophir!' what if I to-day
A like token recover, and tell.

Chorus of Angels

The fire of our heart presages
(And gins to dim,)
That though through ageless ages
We wait for him,
He comes; our glory retires,
And shrinks from strife,
Folding in closer fires
The Tree of Life.

Prophet

Goeth up a mist,
To water the ground from the four streams at even;
Wrapt in a veil of amethyst
The trees and thickets wait for Spring to appear,
An angel out of heaven,
Bringing apparel new for the new year;
In the soft light the birds
Reset to the loved air the eternal words,
And in the woods primroses peer.

Angel of the Spring

He hath seen me with eyes of wonder
 And named my name,
My shield is riven in sunder,
 And quencht my frame:
My task is done, and rewarded,
 If faithfully;
By others now is guarded
 The Mystic Tree.

II. Summer

Prophet

O Tree of Life, blessed tree,
When shall I thy beauty attain to see?
New fledged ev'n now, new canopied with green,
(Not darkening ever as these in brooding heat,)
 To beasts of the field a screen,
A shadowy bower for weary eyes and feet:
 Tree by tree musing, I find not thee.

See, in the rippling water the children at play,
Flashing hither and thither, diamonded with spray;
Lithe and fair their limbs, their hearts light and gay—
 As fair as they of Niobe;

Sinite parvulos, etc.

Divinely fair, but too divinely famed;
    Not so now let it be.
Children of Adam these by birth proclaimed,
Clasping a mother's breast, a father's knee,
    By father's father named.
      Ay, but see, but see,
Their mien how high, how free their spirit!
    They are naked and not ashamed
Of that translucent veil, that symmetry.
    How they shout for glee!
It is the primal joy, and not the curse they inherit.
    A child of Adam, a child of God can he be?
    O look, look and see!

The Angels of Children

    His ear through nature's noises,
      Where'er he trod,
    Could hear in the children's voices
      The praise of God.
    Our task is done, and rewarded,
      If faithfully;
    By others now is guarded
      The Mystic Tree.

III. Autumn

Prophet

Say who are ye upon this bank reclining,
    At random laid,
Where loaded boughs a diaper intertwining
    Of fragrant shade,
Stretch down their fruits to cheer the heart's repining.

Dicit enim
Vetus
melius est.

They hear me not, asleep, or drunken, or (ah!) dead.
O Tree of Knowledge, 'tis thou, tree divine
Of good and ill;—trembling, I view thee.
To me, as them, thy golden apples incline,
Able to slake my thirst, or else undo me.

Which shall I pluck, which dread
Of all their goodlihead?
If roots be twain, from which there flows
To these elixir, poison to those,
How can I track their currents through the stem
Which bears and buries them?
Nay, but it cannot be the tree of good;
'Tis utter evil; to nearer view
The fruit dislustres, dull of hue,
All its ripe vermilion vanished,
Dead fruit, not human food;
And these mistaking souls from life are banished.
But see,—a wonder,—lo, on each branch swells
A new fruit ruddy-rinded, that smells
Freshly, and from their places in decay
The old shrivel, and drop away.
The ripeness allures to taste, O what should stay me?
Ill was the old, but the new is goodly and sweet;
A blessing is in it, desire to greet,
Not a curse to slay me;
(O divine the taste!)
Of the blind to open the eyes,
Deaf ears to unstop, make wise
The feeble-hearted, and to-day (O haste!)
For these poor dead the tree of life display!

Angel of the Tree of Divine Knowledge

The old fruit which evil bringeth
  He hath eschewed;
I breathe, and a new fruit springeth;
  He saw it good.
My task is done; and rewarded,
  If faithfully;
By others now is guarded
  The Mystic Tree.

IV. Winter

Prophet

I had thought ere this to have blest mine eyes
With thy vision benign, immortal tree;
For since that fruit, more than with Euphrasy,
My spirits are all alert, my sense more keen.
Nor is the north that chides with the script boughs
        An enemy, if it shows
All these but mortal, though in Paradise.
        But thou, O still unseen,
Come into sight; not yet I faint, but abide
And ever abide, yearning thee to behold.
Thee following, this girdling forest wide,
        My heart by hope made bold,
I have laboured through, and now emerge at length
Torn by the briers, spent my strength;
But branches wintry-bare deny the sheen
Of the amaranthine leaves and fruit of gold.
        Till now at last the light
Fails from my hope as from the heaven,
Where marshal the clouds, blown up with boisterous breath
The trees strain from the blast of death
Shrieking convulsed, so fierce the hail is driven
        Across the vault of night.
        And now the waving brand
        Of a cherub lightens down
        And rends the air with crashing din;
        Ah, if it be by God's command
        To show light in the darkness of nature's frown
        That I my purpose win!

Qui perdiderit animam suam inveniet.

It flashes and still flashes, and now I see
Beyond the blaze glooming a tree, a tree,
Stately and large,—(O light deceive not,
O weary eyes not now believe not!)—
Unseen before; to that I press,
Despite the tempest and limbs' tardiness.

Lighten, O sword divine, to clear my way,
And thou, O happy heart, upstay
Steps that falter and swerve, since few
Remain; come light again, I shall win through.

Angel of Death

My flame he hath not abhorred,
  Nor nature's strife,
But lightened through my sword,
  Hath passed to Life.
My task is done; and rewarded,
  If faithfully;
Henceforth no more is guarded
  The Mystic Tree.

DOUGLAS HYDE

MY GRIEF ON THE SEA

FROM THE IRISH

My grief on the sea,
  How the waves of it roll!
For they heave between me
  And the love of my soul!

Abandon'd, forsaken,
  To grief and to care,
Will the sea ever waken
  Relief from despair?

My grief and my trouble!
  Would he and I were
In the province of Leinster,
  Or County of Clare!

Were I and my darling—
    O heart-bitter wound !—
On board of the ship
    For America bound.

On a green bed of rushes
    All last night I lay,
And I flung it abroad
    With the heat of the day.

And my Love came behind me,
    He came from the South;
His breast to my bosom,
    His mouth to my mouth.

KATHERINE TYNAN HINKSON

THE DOVES

THE house where I was born,
Where I was young and gay,
Grows old amid its corn,
Amid its scented hay.

Moan of the cushat dove,
In silence rich and deep;
The old head I love
Nods to its quiet sleep.

Where once were nine and ten
Now two keep house together;
The doves moan and complain
All day in the still weather.

What wind, bitter and great,
Has swept the country's face,
Altered, made desolate
The heart-remembered place?

What wind, bitter and wild,
Has swept the towering trees
Beneath whose shade a child
Long since gathered heartsease?

Under the golden eaves
The house is still and sad,
As though it grieves and grieves
For many a lass and lad.

The cushat doves complain
All day in the still weather;
Where once were nine or ten
But two keep house together.

CHARLES G. D. ROBERTS

ON THE ROAD

Ever just over the top of the next brown rise
  I expect some wonderful thing to flatter my eyes.
'What 's yonder?' I ask of the first wayfarer I meet.
'Nothing!' he answers, and looks at my travel-worn feet.

'Only more hills and more hills, like the many you 've
    passed,
With rough country between, and a poor enough inn at
    the last.'
But already I am a-move, for I see he is blind,
And I hate that old grumble I 've listened to time out of
    mind.

I 've tramped it too long not to know there is truth in it
    still,
That lure of the turn of the road, of the crest of the hill.
So I breast me the rise with full hope, well assured I shall
    see
Some new prospect of joy, some brave venture a tip-toe
    for me.

For I have come far and confronted the calm and the strife.
I have fared wide, and bit deep in the apple of life.
It is sweet at the rind, but oh, sweeter still at the core;
And whatever be gained, yet the reach of the morrow is
    more.

At the crest of the hill I shall hail the new summits to climb.
The demand of my vision shall beggar the largest of time.
For I know that the higher I press, the wider I view,
The more's to be ventured and visioned, in worlds that are
    new.

So when my feet, failing, shall stumble in ultimate dark
And faint eyes no more the high lift of the pathway shall
    mark,
There under the dew I'll lie down with my dreams, for I
    know
What bright hill-tops the morning will show me, all red in
    the glow.

W. BLISS CARMAN

THE JOYS OF THE ROAD

Now the joys of the road are chiefly these:
A crimson touch on the hard-wood trees;

A vagrant's morning wide and blue,
In early fall, when the wind walks, too;

A shadowy highway, cool and brown,
Alluring up and enticing down

From rippled water to dappled swamp,
From purple glory to scarlet pomp;

The outward eye, the quiet will,
And the striding heart from hill to hill;

The tempter apple over the fence;
The cobweb bloom on the yellow quince;

The palish asters along the wood,—
A lyric touch of the solitude;

An open hand, an easy shoe,
And a hope to make the day go through,—

Another to sleep with, and a third
To wake me up at the voice of a bird;

A scrap of gossip at the ferry;
A comrade neither glum nor merry,

Who never defers and never demands,
But, smiling, takes the world in his hands,—

Seeing it good as when God first saw
And gave it the weight of His will for law.

And O the joy that is never won,
But follows and follows the journeying sun,

By marsh and tide, by meadow and stream,
A will-o'-the-wind, a light-o'-dream,

The racy smell of the forest loam,
When the stealthy, sad-heart leaves go home;

The broad gold wake of the afternoon;
The silent fleck of the cold new moon;

The sound of the hollow sea's release
From the stormy tumult to starry peace;

With only another league to wend;
And two brown arms at the journey's end!

These are the joys of the open road—
For him who travels without a load.

MARY COLERIDGE

EGYPT'S MIGHT IS TUMBLED DOWN

EGYPT's might is tumbled down,
    Down a-down the deeps of thought;
Greece is fallen and Troy town,
Glorious Rome hath lost her crown,
    Venice' pride is nought.

But the dreams their children dreamed,
    Fleeting, unsubstantial, vain,
Shadowy as the shadows seemed,
Airy nothing, as they dreamed,
        These remain.

NIGHT IS FALLEN

NIGHT is fallen, within, without,
    Come, Love, soon!
I am weary of my doubt.
The golden fire of the Sun is out,
    The silver fire of the Moon.

Love shall be
A child in me
    When they are cinders gray,
With the earth and with the sea,
With the star that shines on thee,
    And the night and day.

UNITY

THE sense of fellowship is grown
    A radiant mystery.
The dark is shot with light; the stone
    Is light unto the eyes that see.

No more the wild confusèd main
    Is tossed about with storms of fear.
The sea is singing; and the rain
    Is music to the ears that hear.

SEPTEMBER

Now every day the bracken browner grows,
    Even the purple stars
    Of clematis, that shone about the bars,
Grow browner; and the little autumn rose
    Dons, for her rosy gown,
    Sad weeds of brown.

Now falls the eve; and ere the morning sun,
    Many a flower her sweet life will have lost,
    Slain by the bitter frost,
Who slays the butterflies also, one by one,
    The tiny beasts
    That go about their business and their feasts.

HENRY CUST

NON NOBIS

Not unto us, O Lord,
Not unto us the rapture of the day,
The peace of night, or love's divine surprise,
High heart, high speech, high deeds 'mid honouring eyes;
For at Thy word
All these are taken away.

Not unto us, O Lord:
To us thou givest the scorn, the scourge, the scar,
The ache of life, the loneliness of death,
The insufferable sufficiency of breath;
And with Thy sword
Thou piercest very far.

Not unto us, O Lord:
Nay, Lord, but unto her be all things given—
May light and life and earth and sky be blasted—
But let not all that wealth of love be wasted:
Let Hell afford
The pavement of her Heaven!

MAURICE HEWLETT

———

FROM *THE SONG OF THE PLOW*

The Outlook

O WHAT see you from your gray hill?
The sun is low, the air all gold,
Warm lies the slumbrous land and still.
I see the river with deep and shallow,
I see the ford, I hear the mill;
I see the cattle upon the fallow;
　　And there the manor half in trees,
　　And there the church and the acre hallow
Where lie your dead in their feretories
　　Of clay and dust and crumble of peat,
　　With a stone or two to their memories:
Your dead who with their sweat kept sweet
　　This heritage of gray and green,
　　This England now the richer for it.
I see the yews and the thatch between,
　　The smoke that tells of cottage and hearth,
　　And all as it has ever been
From the beginning on this old earth.
　　And so it is even as it was
　　From the beginning in Hodge's garth,
While kings and statesmen flaunt and pass,
　　Kings and lords and knights of the shire,
　　Bishops in lawn (rare flesh to be grass !),
Priest and schoolman, clerk and esquire;
　　Danes and Normans and Scottishmen,
　　Frenchmen, Brunswickers, son after sire,
They come and conquer, they ruffle and reign,
　　They rule, they ride, they spend, they grudge,
　　They bicker their threescore years and ten,

They slay, and thieve, and go; but Hodge
  The Englishman stoops to fork and flail,
  And serves Saint Use, and will not budge,

aint Use

But drives the furrow and fills the pail,
  Raining sweat lest the land go dry:
  He sees his masters, he gives them hail
With hand to forelock as they ride by—
  They that eat what he doth bake,
  They that hold what he must buy,
They that spend what he doth make,
  They that are rich by other men's toil;
  They of the sword and he of the rake,
The lords of the land, the son of the soil!
  O Christ, the Patron of the Poor,
  Thou who didst suffer harlot's oil
Anoint Thy feet, O narrow Door!
  Thou who didst sanctify our dearth
  With bitter pain and anguish sore,
A barefoot King held nothing worth—
  Here's misery for Thy chrism to mend:
  A thousand years to plow the earth,
And be worse off at journey's end!

uestion

Thou mute and patient sojourner
  (So let us ask him, being his friend),
From what dim nation, by what spur
  Cam'st thou to serve this long duress?
  Whence came your fathers, hoping here
To win the land and to possess,
  And gained you for your broad domain
  A hireling's hire and wretchedness
After ten centuries of pain?

Pedigree

'No man can tell how old my stock.
My sires were here before the grain;
They reared that temple of gray rock
  Which in a hollow of the hills
  Seemeth our constancy to mock,
So little hurt crude usage skills
  To it, so much to mortal men.
  They shap't the mist-pool where distils
The blessed dew; they died and then
    They served their dead with barrow and mound.
    With wattled burghs on dun and pen
They made this Albion holy ground,
    Naming the mountains, pen and dun,
    Naming the waters.   First, they found
The lovely service of the sun.
    Then bowed their backs to Roman goads
    From sea to sea the Wall to run;
The furrows of the long white roads
    Are of their driven husbandry:
    We bruise their dust still with our loads.
Then came the English oversea
    Of onset wilder than was Rome's,
    And slew or made our men unfree,
But led our women to their homes
    To serve their needs of board and bed,
    And get them theows—and so it comes
That I am sprung unwarranted
    By priest or book or marriage line;
    Yet south and north my folk are spread
From Thames' mouth to the wells of Tyne.
    They moil aland like busy ants
    With pick and pack, and make no sign,
To sow and garner for the wants
    Of man and beast.   This is their hire,
    To cling about their ancient haunts
Tho' son be poorer than his sire.
    Now therefore you shall understand

My folk yet people every shire
From Lizard to Northumberland.
 They till the levels of the east,
  Where blown grass borders the sea-strand,
And in the dunes for man and beast
 They win their fodder. They make fat
 The lean, themselves they profit least;
But this is not to wonder at.
 Where Ouse and Trent and Humber coil
  'Twixt reedy marsh and meadow flat,
Where Thames grows turbid with the moil
 Of London's pool and London's mart,
 They bank the water into soil,
And spread the dung and lead the cart.
 Find you them in the stormy west
  Where from long Cleator to the Start
The land meets ocean, crest with crest,
 Throwing her rocky bastions up:
 There is my kindred's upland nest
Who lead their sheep for bite and sup
 By mountain path and waterfall
  To where the grass grows in a cup
Of rearing cliff and craggy wall.
 And thence the upland rivers race
  A nobler course; thence best of all
Flings Severn down, to earn her grace
 There where she broadens to the main
 And giveth Bristol pride of place.
Go seek my kith on hill and plain,
 Whether in Cumberland's deep dales,
  In York's dark moors or Lincoln's fen,
In Westmorland's hill-shadowed vales;
 From the scarred Peak and splintry Edge,
 By Salop's stony march with Wales,
To grassy boss and grassy ledge,
 To pastoral Wilts, to Somerset,
 To Dartmoor holding up her ridge
Against the west wind and the wet;

In billowy breadths of open down
  Where the bright rivers ripple and fret,
And each hill wears a beechen crown,
  And every village hides in trees;
  And on the heath, by market town,
By holt and brake, from Axe to Tees—
  Seek there, for there my root is thrown
  Between the Eastern and Western seas.
And whence my masters, whence their own,
  And wherefore over us they lord it
  Who are of England's marrow and bone,
The Use is so and doth award it.
  To them the land, to us the plow;
  They take the fruits when we have scored it,
But I eat bread in the sweat of my brow
  And hold my wife against my side,
  And love her when the lights are low,
And call her mine, and bid her bide
  The better or worse of tricksome years,
  As she promised when she was bride.
And so I, Hodge, make shift with my peers.'

Quousque Tandem?

Is it not his yet, this dear soil,
  Rich with his blood and sweat and tears?
Warm with his love, quick with his toil,
  Where kings and their stewards come and go,
  And take his earnings as tribute royal,
And suffer him keep a shilling or so?
  They come, they pass, their names grow dim;
  He bends to plow, or plies his hoe;
And what were they to the land or him?
  They shall perish but he endure
  (Thus saith the Scripture old and grim),
He shall shed them like a vesture;
  But he is the same, his tale untold;
  And to his son's sons shall inure
The land whereon he was bought and sold.

HENRY NEWBOLT

DRAKE'S DRUM

DRAKE he 's in his hammock an' a thousand mile away,
  (Capten, art tha sleepin' there below?),
Slung atween the round shot in Nombre Dios Bay,
  An' dreamin' arl the time o' Plymouth Hoe.
Yarnder lumes the Island, yarnder lie the ships,
  Wi' sailor-lads a-dancin' heel-an'-toe,
An' the shore-lights flashin', and the night-tide dashin',
  He sees et arl so plainly as he saw et long ago.

Drake he was a Devon man, an' ruled the Devon seas,
  (Capten, art tha sleepin' there below?),
Rovin' tho' his death fell, he went wi' heart at ease,
  An' dreamin' arl the time o' Plymouth Hoe.
'Take my drum to England, hang et by the shore,
  Strike et when your powder 's runnin' low;
If the Dons sight Devon, I 'll quit the port o' Heaven,
  An' drum them up the Channel as we drummed them
    long ago.'

Drake he 's in his hammock till the great Armadas come,
  (Capten, art tha sleepin' there below?),
Slung atween the round shot, listenin' for the drum,
  An' dreamin' arl the time o' Plymouth Hoe.
Call him on the deep sea, call him up the Sound,
  Call him when ye sail to meet the foe;
Where the old trade 's plyin' an' the old flag flyin'
  They shall find him ware an' wakin', as they found him
    long ago!

SRÁHMANDÁZI

DEEP embowered beside the forest river,
  Where the flame of sunset only falls,
Lapped in silence lies the House of Dying,
  House of them to whom the twilight calls.

There within when day was near to ending,
   By her lord a woman young and strong,
By his chief a songman old and stricken
   Watched together till the hour of song.

'O my songman, now the bow is broken,
   Now the arrows one by one are sped,
Sing to me the Song of Sráhmandázi,
   Sráhmandázi, home of all the dead.'

Then the songman, flinging wide his songnet,
   On the last token laid his master's hand,
While he sang the song of Sráhmandázi,
   None but dying men can understand.

'Yonder sun that fierce and fiery-hearted
   Marches down the sky to vanish soon,
At the self-same hour in Sráhmandázi
   Rises pallid like the rainy moon.

'There he sees the heroes by their river,
   Where the great fish daily upward swim;
Yet they are but shadows hunting shadows,
   Phantom fish in waters drear and dim.

'There he sees the kings among their headmen,
   Women weaving, children playing games;
Yet they are but shadows ruling shadows,
   Phantom folk with dim forgotten names.

'Bid farewell to all that most thou lovest,
   Tell thy heart thy living life is done;
All the days and deeds of Sráhmandázi
   Are not worth an hour of yonder sun.'

Dreamily the chief from out the songnet
   Drew his hand and touched the woman's head:
'Know they not, then, love in Sráhmandázi?
   Has a king no bride among the dead?'

Then the songman answered, 'O my master,
  Love they know, but none may learn it there;
Only souls that reach that land together
  Keep their troth and find the twilight fair.

'Thou art still a king, and at thy passing
  By thy latest word must all abide:
If thou willest, here am I, thy songman;
  If thou lovest, here is she, thy bride.'

Hushed and dreamy lay the House of Dying,
  Dreamily the sunlight upward failed,
Dreamily the chief on eyes that loved him
  Looked with eyes the coming twilight veiled.

Then he cried, 'My songman, I am passing;
  Let her live, her life is but begun;
All the days and nights of Sráhmandázi
  Are not worth an hour of yonder sun.'

Yet, when there within the House of Dying
  The last silence held the sunset air,
Not alone he came to Sráhmandázi,
  Not alone she found the twilight fair:

While the songman, far beneath the forest,
  Sang of Sráhmandázi all night through,
'Lovely be thy name, O Land of Shadows,
  Land of meeting, Land of all the true!'

COMMEMORATION

I SAT by the granite pillar, and sunlight fell
  Where the sunlight fell of old,
And the hour was the hour my heart remembered well,
  And the sermon rolled and rolled
As it used to roll when the place was still unhaunted,
And the strangest tale in the world was still untold.

And I knew that of all this rushing of urgent sound
    That I so clearly heard,
The green young forest of saplings clustered round
    Was heeding not one word:
Their heads were bowed in a still serried patience
Such as an angel's breath could never have stirred.

For some were already away to the hazardous pitch,
    Or lining the parapet wall,
And some were in glorious battle, or great and rich,
    Or throned in a college hall:
And among the rest was one like my own young phantom,
Dreaming for ever beyond my utmost call.

'O Youth,' the preacher was crying, 'deem not thou
    Thy life is thine alone;
Thou bearest the will of the ages, seeing how
    They built thee bone by bone,
And within thy blood the Great Age sleeps sepulchred
Till thou and thine shall roll away the stone.

'Therefore the days are coming when thou shalt burn
    With passion whitely hot;
Rest shall be rest no more; thy feet shall spurn
    All that thy hand hath got;
And One that is stronger shall gird thee, and lead thee swiftly
Whither, O heart of Youth, thou wouldest not.'

And the School passed; and I saw the living and dead
    Set in their seats again,
And I longed to hear them speak of the word that was said,
    But I knew that I longed in vain.
And they stretched forth their hands, and the wind of the
       spirit took them
Lightly as drifted leaves on an endless plain.

THE DEATH OF ADMIRAL BLAKE
(*August 7th,* 1657)

LADEN with spoil of the South, fulfilled with the glory of
    achievement,
    And freshly crowned with never-dying fame,
Sweeping by shores where the names are the names of the
    victories of England
    Across the Bay the squadron homeward came.

Proudly they came, but their pride was the pomp of a funeral
    at midnight,
    When dreader yet the lonely morrow looms;
Few are the words that are spoken, and faces are gaunt
    beneath the torchlight
    That does but darken more the nodding plumes.

Low on the field of his fame, past hope lay the Admiral
    triumphant,
    And fain to rest him after all his pain;
Yet for the love that he bore to his own land, ever un-
    forgotten,
    He prayed to see the western hills again.

Fainter than stars in a sky long gray with the coming of the
    daybreak,
    Or sounds of night that fade when night is done,
So in the death-dawn faded the splendour and loud renown
    of warfare,
And life of all its longings kept but one.

Oh! to be there for an hour when the shade draws in beside
    the hedgerows,
    And falling apples wake the drowsy noon:
Oh! for the hour when the elms grow sombre and human
    in the twilight,
    And gardens dream beneath the rising moon.

'Only to look once more on the land of the memories of
        childhood,
    Forgetting weary winds and barren foam:
Only to bid farewell to the combe and the orchard and the
        moorland,
    And sleep at last among the fields of home!'

So he was silently praying, till now, when his strength was
        ebbing faster,
    The Lizard lay before them faintly blue;
Now on the gleaming horizon the white cliffs laughed along
        the coast-line,
    And now the forelands took the shapes they knew.

There lay the Sound and the Island with green leaves down
        beside the water,
    The town, the Hoe, the masts with sunset fired—
Dreams! ay, dreams of the dead! for the great heart faltered
        on the threshold,
    And darkness took the land his soul desired.

ARTHUR CHRISTOPHER BENSON

THE HAWK

THE hawk slipt out of the pine, and rose in the sunlit air:
Steady and still he poised; his shadow slept on the grass:
And the bird's song sickened and sank: she cowered with
        furtive stare,
Dumb, till the quivering dimness should flicker and shift
        and pass.

Suddenly down he dropped. She heard the hiss of his
        wing,
Fled with a scream of terror: oh, would she had dared
        to rest!
For the hawk at eve was full, and there was no bird to sing,
And over the heather drifted the down from a bleeding
        breast.

IN A COLLEGE GARDEN

Birds, that cry so loud in the old
  green bowery garden,
  Your song is of *Love! Love! Love!* Will
   ye weary not nor cease?
For the loveless soul grows sick, the heart
   that the grey days harden;
  I know too well that ye love!   I would ye
   should hold your peace.

I too have seen Love rise like a star: I have
   marked his setting;
  I dreamed in my folly and pride that Life
   without Love were peace.
But if Love should await me yet, in the land
   of sleep and forgetting—
  Ah, bird, could you sing me this, I would
   not your song should cease!

EVENSONG

Thrush, sing clear, for the spring is here:
Sing, for the summer is near, is near,

All day long thou hast plied thy song,
Hardly hid from the hurrying throng:

Now the shade of the trees is laid
Down the meadow and up the glade:

Now when the air grows cool and rare
Birds of the cloister fall to prayer:

Here is the bed of the patient dead,
Shoulder by shoulder, head by head.

Sweet bells swing in the tower, and ring
Men to worship before their King.

See they come as the grave bells hum,
Restless voices awhile are dumb:

More and more on the sacred floor,
Feet that linger about the door:

Sweet sounds swim through the vaulting dim,
Psalm and canticle, vesper hymn.

That is the way that mortals pray:
Which is the sweeter? brown bird, say!

Which were best for me? both are blest;
Sing thy sweetest and leave the rest.

NORMAN GALE

THE COUNTRY FAITH

HERE in the country's heart,
Where the grass is green,
Life is the same sweet life
As it e'er hath been.

Trust in a God still lives,
And the bell at morn
Floats with a thought of God
O'er the rising corn.

God comes down in the rain,
And the crop grows tall—
This is the country faith,
And the best of all.

THE SHADED POOL

A LAUGHING knot of village maids
Goes gaily tripping to the brook,
For water-nymphs they mean to be,
And seek some still, secluded nook.
Here Laura goes, my own delight,
And Colin's love, the madcap Jane,
And half a score of goddesses
Trip over daisies in the plain:
Already now thy loose their hair
And peep from out the tangled gold,
Or speed the flying foot to reach
The brook that 's only summer-cold;
The lovely locks stream out behind
The shepherdesses on the wing,
And Laura's is the wealth I love,
And Laura's is the gold I sing.

A-row upon the bank they pant,
And all unlace the country shoe;
Their fingers tug the garter-knots
To loose the hose of varied hue.
The flashing knee at last appears,
The lower curves of youth and grace,
Whereat the girls intently scan
The mazy thickets of the place.
But who 's to see except the thrush
Upon the wild crab-apple tree?
Within his branchy haunt he sits—
A very Peeping Tom is he!
Now music bubbles in his throat,
And now he pipes the scene in song—
The virgins slipping from their robes,
The cheated stockings lean and long,
The swift-descending petticoat,
The breasts that heave because they ran,
The rounded arms, the brilliant limbs,
The pretty necklaces of tan.

Did ever amorous god in Greece,
In search of some young mouth to kiss,
By any river chance upon
A sylvan scene as bright as this?
But though each maid is pure and fair,
For one alone my heart I bring,
And Laura's is the shape I love,
And Laura's is the snow I sing.

And now upon the brook's green brink,
A milk-white bevy, lo, they stand,
Half shy, half frighten'd, reaching back
The beauty of a poising hand!
How musical their little screams
When ripples kiss their shrinking feet!
And then the brook embraces all
Till gold and white the water meet!
Within the streamlet's soft cool arms
Delight and love and gracefulness
Sport till a flock of tiny waves
Swamps all the beds of floating cress;
And on his shining face are seen
Great yellow lilies drifting down
Beyond the ringing apple-tree,
Beyond the empty homespun gown.
Did ever Orpheus with his lute,
When making melody of old,
E'er find a stream in Attica
So ripely full of pink and gold?

At last they climb the sloping bank
And shake upon the thirsty soil
A treasury of diamond-drops
Not gained by aught of grimy toil.
Again the garters clasp the hose,
Again the velvet knee is hid,
Again the breathless babble tells
What Colin said, what Colin did.

In grace upon the grass they lie
And spread their tresses to the sun,
And rival, musical as they,
The blackbird's alto shake and run.
Did ever Love, on hunting bent,
Come idly humming through the hay,
And, to his sudden joyfulness,
Find fairer game at close of day?
Though every maid 's a lily-rose,
And meet to sway a sceptred king,
Yet Laura's is the face I love,
And Laura's are the lips I sing.

SONG

FIRST the fine, faint, dreamy motion
    Of the tender blood
Circling in the veins of children—
    This is Life, the bud.

Next the fresh, advancing beauty
    Growing from the gloom,
Waking eyes and fairer bosom—
    This is Life, the bloom.

Then the pain that follows after,
    Grievous to be borne,
Pricking, steeped in subtle poison—
    This is Love, the thorn.

TO THE SWEETWILLIAM

I SEARCH the poets' honied lines,
And not in vain, for columbines;
And not in vain for other flowers
That sanctify the many bowers
Unsanctified by human souls.
See where the larkspur lifts among

The thousand blossoms finely sung,
Still blossoming in the fragrant scrolls!
   Charity, eglantine, and rue
   And love-in-a-mist are all in view,
     With coloured cousins; but where are you,
        Sweetwilliam?

The lily and the rose have books
Devoted to their lovely looks,
And wit has fallen in vital showers
Through England's most miraculous hours
To keep them fresh a thousand years.
The immortal library can show
The violet's well-thumbed folio
Stained tenderly by girls in tears.
   The shelf where Genius stands in view
   Has briar and daffodil and rue
     And love-lies-bleeding; but not you,
        Sweetwilliam.

Thus, if I seek the classic line
For marybuds, 'tis Shakespeare, thine!
And ever is the primrose born
'Neath Goldsmith's overhanging thorn.
In Herrick's breastknot I can see
The apple blossom, fresh and fair
As when he plucked and put it there,
Heedless of Time's anthology.
   So flower by flower comes into view,
   Kept fadeless by the Olympian dew
     For startled eyes; and yet not you,
        Sweetwilliam.

Too seldom named! And never so
As makes the astonished heart to go
With deer-like leapings! Horace found
A name unsuited to the bound
His gleaming satires had to bear:

Even so, methinks, a want of grace
In country calling lost a place
In poesy for one so fair.
   How chancily a blossom slips
   From ballad sunshine to eclipse,
   Being short of honey for the lips,
            Sweetwilliam!

Though gods of song have let you be,
Bloom in my little book for me.
Unwont to stoop or lean, you show
An undefeated heart, and grow
As pluckily as cedars.   Heat
And cold, and winds that make
Tumbledown sallies, cannot shake
Your resolution to be sweet.
   Then take this song, be it born to die
   Ere yet the unwedded butterfly
   Has glimpsed a darling in the sky,
            Sweetwilliam!

ARTHUR QUILLER-COUCH

UPON ECKINGTON BRIDGE, RIVER AVON

O PASTORAL heart of England! like a psalm
   Of green days telling with a quiet beat—
O wave into the sunset flowing calm!
   O tirèd lark descending on the wheat!
Lies it all peace beyond that western fold
   Where now the lingering shepherd sees his star
Rise upon Malvern?   Paints an Age of Gold
      Yon cloud with prophecies of linkèd ease—
      Lulling this Land, with hills drawn up like knees,
   To drowse beside her implements of war?

Man shall outlast his battles.   They have swept
   Avon from Naseby Field to Severn Ham;

And Evesham's dedicated stones have stepp'd
  Down to the dust with Montfort's oriflame.
Nor the red tear nor the reflected tower
  Abides; but yet these eloquent grooves remain,
Worn in the sandstone parapet hour by hour
    By labouring bargemen where they shifted ropes.
    E'en so shall man turn back from violent hopes
To Adam's cheer, and toil with spade again.

Ay, and his mother Nature, to whose lap
  Like a repentant child at length he hies,
Not in the whirlwind or the thunder-clap
  Proclaims her more tremendous mysteries:
But when in winter's grave, bereft of light,
  With still, small voice divinelier whispering
—Lifting the green head of the aconite,
    Feeding with sap of hope the hazel-shoot—
    She feels God's finger active at the root,
Turns in her sleep, and murmurs of the Spring.

CLOUDESLEY BRERETON

BALLAD OF EXTREME OLD AGE

THE World sweeps past me now, and other wars
      Set men aflame,
The fights we fought forgot, the sacred cause
      No more the same!
The pass-words of our day are dead and gone,
      Or only found
Graven upon the tombs that mark moss-grown
      Our burial ground,
Where those we fought and those who fought for us
      Together lie
Neglected, vanquished and victorious—
      And none come nigh!
I judge not, nor condemn.   How can I judge
      This alien age

With other thoughts and hopes? Why should I grudge
  Their lot or rage?
One prayer alone I make—a humble one—
  Ye powers! dispense
That I may sit a little in the sun
  Ere I go hence.

GEORGE SANTAYANA

ODE

GATHERING the echoes of forgotten wisdom,
And mastered by a proud, adventurous purpose,
Columbus sought the golden shores of India
  Opposite Europe.

He gave the world another world, and ruin
Brought upon blameless, river-loving nations,
Cursed Spain with barren gold, and made the Andes
  Fiefs of St. Peter;

While in the cheerless North the thrifty Saxon
Planted his corn, and, narrowing his bosom,
Made Covenant with God, and by keen virtue
  Trebled his riches.

What virtue hast thou left us, bold Columbus?
What honour left thy brothers, brave Magellan?
Daily the children of the rich for pastime
  Circle the planet.

And what good comes to us of all your dangers?
A smaller earth and smaller hope of heaven.
Ye have but cheapened gold, and, measuring ocean,
  Counted the islands.

No Ponce de Leon shall drink in fountains,
On any flowering Easter, youth eternal;
No Cortes look upon another ocean;
  No Alexander

Found in the Orient dim a boundless kingdom,
And, clothing his great strength in barbarous splendour
Build by the sea his throne, while sacred Egypt
   Honours his godhead.

The earth, the mother once of godlike Theseus
And mighty Heracles, at length is weary,
And now brings forth a spawn of antlike creatures,
   Blackening her valleys.

Inglorious in their birth and in their living,
Curious and querulous, afraid of battle,
Rummaging earth for cones, in camps of hovels
   Crouching from winter,

As if grim fate, amid our boastful prating,
Made us the image of our brutish fathers,
When from their caves they issued, crazed with terror,
   Howling and hungry.

For all things come about in sacred cycles,
And life brings death, and light eternal darkness,
And now the world grows old apace; its glory
   Passes for ever.

Perchance the earth will yet for many ages
Bear her dead child, her moon, around her orbit;
Strange craft may tempt the ocean streams, new forest
   Cover the mountains.

If in those latter days men still remember
Our wisdom and our travail and our sorrow,
They never can be happy, with that burden
   Heavy upon them.

Knowing the hideous past, the blood, the famine,
The ancestral hate, the eager faith's disaster,
All ending in their little lives, and vulgar
   Circle of troubles.

But if they have forgot us, and the shifting
Of sands has buried deep our thousand cities,
Fell superstition then will seize upon them;
   Protean error

Will fill their panting hearts with sickly phantoms
Of sudden blinding good and monstrous evil;
There will be miracles again, and torment,
   Dungeon, and fagot,—

Until the patient earth, made dry and barren,
Sheds all her herbage in a final winter,
And the gods turn their eyes to some far distant
   Bright constellation.

WILLIAM BUTLER YEATS

THE LAKE ISLE OF INNISFREE

WILL arise and go now, and go to Innisfree,
nd a small cabin build there, of clay and wattles made;
ine bean rows will I have there, a hive for the honey-bee,
nd live alone in the bee-loud glade.

nd I shall have some peace there, for peace comes dropping
 slow,
ropping from the veils of the morning to where the cricket
 sings;
here midnight's all a glimmer, and noon a purple glow,
ne evening full of the linnet's wings.

will arise and go now, for always night and day
hear lake water lapping with low sounds by the shore;
Vhile I stand on the roadway, or on the pavements gray,
hear it in the deep heart's core.

WHEN YOU ARE OLD

When you are old and gray and full of sleep,
And nodding by the fire, take down this book,
And slowly read, and dream of the soft look
Your eyes had once, and of their shadows deep;

How many loved your moments of glad grace,
And loved your beauty with love false or true;
But one man loved the pilgrim soul in you,
And loved the sorrows of your changing face.

And bending down beside the glowing bars
Murmur, a little sadly, how love fled
And paced upon the mountains overhead,
And hid his face amid a crowd of stars.

THE MAN WHO DREAMED OF FAERYLAND

He stood among a crowd at Drumahair;
His heart hung all upon a silken dress,
And he had known at last some tenderness,
Before earth made of him her sleepy care;
But when a man poured fish into a pile,
It seemed they raised their little silver heads
And sang how day a Druid twilight sheds
Upon a dim, green, well-beloved isle,
Where people love beside star-laden seas;
How Time may never mar their faery vows
Under the woven roofs of quicken boughs:
The singing shook him out of his new ease.

He wandered by the sands of Lisadill;
His mind ran all on money cares and fears,
And he had known at last some prudent years
Before they heaped his grave under the hill;

But while he passed before a plashy place,
A lug-worm with its gray and muddy mouth
Sang how somewhere to north or west or south
There dwelt a gay, exulting, gentle race;
And how beneath those three times blessed skies
A Danaan fruitage makes a shower of moons,
And as it falls awakens leafy tunes:
And at that singing he was no more wise.

He mused beside the well of Scanavin,
He mused upon his mockers; without fail
His sudden vengeance were a country tale,
Now that deep earth has drunk his body in;
But one small knot-grass growing by the pool
Told where, ah, little, all-unneeded voice!
Old Silence bids a lonely folk rejoice,
And chaplet their calm brows with leafage cool;
And how, when fades the sea-strewn rose of day,
A gentle feeling wraps them like a fleece,
And all their trouble dies into its peace:
The tale drove his fine angry mood away.

He slept under the hill of Lugnagall;
And might have known at last unhaunted sleep
Under that cold and vapour-turbaned steep,
Now that old earth had taken man and all:
Were not the worms that spired about his bones
A-telling with their low and reedy cry,
Of how God leans His hands out of the sky,
To bless that isle with honey in His tones;
That none may feel the power of squall and wave,
And no one any leaf-crowned dancer miss
Until He burn up Nature with a kiss:
The man has found no comfort in the grave.

DOWN BY THE SALLEY GARDENS

Down by the salley gardens my love and I did meet;
She pass'd the salley gardens with little snow-white feet.
She bid me take love easy, as the leaves grow on the
    tree;
But I, being young and foolish, with her would not agree

In a field by the river my love and I did stand,
And on my leaning shoulder she laid her snow-white
    hand.
She bid me take life easy, as the grass grows on the weirs
But I was young and foolish, and now am full of tears.

AEDH WISHES FOR THE CLOTHS OF HEAVEN

Had I the heavens' embroidered cloths,
Enwrought with golden and silver light,
The blue and the dim and the dark cloths
Of night and light and the half-light,
I would spread the cloths under your feet:
But I, being poor, have only my dreams;
I have spread my dreams under your feet;
Tread softly because you tread on my dreams.

THE HOST OF THE AIR

O'Driscoll drove with a song
The wild duck and the drake
From the tall and the tufted reeds
Of the drear Hart Lake.

And he saw how the reeds grew dark
At the coming of night tide,
And dreamed of the long dim hair
Of Bridget his bride.

He heard while he sang and dreamed
A piper piping away,
And never was piping so sad,
And never was piping so gay.

And he saw young men and young girls
Who danced on a level place,
And Bridget his bride among them,
With a sad and a gay face.

The dancers crowded about him,
And many a sweet thing said,
And a young man brought him red wine
And a young girl white bread.

But Bridget drew him by the sleeve,
Away from the merry bands,
To old men playing at cards
With a twinkling of ancient hands.

The bread and the wine had a doom,
For these were the host of the air;
He sat and played in a dream
Of her long dim hair.

He played with the merry old men
And thought not of evil chance,
Until one bore Bridget his bride
Away from the merry dance.

He bore her away in his arms,
The handsomest young man there,
And his neck and his breast and his arms
Were drowned in her long dim hair.

O'Driscoll scattered the cards
And out of his dream awoke:
Old men and young men and young girls
Were gone like a drifting smoke;

But he heard high up in the air
A piper piping away,
And never was piping so sad,
And never was piping so gay.

THE OLD MEN ADMIRING THEMSELVES
IN THE WATER

I HEARD the old, old men say,
'Everything alters,
And one by one we drop away.'
They had hands like claws, and their knees
Were twisted like the old thorn trees
By the waters.
I heard the old, old men say,
'All that's beautiful drifts away
Like the waters.'

DORA SIGERSON SHORTER

THE COMFORTERS

WHEN I crept over the hill, broken with tears,
    When I crouched down on the grass, dumb in despair,
I heard the soft croon of the wind bend to my ears,
    I felt the light kiss of the wind touching my hair.

When I stood lone on the height my sorrow did speak,
    As I went down the hill, I cried and I cried,
The soft little hands of the rain stroking my cheek,
    The kind little feet of the rain ran by my side.

When I went to thy grave, broken with tears,
    When I crouched down in the grass, dumb in despair,
I heard the sweet croon of the wind soft in my ears,
    I felt the kind lips of the wind touching my hair.

When I stood lone by thy cross, sorrow did speak.
    When I went down the long hill, I cried and I cried.
The soft little hands of the rain stroked my pale cheek,
    The kind little feet of the rain ran by my side.

RUDYARD KIPLING

A DEDICATION

My new-cut ashlar takes the light
Where crimson-blank the windows flare.
By my own work before the night,
Great Overseer, I make my prayer.

If there be good in that I wrought,
Thy hand compelled it, Master, Thine—
Where I have failed to meet Thy thought
I know, through Thee, the blame is mine.

One instant's toil to Thee denied
Stands all Eternity's offence;
Of that I did with Thee to guide
To Thee, through Thee, be excellence.

Who, lest all thought of Eden fade,
Bring'st Eden to the craftsman's brain—
Godlike to muse o'er his own Trade
And manlike stand with God again!

The depth and dream of my desire,
The bitter paths wherein I stray—
Thou knowest Who hast made the Fire,
Thou knowest Who hast made the Clay.

One stone the more swings into place
In that dread Temple of Thy worth.
It is enough that, through Thy Grace,
I saw naught common on Thy Earth.

Take not that vision from my ken.
Oh, whatsoe'er may spoil or speed—
Help me to need no aid from men,
That I may help such men as need!

SUSSEX

GOD gave all men all earth to love,
　But since our hearts are small,
Ordained for each one spot should prove
　Belovèd over all;
That as He watched Creation's birth,
　So we, in godlike mood,
May of our love create our earth
　And see that it is good.

So one shall Baltic pines content,
　As one some Surrey glade,
Or one the palm-grove's droned lament
　Before Levuka's Trade.
Each to his choice, and I rejoice
　The lot has fallen to me
In a fair ground—in a fair ground—
　Yea, Sussex by the sea !

No tender-hearted garden crowns,
　No bosomed woods adorn
Our blunt, bow-headed, whale-backed Downs
　But gnarled and writhen thorn—
Bare slopes where chasing shadows skim,
　And, through the gaps revealed,
Belt upon belt, the wooded, dim,
　Blue goodness of the Weald.

Clean of officious fence or hedge,
　Half-wild and wholly tame,
The wise turf cloaks the white cliff edge
　As when the Romans came.
What sign of those that fought and died
　At shift of sword and sword?
The barrow and the camp abide,
　The sunlight and the sward.

Here leaps ashore the full Sou'west
 All heavy-winged with brine,
Here lies above the folded crest
 The Channel's leaden line;
And here the sea-fogs lap and cling,
 And here, each warning each,
The sheep-bells and the ship-bells ring
 Along the hidden beach.

We have no waters to delight
 Our broad and brookless vales—
Only the dewpond on the height
 Unfed, that never fails
Whereby no tattered herbage tells
 Which way the season flies—
Only our close-bit thyme that smells
 Like dawn in Paradise.

Here through the strong and shadeless days
 The tinkling silence thrills;
Or little, lost, Down churches praise
 The Lord who made the hills:
But here the Old Gods guard their round,
 And, in her secret heart,
The heathen kingdom Wilfrid found
 Dreams, as she dwells, apart.

Though all the rest were all my share,
 With equal soul I 'd see
Her nine-and-thirty sisters fair,
 Yet none more fair than she.
Choose ye your need from Thames to Tweed,
 And I will choose instead
Such lands as lie 'twixt Rake and Rye
 Black Down and Beachy Head.

I will go out against the sun
  Where the rolled scarp retires,
And the Long Man of Wilmington
  Looks naked toward the shires;
And east till doubling Rother crawls
  To find the fickle tide,
By dry and sea-forgotten walls,
  Our ports of stranded pride.

I will go north about the shaws
  And the deep ghylls that breed
Huge oaks and old, the which we hold
  No more than 'Sussex weed';
Or south where windy Piddinghoe's
  Begilded dolphin veers
And red beside wide-bankèd Ouse
  Lie down our Sussex steers.

So to the land our hearts we give
  Till the sure magic strike,
And Memory, Use, and Love make live
  Us and our fields alike—
That deeper than our speech and thought,
  Beyond our reason's sway,
Clay of the pit whence we were wrought
  Yearns to its fellow-clay.

God gives all men all earth to love,
  But since man's heart is small,
Ordains for each one spot shall prove
  Beloved over all.
Each to his choice, and I rejoice
  The lot has fallen to me
In a fair ground—in a fair ground—
  Yea, Sussex by the sea!

THE SONG OF DIEGO VALDEZ

THE God of Fair Beginnings
  Hath prospered here my hand—
The cargoes of my lading,
  And the keels of my command.
For out of many ventures
  That sailed with hope as high,
My own have made the better trade,
  And Admiral am I.

To me my King's much honour,
  To me my people's love—
To me the pride of Princes
  And power all pride above;
To me the shouting cities,
  To me the mob's refrain:—
'Who knows not noble Valdez,
  Hath never heard of Spain.'

But I remember comrades—
  Old playmates on new seas—
Whenas we traded orpiment
  Among the savages—
A thousand leagues to south'ard
  And thirty years removed—
They knew not noble Valdez,
  But me they knew and loved.

Then they that found good liquor,
  They drank, it not alone,
And they that found fair plunder,
  They told us every one,
About our chosen islands
  Or secret shoals between,
When, weary from far voyage,
  We gathered to careen.

There burned our breaming-fagots
  All pale along the shore:
There rose our worn pavilions—
  A sail above an oar:
As flashed each yearning anchor
  Through mellow seas afire,
So swift our careless captains
  Rowed each to his desire.

Where lay our loosened harness?
  Where turned our naked feet?
Whose tavern 'mid the palm-trees?
  What quenchings of what heat?
Oh fountain in the desert!
  Oh cistern in the waste!
Oh bread we ate in secret!
  Oh cup we spilled in haste!

The youth new-taught of longing,
  The widow curbed and wan,
The goodwife proud at season,
  And the maid aware of man—
All souls unslaked, consuming
  Defrauded in delays,
Desire not more their quittance
  Than I those forfeit days!

I dreamed to wait my pleasure
  Unchanged my spring would bide:
Wherefore, to wait my pleasure,
  I put my spring aside
Till, first in face of Fortune,
  And last in mazed disdain,
I made Diego Valdez
  High Admiral of Spain.

Then walked no wind 'neath Heaven
  Nor surge that did not aid—
I dared extreme occasion,
  Nor ever one betrayed.

They wrought a deeper treason—
  (Led seas that served my needs!)
They sold Diego Valdez
  To bondage of great deeds.

The tempest flung me seaward,
  And pinned and bade me hold
The course I might not alter—
  And men esteemed me bold!
The calms embayed my quarry,
  The fog-wreath sealed his eyes;
The dawn-wind brought my topsails—
  And men esteemed me wise!

Yet 'spite my tyrant triumphs,
  Bewildered, dispossessed—
My dream held I before me—
  My vision of my rest;
But, crowned by Fleet and People,
  And bound by King and Pope—
Stands here Diego Valdez
  To rob me of my hope.

No prayer of mine hall move him,
  No word of his set free
The Lord of Sixty Pennants
  And the Steward of the Sea.
His will can loose ten thousand
  To seek their loves again—
But not Diego Valdez,
  High Admiral of Spain.

There walks no wind 'neath Heaven
  Nor wave that shall restore
The old careening riot
  And the clamorous, crowded shore—
The fountain in the desert,
  The cistern in the waste,
The bread we ate in secret,
  The cup we spilled in haste.

Now call I to my Captains—
    For council fly the sign,
Now leap their zealous galleys,
    Twelve-oared, across the brine.
To me the straiter prison,
    To me the heavier chain—
To me Diego Valdez,
    High Admiral of Spain!

THE FLOWERS

Buy my English posies!
    Kent and Surrey may—
Violets of the Undercliff
    Wet with Channel spray;
Cowslips from a Devon combe—
    Midland furze afire—
Buy my English posies
    And I'll sell your heart's desire!

Buy my English posies!
    You that scorn the May,
Won't you greet a friend from home
    Half the world away?
Green against the draggled drift,
    Faint and frail and first—
Buy my Northern blood-root
    And I'll know where you were nursed!
Robin down the logging-road whistles, 'Come to me!
Spring has found the maple-grove, the sap is running free
All the winds of Canada call the ploughing-rain.
Take the flower and turn the hour, and kiss your love
    again!

Buy my English posies!
    Here's to match your need—
Buy a tuft of royal heath,
    Buy a bunch of weed

White as sand of Muisenberg
    Spun before the gale—
Buy my heath and lilies
    And I 'll tell you whence you hail!
Under hot Constantia broad the vineyards lie—
Throned and thorned the aching berg props the speckless sky—
Low below the Wynberg firs trails the tilted wain—
Take the flower and turn the hour, and kiss your love again!

Buy my English posies!
    You that will not turn—
Buy my hot-wood clematis,
    Buy a frond o' fern
Gather'd where the Erskine leaps
    Down the road to Lorne—
Buy my Christmas creeper
    And I 'll say where you were born!
West away from Melbourne dust holidays begin—
They that mock at Paradise woo at Cora Lynn—
Through the great South Otway gums sings the great South Main—
Take the flower and turn the hour, and kiss your love again!

Buy my English posies!
    Here 's your choice unsold!
Buy a blood-red myrtle-bloom,
    Buy the kowhai's gold
Flung for gift on Taupo's face,
    Sign that spring is come—
Buy my clinging myrtle
    And I 'll give you back your home!
Broom behind the windy town; pollen of the pine—
Bell-bird in the leafy deep where the *ratas* twine—
Fern above the saddle-bow, flax upon the plain—
Take the flower and turn the hour, and kiss your love again!

Buy my English posies!
  Ye that have your own
Buy them for a brother's sake
  Overseas, alone!
Weed ye trample underfoot
  Floods his heart abrim—
Birds ye never heeded,
  Oh, she calls his dead to him!
Far and far our homes are set round the Seven Seas;
Woe for us if we forget, we who hold by these!
Unto each his mother-beach, bloom and bird and land—
Masters of the Seven Seas, oh, love and understand!

'CITIES AND THRONES AND POWERS'

CITIES and Thrones and Powers,
  Stand in Time's eye,
Almost as long as flowers,
  Which daily die:
But, as new buds put forth
  To glad new men,
Out of the spent and unconsidered Earth,
  The Cities rise again.

This season's Daffodil,
  She never hears,
What change, what chance, what chill,
  Cut down last year's;
But with bold countenance,
  And knowledge small,
Esteems her seven days' continuance,
  To be perpetual.

So Time that is o'er kind
  To all that be,
Ordains us e'en as blind,
  As bold as she:

That in our very death,
  And burial sure,
Shadow to shadow, well persuaded, saith,
  'See how our works endure!'

ARTHUR SYMONS

LAUS VIRGINITATIS

THE mirror of men's eyes delights me less,
O mirror, than the friend I find in thee;
Thou lovest, as I love, my loveliness,
Thou givest my beauty back to me.

I to myself suffice; why should I tire
The heart with roaming that would rest at home?
Myself the limit to my own desire,
I have no desire to roam.

I hear the maidens crying in the hills:
'Come up among the bleak and perilous ways,
Come up and follow after Love, who fills
The hollows of our nights and days;

'Love the deliverer, who is desolate,
And saves from desolation; the divine
Out of great suffering; Love, compassionate,
Who is thy bread and wine,

'O soul, that faints in following after him.'
I hear; but what is Love that I should tread
Hard ways among the perilous passes dim,
Who need no succouring wine and bread?

Enough it is to dream, enough to abide
Here where the loud world's echoes fall remote,
Untroubled, unawakened, satisfied;
As water-lilies float

Lonely upon a shadow-sheltered pool,
Dreaming of their own whiteness; even so,
I dwell within a nest of shadows cool,
And watch the vague hours come and go.

They come and go, but I my own delight
Remain, and I desire no change in aught:
Might I escape indifferent Time's despite,
That ruins all he wrought!

This dainty body formed so curiously,
So delicately and wonderfully made,
My own, that none hath ever shared with me,
My own, and for myself arrayed;

All this that I have loved and not another,
My one desire's delight, this, shall Time bring
Where Beauty hath the abhorred worm for brother,
The dust for covering?

At least I bear it virgin to the grave,
Pure, and apart, and rare, and casketed;
What, living, was my own and no man's slave,
Shall be my own when I am dead.

But thou, my friend, my mirror, dost possess
The shadow of myself that smiles in thee,
And thou dost give, with thy own loveliness,
My beauty back to me.

CREDO

EACH, in himself, his hour to be and cease
Endures alone, but who of men shall dare,
Sole with himself, this single burden bear,
All the long day until the night's release?

Yet ere night falls, and the last shadows close,
This labour of himself is each man's lot;
All he has gained of earth shall be forgot,
Himself he leaves behind him when he goes.
If he has any valiancy within,
If he has made his life his very own,
If he has loved or laboured, and has known
A strenuous virtue, or a strenuous sin;
Then, being dead, his life was not all vain,
For he has saved what most desire to lose,
And he has chosen what the few must choose,
Since life, once lived, shall not return again.
For of our time we lose so large a part
In serious trifles, and so oft let slip
The wine of every moment, at the lip
Its moment, and the moment of the heart.
We are awake so little on the earth,
And we shall sleep so long, and rise so late,
If there is any knocking at that gate
Which is the gate of death, the gate of birth.

THE OLD WOMEN

THEY pass upon their old, tremulous feet,
Creeping with little satchels down the street,
And they remember, many years ago,
Passing that way in silks.   They wander, slow
And solitary, through the city ways,
And they alone remember those old days
Men have forgotten.   In their shaking heads
A dancer of old carnivals yet treads
The measure of past waltzes, and they see
The candles lit again, the patchouli
Sweeten the air, and the warm cloud of musk
Enchant the passing of the passionate dusk.
Then you will see a light begin to creep
Under the earthen eyelids, dimmed with sleep,

And a new tremor, happy and uncouth,
Jerking about the corners of the mouth.
Then the old head drops down again, and shakes,
Muttering.

          Sometimes, when the swift gaslight wake.
The dreams and fever of the sleepless town,
A shaking huddled thing in a black gown
Will steal at midnight, carrying with her
Violet little bags of lavender,
Into the tap-room full of noisy light;
Or, at the crowded earlier hour of night,
Sidle, with matches, up to some who stand
About a stage-door, and, with furtive hand,
Appealing: 'I too was a dancer, when
Your fathers would have been young gentleman !'
And sometimes, out of some lean ancient throat
A broken voice, with here and there a note
Of unspoilt crystal, suddenly will arise
Into the night, while a cracked fiddle cries
Pantingly after; and you know she sings
The passing of light, famous, passing things.
And sometimes, in the hours past midnight, reels
Out of an alley upon staggering heels,
Or into the dark keeping of the stones
About a doorway, a vague thing of bones
And draggled hair.

          And all these have been loved,
And not one ruinous body has not moved
The heart of man's desire, nor has not seemed
Immortal in the eyes of one who dreamed
The dream that men call love.   This is the end
Of much fair flesh; it is for this you tend
Your delicate bodies many careful years,
To be this thing of laughter and of tears,
To be this living judgment of the dead,
An old grey woman with a shaking head.

THE DANCE OF THE DAUGHTERS OF HERODIAS

Is it the petals falling from the rose?
For in the silence I can hear a sound
Nearer than my own heart-beat, such a word
As roses murmur, blown by a great wind.
I see a pale and windy multitude
Beaten about the air, as if the smoke
Of incense kindled into visible life
Shadowy and invisible presences;
And, in the cloudy darkness, I can see
The thin white feet of many women dancing,
And in their hands . . . I see it is the dance
Of the daughters of Herodias; each of them
Carries a beautiful platter in her hand,
Smiling, because she holds against her heart
The secret lips and the unresting brow
Some John the Baptist's head makes lamentable;
Smiling as innocently as if she carried
A wet red quartered melon on a dish.
For they are stupid, and they do not know
That they are slaying the messenger of God.
Here is Salome.   She is a young tree
Swaying in the wind; her arms are slender branches,
And the heavy summer leafage of her hair
Stirs as if rustling in a silent wind;
Her narrow feet are rooted in the ground,
But, when the dim wind passes over her,
Rustlingly she awakens, as if life
Thrilled in her body to its finger-tips.
Her little breasts arise as if a thought
Beckoned, her body quivers; and she leans
Forward, as if she followed, her wide eyes
Swim open, her lips seek; and now she leans
Backward, and her half-parted lips are moist,
And her eyelashes mingle.   The gold coins

Tinkle like little bells about her waist,
Her golden anklets clash once, and are mute.
The eyes of the blue-lidded turquoises,
The astonished rubies, waked from dreams of fire,
The emeralds coloured like the under-sea,
Pale chrysoprase and flaming chrysolite,
The topaz twofold, twofold sardonyx,
Open, from sleeping long between her breasts;
And those two carbuncles, which are the eyes
Of the gold serpent nestling in her hair,
Shoot starry fire; the bracelets of wrought gold
Mingle with bracelets of carved ivory
Upon her drooping wrists.   Herodias smiles,
But the grey face of Herod withers up,
As if it dropped to ashes; the parched tongue
Labours to moisten his still-thirsting lips;
The rings upon his wrinkled fingers strike,
Ring against ring, between his knees.   And she,
Salome, has forgotten everything,
But that the wind of dancing in her blood
Exults, crying a strange, awakening song;
And Herod has forgotten everything,
He has forgotten he is old and wise.
He does not hear the double-handed sword
Scrape on the pavement, as Herodias beckons
The headsman, from behind him, to come forth.

They dance, the daughters of Herodias,
With their eternal, white, unfaltering feet,
And always, when they dance, for their delight,
Always a man's head falls because of them.
Yet they desire not death, they would not slay
Body or soul, no, not to do them pleasure:
They desire love, and the desire of men;
And they are the eternal enemy.
They know that they are weak and beautiful,
And that their weakness makes them beautiful,
For pity, and because man's heart is weak.

To pity woman is an evil thing;
She will avenge upon you all your tears,
She would not that a man should pity her.
But to be loved by one of these beloved
Is poison sweeter than the cup of sleep
At midnight: death, or sorrow worse than death,
Or that forgetfulness, drowning the soul,
Shall heal you of it, but no other thing:
For they are the eternal enemy.
They do not understand that in the world
There grows between the sunlight and the grass
Anything save themselves desirable.
It seems to them that the swift eyes of men
Are made but to be mirrors, not to see
Far-off, disastrous, unattainable things.
'For are not we,' they say, 'the end of all?
Why should you look beyond us?   If you look
Into the night, you will find nothing there:
We also have gazed often at the stars.
We, we alone among all beautiful things,
We only are real: for the rest are dreams.
Why will you follow after wandering dreams
When we await you?   And you can but dream
Of us, and in our image fashion them!'
They do not know that they but speak in sleep,
Speaking vain words as sleepers do; that dreams
Are fairer and more real than they are;
That all this tossing of our freighted lives
Is but the restless shadow of a dream;
That the whole world, and we that walk in it,
Sun, moon, and stars, and the unageing sea,
And all the happy humble life of plants,
And the unthoughtful eager life of beasts,
And all our loves, and birth, and death, are all
Shadows, and a rejoicing spectacle
Dreamed out of utter darkness and the void
By that first, last, eternal soul of things,
The shadow of whose brightness fashions us,

That, for the day of our eternity,
It may behold itself as in a mirror.
Shapes on a mirror, perishable shapes,
Fleeting, and without substance, or abode
In a fixed place, or knowledge of ourselves,
Poor, fleeting, fretful, little arrogant shapes;
Let us dream on, forgetting that we dream!

They dance, the daughters of Herodias,
Everywhere in the world, and I behold
Their rosy-petalled feet upon the air
Falling and falling in a cadence soft
As thoughts of beauty sleeping.   Where they pass,
The wisdom which is wiser than things known,
The beauty which is fairer than things seen,
Dreams which are nearer to eternity
Than that most mortal tumult of the blood
Which wars on itself in loving, droop and die.
But they smile innocently, and dance on,
Having no thought but this unslumbering thought:
'Am I not beautiful?   Shall I not be loved?'
Be patient, for they will not understand,
Not till the end of time will they put by
The weaving of slow steps about men's hearts.
They shall be beautiful, they shall be loved.
And though a man's head falls because of them
Whenever they have danced his soul asleep,
It is not well that they should suffer wrong;
For beauty is still beauty, though it slay,
And love is love, although it love to death.
Pale, windy, and ecstatic multitude
Beaten about this mortal air with winds
Of an all but immortal passion, borne
Upon the flight of thoughts that drooped their wings
Into the cloud and twilight for your sake,
Yours is the beauty of your own desire,
And it shall wither only with that love
Which gave it being.   Dance in the desolate air,

Dance always, daughters of Herodias,
With your eternal, white, unfaltering feet.
But dance, I pray you, so that I from far
May hear your dancing fainter than the drift
Of the last petals falling from the rose.

RICHARD LE GALLIENNE

THE SECOND CRUCIFIXION

LOUD mockers in the roaring street
 Say Christ is crucified again:
Twice pierced His gospel-bearing feet,
 Twice broken His great heart in vain.

I hear, and to myself I smile,
For Christ talks with me all the while.

No angel now to roll the stone
 From off His unawaking sleep,
In vain shall Mary watch alone,
 In vain the soldiers vigil keep.

Yet while they deem my Lord is dead
My eyes are on His shining head.

Ah! never more shall Mary hear
 That voice exceeding sweet and low
Within the garden calling clear:
 Her Lord is gone, and she must go.

Yet all the while my Lord I meet
In every London lane and street.

Poor Lazarus shall wait in vain,
 And Bartimaeus still go blind;
The heeling hem shall ne'er again
 Be touch'd by suffering humankind.

Yet all the while I see them rest,
The poor and outcast, on His breast.

No more unto the stubborn heart
   With gentle knocking shall He plead,
No more the mystic pity start,
   For Christ twice dead is dead indeed.

So in the street I hear men say:
Yet Christ is with me all the day.

HERBERT TRENCH

SHE COMES NOT WHEN NOON IS ON THE ROSES

SHE comes not when Noon is on the roses—
      Too bright is Day.
She comes not to the soul till it reposes
      From work and play.

But when Night is on the hills, and the great Voices
      Roll in from sea,
By starlight and by candlelight and dreamlight
      She comes to me.

A SONG TO AROLILIA

DWELLER BY THE FOUNTAIN

WHEN you were born, the Earth obeyed,
      (*Call her, Echo!*)
Fragrancies from the distance blew,
Beanfields and violets were made
And jasmine by the cypress grew—
Jasmine by the cloudy yew—
      (*Call her, Echo!*
   Call Arolilia by her name!)

When you were born, despairs must die,
  (*Call her, Echo!*)
Sweet tongues were loosened from a spell—
Snow mountains glistened from on high
And torrents to the valleys fell—
A song into Man's bosom fell—
  (*Call her, Echo!*
 Call Arolilia by her name!)

When you were born, hid lightning's shape
  (*Call her, Echo!*)
Took up the poor man's altar coal,
His green vine throbbed into the grape
 And in the dastard sprang a soul—
 Even in the dastard sprang a soul—
  (*Call her, Echo!*
 Call Arolilia by her name!)

When you were born, all golden shot
  (*Call her, Echo!*)
Fountains of daybreak from the sea,
And still, if near I find you not—
If steps I hear, but you come not—
Darkness lies on the world for me!
  (*Call her, Echo!*
 Call Arolilia by her name!)

COME, LET US MAKE LOVE DEATHLESS

Come, let us make love deathless, thou and I,
 Seeing that our footing on the Earth is brief—
Seeing that her multitudes sweep out to die
 Mocking at all that passes their belief.
For standard of our love not theirs we take;
 If we go hence to-day
Fill the high cup that is so soon to break
 With richer wine than they!

Ay, since beyond these walls no heavens there be
    Joy to revive or wasted youth repair,
I 'll not bedim the lovely flame in thee
    Nor sully the sad splendour that we wear.
Great be the love, if with the lover dies
    Our greatness past recall,
And nobler for the fading of those eyes
    The world seen once for all!

BITTER SERENADE

Venice, 15—

(He speaks, touching the chords)
LANTERNS of silk down the lagoons are vanish'd,
    Brilliance, uproar and sweep of masquerade;
Their eddies swell—the firefly world is banish'd,
    All your canal is shade.

Magnolia-bloom is here my only candle,
    White petals wash, and break, along the wall;
The clumsy lute, the lute with the scorched handle,
    Is here to tell you all.

Do you remember—yes, you will remember—
    That ballad of a lute of curious tone
Wrought—a charr'd log—out of a great hearth's ember?
    The great hearth was your own.

Firelight was all our light.   Your endless gazes—
    Contemptuous of all living—forth would float,
Half-terrible in beauty, down those mazes
    As in a flame-winged boat.

Urania's locks, with horror in their starkness,
    Enlapt you, pale as an Aegean gem,
Enwound your ears with silence, and of darkness
    Made you a diadem.

What eyes were yours, that made the witless falter—
   The beating of the heart forget to beat—
Some Arab prisoner's on a Libyan altar
   And sleepless with defeat.

Yet with that smile that seemed no smile of woman
   Frowningly once—floating on light—you cried
As in a vision: '*Friend, not like your Roman*
   Cynthia, by the roadside

Would I be tomb'd—close to the dust and rumbling—
   But childless, by some playground; that at hours
Oft I may hear the wicked children tumbling
   Forth, like a tide of flowers! . . .'

By God! to the chords wherewith you then endowed us
   (Something in you gave frame and strings a voice)
Now you must listen, in the hours allowed us,
   Listen, you have no choice! . . .

   (*He sings*)

The Song

   O heart thrice-noble, to the quick bereaved,
      In beauty wasted, and in weakness dire
   Maintaining 'gainst the Gods that have deceived
      Such cold unwavering ire!

   The very stars grow dread with tense fore-feeling
      Of dawn; the bell-towers darken in the sky
   As they would groan before they strike, revealing
      New day to such as I!

   There comes a day too merciless in clearness,
      Worn to the bone the stubborn must give o'er;
   There comes a day when to endure in nearness
      Can be endured no more.

   A man can take the buffets of the tourney,
      But there's a hurt, lady, beyond belief;
   A grief the Sun finds not upon his journey
      Marked on the map of grief.

Fate smote you young.   Death young would now frustrate
   you.
  I have but lived—as alchemists for gold—
In my mad pity's flame to re-create you,
   Heavenly one, waning, cold!

Planet dark!   Strange and hostile desolation
   Whereto no ray serene hath ever gone
Nor touched with the one kiss of evocation—
   You might have loved and shone!

Was I not bred of the same clay and vapour
   And lightning of the universe as you?
Had I the self-same God to be my shaper,
   Or cracks the world in two?

It cannot be, though I have nought of merit,
   That man may hold so dear, and with such pain
Enfold with all the tendrils of the spirit
   Yet not be loved again;

It cannot be that such intensest yearning,
   Such fierce and incommunicable care
Starr'd on your face, as through a crystal burning,
   Is wasted on the air;

It cannot be I gave my soul, unfolding
   To you its very inmost, like a child
Utterly giving faith—no jot withholding—
   By you to be beguiled;

It cannot be to look on us, despising,
   That yonder great-puls'd Sun englobes the wave
With crocus fire—releasing and arising—
   To break upon the slave;

No.   In rich Venice, riotous and human,
   That shrinks for me to sandbanks and a sky,
You hold the love I bear you a thing common.
   Enough.   So let it die;

Die from your waves away—O, pale, pale wonder!
  The gaunt ships out—toss'd petals—to the main
Be suck'd—the iron bands be snapt asunder!
  But Night, Death, you—remain.

(*He ceases to sing, and speaks, touching the chords*)

In the outer flood, and plunging at his tether,
  One sullen hulk complains against the quays;
Rusty, and timbered ill for such fine weather,
  He thinks on the high seas.

My hand forgets the strings.   May be for travel
  It trembles to be gone, to steer the fleet!
There's the secret of the Indies to unravel,
  And then the Turks to beat!

SONG OF THE VINE, IN ENGLAND

Man

O Vine along my garden wall
  Could I thine English slumber break,
And thee from wintry exile disenthral
  Where would thy spirit wake?

Vine

I would wake at the hour of dawning in May in Italy,
When rose mists rise from the Magra's valley plains
In the fields of maize and olives around Pontrémoli
When peaks grow golden and clear and the starlight wanes:
I would wake to the dance of the sacred mountains, boundlessly
Kindling their marble snows in the rite of fire,
To them my newborn tendrils softly and soundlessly
  Would uncurl and aspire.

I would hang no more on thy wall a rusted slumberer,
Listless and fruitless, strewing the pathways cold,
I would seem no more in thine eyes an idle cumberer,
Profitless alien, bitter and sere and old.
In some warm terraced dell where the Roman rioted
And still in tiers his stony theatre heaves,
Would I festoon with leaf-light his glory quieted,
          And flake his thrones with leaves.

Doves from the mountain belfries would seek and cling
     to me
To drink from the altar, winnowing the fragrant airs;
Women from olived hillsides by turns would sing to me
Beating the olives, or stooping afield in pairs;
On gala evenings the gay little carts of labourers
Swinging from axles their horns against evil eye
And crowded with children, revellers, pipers and taborers
          Chanting would pass me by. . . .

There go the pale blue shadows, so light and showery,
Over sharp Apuan peaks—rathe mists unwreathe—
Almond trees wake, and the paven yards grow flowery—
Crocuses cry from the earth at the joy to breathe;
There through the deep-eaved gateways of haughty
     turreted
Arno—house-laden bridges of strutted stalls—
Mighty white oxen drag in the jars rich-spirited,
          Grazing the narrow walls!

Wine-jars I too have filled, and the heart was thrilled with
     me!
Brown-limbed on shady turf the families lay,
Shouting they bowled the bowls, and old men filled with m
Roused the September twilight with songs that day.
Lanterns of sun and moon the young children flaunted me
Plaiters of straw from doorway to window cried—
Borne through the city gates the great oxen vaunted me,
          Swaying from side to side.

Vine-jars out of my leafage that once so vitally
Throbbed into purple, of me thou shalt never take:
Thy heart would remember the towns on the branch of Italy,
And teaching to throb I should teach it, perchance, to
    break.
It would beat for those little cities, rock - hewn and
    mellowing,
Festooned from summit to summit, where still sublime
Murmur her temples, lovelier in their yellowing
        Than in the morn of time.

from the scorn of frost and the wind's iniquity
Barren, aloft in that golden air would thrive:
My passionate rootlets draw from that hearth's antiquity
Whirls of profounder fire in us to survive—
Serried realms of our fathers would swell and foam with us—
Juice of the Latin sunrise; your own sea-flung
Rude and far-wandered race might again find home with us,
        Leaguing with old Rome, young.

STANZAS TO TOLSTOI IN HIS OLD AGE [1]

I

Is this some glowering Titan, inly bright,
   Angered that summer grasses bloom and seethe
Only to taunt him—strange to the upper light—
   Born at the mouth of Tartarus to breathe,
     And lodged where vapour-dripping chasms ensheathe
     The groping ire of his tremendous hands?
     Are these the thews that kept in swaddling-bands
The wingèd Reason, and would now compel
       Beauty, that Spirit clear,
And every art wherein the few excel
   Under a peasant's smock to serve as drudges.
Is it one forgetful of a long career
   Through many wars and loves, who now begrudges

[1] This ode was printed in an English review, and received by L. Tolstoi many years before his attempted pilgrimage and death.

To youth its fair love-season—one who quarrels
   With all not abject—one whose mood would bind
Under one law the wearers of the laurels
   With feet upon the uplands, in the wind?

II

Or may this peasant demiurge not mask
   Mimir himself—the friend of right in hell,
Him that gave Odin on his awful task
   Water of insight from the world-deep well,
   And stayed as the god's hostage, and so fell?
      Perhaps this soul, half-savage, half-divine,
      Is some freed ghost—the slave from Palestine,
Grim Christopher, who strove as he had sworn
        To bear through the mid-flood
That little Child—so hardly to be borne? . . .
   No, no, *this is the prophet of the poor!*
That face is theirs—that heart hath understood
   Their piteous certainty in things unsure.
And stay!—those shaggy brows, and haunting them
   Unrest, unrest—O in the Dolorous Street
Have I not seen thee in Jerusalem,
With sheepskin coat and hat and dusty feet,

III

Like a poor herdsman, pilgrim from the snows
   Far north of Volga, where his little hut
Lay warm, who on some glittering night arose
   And blessed his old wife in the dark, and shut
   On her the door, and took his newly-cut
      Staff from the eaves—a sapling iron-shod—
      And set forth for the sepulchre of God?
Yes, thence by great plains, Taurus passes bleak,
        And fire-lit caravanserai
On, on—though fever sapped his bony cheek
   Month after month, intent and still unbaulked,
Counting the dawns that met his wind-clear eye—
   Thousands of miles to find it had he walked!

But now—since thou hast kissed the very stone,
　　Why restless still, gaunt shepherd come so far?
Why mourn because the ray that led thee on
　　Shines from a long-annihilated star?

IV

The Man upraised on the Judaean crag
　　Captains for us the war with death no more.
His kingdom hangs as hangs the tattered flag
　　Over the tomb of a great knight of yore;
　　Nor shall one law to unity restore
　　　　Races or souls—no staff of thine can urge
　　　　Nor knotted club compel them to converge,
Nor any backward summit lead them up:
　　　　　　The world-spring wherein hides
Formless the God that forms us, bursts its cup—
　　Is seen a Fountain—breaking like a flower
High into light—that at its height divides;
　　Changelessly scattering forth,—in blaze and shower—
In drops of a trembling diaphaneity—
　　Dreams the God-breathings momently up-buoy
To melt a myriad ways.　Those dreams are we,
　　Chanted from some unfathomable joy.

V

What ! Wouldst to *one* conception mould mankind?
　　Hast thou not felt—on thy lone mountain track
Seeing, from some ridge of forest-rushing wind
　　Where the oak-boughs overhead wrestle and crack,
　　Night-plains be-starred with cities mirror back
　　　　The naked deeps of stars—hast thou not felt
　　　　The whole high-scheme wherein we move and melt
With the swift world—that its last secret is
　　　　　　Not Good, nor Immortality,
But Beauty,—once to behold the immensities
　　Filled with one soul, then to make room and die?

Hence the true faith:—to the uttermost to be
    Thyself—to follow up that ecstasy
Compelling—to let being take its course,
    Rise like a song, and like a dream be free,
Poised on the breath of its own soul and source:
    Enough—the Fountain will re-gather thee!

VI

Rejoice then, Master, at the multitude
    Of wills in the many-coloured nations—yea
At the clouds of destinies distinct—the flood
    Of exploring visions—all the radiant spray
    Of hostile forces on their upward way,
        Spirals of the interweaving elements
        And species, these are but the long ascents
Of the self-poised waters of the Universe
        Opening like a rose,
Ingathering all it loses—to disperse
    Its soul in fragrance on the night's abyss,
Yet to build for aye the rainbow as it flows;
    Rejoice that we have spectacle of this—
Of the Fountain opening, opening like a rose
    And Eternal Wisdom rising from its core;
For the light increases, and the rapture grows,
    And the love, in them that perish, waxes more.

REQUIEM OF ARCHANGELS FOR THE WORLD

HEARTS, beat no more! Earth's Sleep has come,
    All iron stands her wrinkled tree,
The streams that sang are stricken dumb,
    The snowflake fades into the sea.
Hearts, throb no more! your time is past;
    Thousands of years for this pent field
Ye have done battle.   Now at last
    The flags may sink, the captains yield.

Sleep, ye great Wars, just and unjust !
   Sleep takes the gate and none defends.
Soft on your craters' fire and lust,
   Civilisations, Sleep descends.
Time it is, time to cease carouse.
   Let the nations and their noise grow dim !
Let the lights wane within the house
   And darkness cover, limb by limb !
Across your passes, Alps and plains
   A planetary vapour flows,
A last invader, and enchains
   The vine, the woman, and the rose.
Sleep, Forests old ! Sleep in your beds
   Wild-muttering Oceans and dark Wells !
Sleep be upon your shrunken heads,
   Blind, everlasting Pinnacles !
Sleep now, most dread high-shining Kings,
   Your torrent glories snapt in death.
Sleep, simple men—sunk water-springs,
   And all the ground Man laboureth.
Sleep, Heroes, in your mountain walls—
   The trumpet shall not wake again;
And ranged on sea-worn pedestals,
   Sleep now, O sleepless Gods of men,
Nor keep wide your unchallenged orbs.
   These troubled clans that make and mourn
Some heavy-lidded Cloud absorbs,
   And the lulling snows of the Unborn.
Make ready thou, tremendous Night,
   Stoop to the Earth, and shroud her scars,
And bid with chanting to the rite
   The torches of thy train of stars !

   .   .   .   .   .

Gloriously hath she offered up
   From the thousand heaving plains of Time
Her sons, like incense from a cup,
   Souls, that were made out of the slime.

She darkens, and yet all her dusk
　Is but the sigh of him that breathes;
The thing unborn bursts from its husk,
　The flash of the sublime unsheathes.
They strove, the Many and the One,
　And all their strivings intervolved
Enlarged Thy Self-dominion;
　Absolute, let them be absolved!
Fount of the time-embranching fire,
　O waneless One, that art the core
Of every heart's unknown desire,
　Take back the hearts that beat no more!

A. E.
(GEORGE WILLIAM RUSSELL)

BY THE MARGIN OF THE GREAT DEEP

When the breath of twilight blows to flame the misty skie
All its vaporous sapphire, violet glow and silver gleam
With their magic flood me through the gateway of the eye
　I am one with the twilight's dream.

When the trees and skies and fields are one in dusky mood,
Every heart of man is rapt within the mother's breast:
Full of peace and sleep and dreams in the vasty quietude,
　I am one with their hearts at rest.

From our immemorial joys of hearth and home and love
Strayed away along the margin of the unknown tide,
All its reach of soundless calm can thrill me far above
　Word or touch from the lips beside.

Aye, and deep and deep and deeper let me drink and draw
From the olden fountain more than light or peace or drean
Such primeval being as o'erfills the heart with awe,
　Growing one with its silent stream.

BABYLON

The blue dusk ran between the streets: my love was winged
    within my mind,
It left to-day and yesterday and thrice a thousand years
    behind.
To-day was past and dead for me, for from to-day my feet
    had run
Through thrice a thousand years to walk the ways of ancient
    Babylon.
On temple top and palace roof the burnished gold flung
    back the rays
Of a red sunset that was dead and lost beyond a million
    days.
The tower of heaven turns darker blue, a starry sparkle
    now begins;
The mystery and magnificence, the myriad beauty and the
    sins
Come back to me. I walk beneath the shadowy multitude
    of towers;
Within the gloom the fountain jets its pallid mist in lily
    flowers.
The waters lull me and the scent of many gardens, and I
    hear
Familiar voices, and the voice I love is whispering in my
    ear.
Oh real as in dream all this; and then a hand on mine is
    laid:
The wave of phantom time withdraws; and that young
    Babylonian maid,
One drop of beauty left behind from all the flowing of that
    tide,
Is looking with the self-same eyes, and here in Ireland by my
    side.
Oh light our life in Babylon, but Babylon has taken wings,
While we are in the calm and proud procession of eternal
    things.

THE MAN TO THE ANGEL

I HAVE wept a million tears:
Pure and proud one, where are thine,
What the gain though all thy years
In unbroken beauty shine?

All your beauty cannot win
Truth we learn in pain and sighs:
You can never enter in
To the circle of the wise.

They are but the slaves of light
Who have never known the gloom,
And between the dark and bright
Willed in freedom their own doom.

Think not in your pureness there,
That our pain but follows sin:
There are fires for those who dare
Seek the throne of might to win.

Pure one, from your pride refrain:
Dark and lost amid the strife
I am myriad years of pain
Nearer to the fount of life.

When defiance fierce is thrown
At the god to whom you bow,
Rest the lips of the Unknown
Tenderest upon my brow.

THE EARTH BREATH

FROM the cool and dark-lipped furrows
    Breathes a dim delight
Through the woodland's purple plumage
    To the diamond night.
Aureoles of joy encircle
    Every blade of grass
Where the dew-fed creatures silent
    And enraptured pass.
And the restless ploughman pauses,
    Turns and, wondering,
Deep beneath his rustic habit
    Finds himself a king;
For a fiery moment looking
    With the eyes of God
Over fields a slave at morning
    Bowed him to the sod.
Blind and dense with revelation
    Every moment flies,
And unto the Mighty Mother,
    Gay, eternal, rise
All the hopes we hold, the gladness,
    Dreams of things to be.
One of all thy generations,
    Mother, hails to thee.
Hail, and hail, and hail for ever,
    Though I turn again
From thy joy unto the human
    Vesture of pain.
I, thy child who went forth radiant
    In the golden prime,
Find thee still the mother-hearted
    Through my night in time;
Find in thee the old enchantment
    There behind the veil
Where the gods, my brothers, linger.
    Hail, forever, hail!

LAURENCE HOUSMAN

DEUS NOSTER IGNIS CONSUMENS

To Him be praise who made
    Desire more fair than rest:
Better the prayer while prayed,
    Than the attained request!
Man goes from strength to strength
    Fresh with each draught of pain,
Only to fail at length
    Of heights he could not gain.

The soul of live desire,
    How shall it mate with dust?
To whom was given fire,—
    For ashes shall he lust?
Man's tenure is but breath,
    His flesh, a vesture worn:
Let him that fears not death
    Fear not to rest unborn.

The crown entails the curse;
    Here all the fame that's won,
A harvest for the hearse,
    Falls withered to the sun.
There, weary of reward,
    The victor strips his wreath;
There, sick with deaths, the sword
    Sighs back into the sheath.

ERNEST DOWSON

NON SUM QUALIS ERAM BONAE SUB REGNO CYNARAE

LAST night, ah, yesternight, betwixt her lips and mine
There fell thy shadow, Cynara! thy breath was shed
Upon my soul between the kisses and the wine;

And I was desolate and sick of an old passion,
    Yea, I was desolate and bowed my head:
I have been faithful to thee, Cynara! in my fashion.

All night upon mine heart I felt her warm heart beat,
Night-long within mine arms in love and sleep she lay;
Surely the kisses of her bought red mouth were sweet;
But I was desolate and sick of an old passion,
    When I awoke and found the dawn was gray:
I have been faithful to thee, Cynara! in my fashion.

I have forgot much, Cynara! gone with the wind,
Flung roses, roses riotously with the throng,
Dancing, to put thy pale, lost lilies out of mind;
But I was desolate and sick of an old passion,
    Yea, all the time, because the dance was long:
I have been faithful to thee, Cynara! in my fashion.

I cried for madder music and for stronger wine,
But when the feast is finished and the lamps expire,
Then falls thy shadow, Cynara! the night is thine;
And I am desolate and sick of an old passion,
    Yea, hungry for the lips of my desire:
I have been faithful to thee, Cynara! in my fashion.

VITAE SUMMA BREVIS SPEM NOS VETAT INCHOARE LONGAM

THEY are not long, the weeping and the laughter,
    Love and desire and hate:
I think they have no portion in us after
    We pass the gate.

They are not long, the days of wine and roses:
    Out of a misty dream
Our path emerges for a while, then closes
    Within a dream.

NUNS OF THE PERPETUAL ADORATION

CALM, sad, secure; behind high convent walls,
   These watch the sacred lamp, these watch and pray:
And it is one with them when evening falls,
   And one with them the cold return of day.

These heed not time; their nights and days they make
   Into a long, returning rosary,
Whereon their lives are threaded for Christ's sake:
   Meekness and vigilance and chastity.

A vowed patrol, in silent companies,
   Life-long they keep before the living Christ:
In the dim church, their prayers and penances
   Are fragrant incense to the Sacrificed.

Outside, the world is wild and passionate;
   Man's weary laughter and his sick despair
Entreat at their impenetrable gate:
   They heed no voices in their dream of prayer.

They saw the glory of the world displayed;
   They saw the bitter of it, and the sweet;
They knew the roses of the world should fade,
   And be trod under by the hurrying feet.

Therefore they rather put away desire,
   And crossed their hands and came to sanctuary;
And veiled their heads and put on coarse attire:
   Because their comeliness was vanity.

And there they rest; they have serene insight
   Of the illuminating dawn to be:
Mary's sweet Star dispels for them the night,
   The proper darkness of humanity.

Calm, sad, secure; with faces worn and mild:
   Surely their choice of vigil is the best?
Yea! for our roses fade, the world is wild;
   But there, beside the altar, there, is rest.

EXTREME UNCTION

Upon the eyes, the lips, the feet,
    On all the passages of sense,
The atoning oil is spread with sweet
    Renewal of lost innocence.

The feet, that lately ran so fast
    To meet desire, are soothly sealed;
The eyes, that were so often cast
    On vanity, are touched and healed.

From troublous sights and sounds set free;
    In such a twilight hour of breath,
Shall one retrace his life, or see,
    Through shadows, the true face of death?

Vials of mercy! Sacring oils!
    I know not where nor when I come,
Nor through what wanderings and toils,
    To crave of you Viaticum.

Yet, when the walls of flesh grow weak,
    In such an hour, it well may be,
Through mist and darkness, light will break,
    And each anointed sense will see.

ARTHUR SHEARLY CRIPPS

———

ALL SAINTS' DAY

Magic casements, opening on the foam
Of perilous seas in faery lands forlorn.—Keats.

Ah me!
It was God's choice ere mine that I should be
The one dim casement by whose panes they see—
These maiden knights of mine—their elders' chivalry.

Alas!
How cobweb-hung the frame! How dim the glass
Whereat their bright eyes watch the pageant pass—
Pageant with raiment white and palms of Hallow-Mass!

Make clean,
O glimmering showers of Grace and Dews unseen,
My panes that do deface their rainbow sheen—
Those venturous Sails that furl in haven-pools serene!

Behold!
At my poor breath-dimmed panes what pomps unfold!
See the Host rise a Harvest Moon of gold!
Lo, the Vine's Branches bend with clusters yet untold!

Ah me!
Flawed priest, that God should choose to make of thee
A nursery window, whence His babes may see
Rapture of Saints that are, wonder of Saints to be!

LIONEL JOHNSON

THE DARK ANGEL

Dark Angel, with thine aching lust,
To rid the world of penitence:
Malicious Angel, who still dost
My soul such subtile violence!

Because of thee, no thought, no thing,
Abides for me undesecrate:
Dark Angel, ever on the wing,
Who never reachest me too late!

When music sounds, then changest thou
Its silvery to a sultry fire:
Nor will thine envious heart allow
Delight untortured by desire.

Through thee, the gracious Muses turn
To Furies, O mine Enemy !
And all the things of beauty burn
With flames of evil ecstasy.

Because of thee, the land of dreams
Becomes a gathering place of fears:
Until tormented slumber seems
One vehemence of useless tears.

When sunlight glows upon the flowers,
Or ripples down the dancing sea:
Thou, with thy troop of passionate powers,
Beleaguerest, bewilderest me.

Within the breath of autumn woods,
Within the winter silences:
Thy venomous spirit stirs and broods,
O Master of impieties !

The ardour of red flame is thine,
And thine the steely soul of ice:
Thou poisonest the fair design
Of nature, with unfair device.

Apples of ashes, golden bright;
Waters of bitterness, how sweet !
O banquet of a foul delight,
Prepared by thee, dark Paraclete !

Thou art the whisper in the gloom,
The hinting tone, the haunting laugh:
Thou art the adorner of my tomb,
The minstrel of mine epitaph.

I fight thee, in the Holy Name !
Yet, what thou dost, is what God saith:
Tempter ! should I escape thy flame,
Thou wilt have helped my soul from Death:

The second Death, that never dies,
That cannot die, when time is dead:
Live Death, wherein the lost soul cries,
Eternally uncomforted.

Dark Angel, with thine aching lust!
Of two defeats, of two despairs:
Less dread, a change to shifting dust,
Than thine eternity of cares.

Do what thou wilt, thou shalt not so,
Dark Angel! triumph over me:
Lonely, unto the Lone I go;
Divine, to the Divinity.

BY THE STATUE
OF KING CHARLES AT CHARING CROSS

SOMBRE and rich, the skies,
Great glooms, and starry plains;
Gently the night wind sighs;
Else a vast silence reigns.

The splendid silence clings
Around me: and around
The saddest of all Kings,
Crown'd, and again discrown'd.

Comely and calm, he rides
Hard by his own Whitehall.
Only the night wind glides:
No crowds, nor rebels, brawl.

Gone, too, his Court: and yet,
The stars his courtiers are:
Stars in their stations set;
And every wandering star.

Alone he rides, alone,
The fair and fatal King:
Dark night is all his own,
That strange and solemn thing.

Which are more full of fate:
The stars; or those sad eyes?
Which are more still and great:
Those brows, or the dark skies?

Although his whole heart yearn
In passionate tragedy,
Never was face so stern
With sweet austerity.

Vanquish'd in life, his death
By beauty made amends:
The passing of his breath
Won his defeated ends.

Brief life, and hapless? Nay:
Through death, life grew sublime.
Speak after sentence? Yea:
And to the end of time.

Armour'd he rides, his head
Bare to the stars of doom;
He triumphs now, the dead,
Beholding London's gloom.

Our wearier spirit faints,
Vex'd in the world's employ:
His soul was of the saints;
And art to him was joy.

King, tried in fires of woe!
Men hunger for thy grace:
And through the night I go,
Loving thy mournful face.

Yet, when the city sleeps,
When all the cries are still,
The stars and heavenly deeps
Work out a perfect will.

OXFORD

OVER, the four long years ! And now there rings
One voice of freedom and regret: *Farewell!*
Now old remembrance sorrows, and now sings:
But song from sorrow, now, I cannot tell.

City of weather'd cloister and worn court;
Grey city of strong towers and clustering spires:
Where art's fresh loveliness would first resort;
Where lingering art kindled her latest fires !

Where on all hands, wondrous with ancient grace,
Grace touch'd with age, rise works of goodliest men:
Next Wykeham's art obtain their splendid place
The zeal of Inigo, the strength of Wren.

Where at each coign of every antique street,
A memory hath taken root in stone:
There, Raleigh shone; there, toil'd Franciscan feet;
There, Johnson flinched not, but endured alone.

There, Shelley dream'd his white Platonic dreams;
There, classic Landor throve on Roman thought;
There, Addison pursued his quiet themes;
There, smiled Erasmus, and there, Colet taught.

And there, O memory more sweet than all !
Lived he, whose eyes keep yet our passing light;
Whose crystal lips Athenian speech recall;
Who wears Rome's purple with least pride, most **right.**[1]

[1] Cardinal Newman.

That is the Oxford strong to charm us yet:
Eternal in her beauty and her past.
What, though her soul be vex'd? She can forget
Cares of an hour: only the great things last.

Only the gracious air, only the charm,
And ancient might of true humanities,
These nor assault of man, nor time, can harm:
Not these, nor Oxford with her memories.

Together have we walk'd with willing feet
Gardens of plenteous trees, bowering soft lawn;
Hills whither Arnold wander'd; and all sweet
June meadows, from the troubling world withdrawn;

Chapels of cedarn fragrance, and rich gloom
Pour'd from empurpled panes on either hand;
Cool pavements, carved with legends of the tomb;
Grave haunts, where we might dream, and understand.

Over, the four long years! And unknown powers
Call to us, going forth upon our way:
Ah! Turn we, and look back upon the towers
That rose above our lives, and cheer'd the day.

Proud and serene, against the sky they gleam:
Proud and secure, upon the earth they stand.
Our city hath the air of a pure dream,
And hers indeed is a Hesperian land.

Think of her so! The wonderful, the fair,
The immemorial, and the ever young:
The city sweet with our forefathers' care:
The city where the Muses all have sung.

Ill times may be; she hath no thought of time:
She reigns beside the waters yet in pride.
Rude voices cry: but in her ears the chime
Of full sad bells brings back her old springtide.

Like to a queen in pride of place, she wears
The splendour of a crown in Radcliffe's dome.
Well fare she—well!   As perfect beauty fares,
And those high places that are beauty's home.

STEPHEN PHILLIPS

———

FROM *MARPESSA*

Idas to
Marpessa.
                         I LOVE thee then
Not only for thy body packed with sweet
Of all this world, that cup of brimming June,
That jar of violet wine set in the air,
That palest rose sweet in the night of life;
Not for that stirring bosom all besieged
By drowsing lovers, or thy perilous hair;
Not for that face that might indeed provoke
Invasion of old cities; no, nor all
Thy freshness stealing on me like strange sleep.
Not for this only do I love thee, but
Because Infinity upon thee broods,
And thou art full of whispers and of shadows.
Thou meanest what the sea has striven to say
So long, and yearnèd up the cliffs to tell;
Thou art what all the winds have uttered not,
What the still night suggesteth to the heart.
Thy voice is like to music heard ere birth,
Some spirit lute touched on a spirit sea;
Thy face remembered is from other worlds,
It has been died for, though I know not when,
It has been sung of, though I know not where.

It has the strangeness of the luring West,
And of sad sea-horizons; beside thee
I am aware of other times and lands,
Of births far back, of lives in many stars.
O beauty lone and like a candle clear
In this dark country of the world! Thou art
My woe, my early light, my music dying.

.   .   .   .   .   .

But if I live with Idas, then we two *Marpessa*
On the low earth shall prosper hand in hand *to Apollo.*
In odours of the open field, and live
In peaceful noises of the farm, and watch
The pastoral fields burned by the setting sun.
And he shall give me passionate children, not
Some radiant god that will despise me quite,
But clambering limbs and little hearts that err.
And I shall sleep beside him in the night,
And fearful from some dream shall touch his hand
Secure; or at some festival we two
Will wander through the lighted city streets;
And in the crowd I 'll take his arm and feel
Him closer for the press. So shall we live.
And though the first sweet sting of love be past,
The sweet that almost venom is; though youth,
With tender and extravagant delight,
The first and secret kiss by twilight hedge,
The insane farewell repeated o'er and o'er,
Pass off; there shall succeed a faithful peace;
Beautiful friendship tried by sun and wind,
Durable from the daily dust of life.
And though with sadder, still with kinder eyes,
We shall behold all frailties, we shall haste
To pardon, and with mellowing minds to bless.
Then though we must grow old, we shall grow old
Together, and he shall not greatly miss
My bloom faded, and waning light of eyes,
Too deeply gazed in ever to seem dim;

Nor shall we murmur at, nor much regret
The years that gently bend us to the ground,
And gradually incline our face; that we
Leisurely stooping, and with each slow step,
May curiously inspect our lasting home.
But we shall sit with luminous holy smiles,
Endeared by many griefs, by many a jest,
And custom sweet of living side by side;
And full of memories not unkindly glance
Upon each other.   Last, we shall descend
Into the natural ground—not without tears—
One must go first, ah god! one must go first;
After so long one blow for both were good;
Still, like old friends, glad to have met, and leave
Behind a wholesome memory on the earth.

LAURENCE BINYON

—

THE LITTLE DANCERS: A LONDON VISION

LONELY, save for a few faint stars, the sky
Dreams; and lonely, below, the little street
Into its gloom retires, secluded and shy.
Scarcely the dumb roar enters this soft retreat;
And all is dark, save where come flooding rays
From a tavern window: there, to the brisk measure
Of an organ that down in an alley merrily plays,
Two children, all alone and no one by,
Holding their tatter'd frocks, through an airy maze
Of motion, lightly threaded with nimble feet,
Dance sedately: face to face they gaze,
Their eyes shining, grave with a perfect pleasure.

THE BACCHANAL OF ALEXANDER

I

A WONDROUS rumour fills and stirs
The wide Carmanian Vale;
On leafy hills the sunburnt vintagers
Stand listening; silent is the echoing flail
Upon the threshing floors:
Girls in the orchards one another hail
Over their golden stores.
'Leave the dewy apples hanging flushed,
Ripe to drop
In our baskets! Leave the heavy grapes uncrushed,
Leave the darkened figs, a half-pulled crop,
Olive-boughs by staves unbeaten, come,
All our hills be hushed!
For a Conqueror, nay a God,
Comes into our land this day,
From the Eastern desert dumb,
That no mortal ever trod:
Come we down to meet him on his way!'

From reddening vineyards steeped in sun,
Trees that with riches droop,
Down the green upland men and maidens run
Or under the low leaves with laughter stoop.
But now they pause, they hear
Far trampling sounds; and many a soft-eyed troop
Murmurs a wondering fear.
'Wherefore hast thou summoned us afar,
Voice so proud?
Who are ye that so imperious are?
Is it he to whom all India bowed,
Bacchus, and the great host that pursue
Triumphing, his car;
Whom our fathers long foretold?
O if it be he, the God indeed,

May his power our vines endue
With prosperity fourfold.
Bring we all ripe offerings for his need!'

Slowly along the vine-robed vale move on,
Like those that walk in dream,
The ranks of Macedon.
O much-proved men, why doubt ye truth so sweet?
This is that fair Carmania, that did seem
So far to gain, yet now is at your feet.
'Tis no Circean magic greenly crowds
This vale of elms, the laden vines uprearing,
The small flowers in the grass, the illumined clouds,
Trembling streams with rushes lined,
All in strangeness reappearing
Like a blue morn to the blind!
Worn feet go happy, and parched throats may laugh,
Or blissful cold drops from dipt helmets quaff;
Dear comrades, flinging spears down, stand embraced
And heap this rich oblivion on the waste
Of torment whence they came;
That land of salt sand vaulted o'er with flame,
That furnace, which for sixty days they pierced,
Wrapt in a hot slow cloud of pricking grains,
On ever crumbling mounds through endless plains
And ravening hands scooped fire, not water, for their thirst
Streams of Carmania, never have ye seen
Such mirrored rapture of strong limbs unclad,
Lips pressing, lover-like, delicious green
Of leaves, or breaking into laughter mad;
Out-wearied ranks, that couched in gloom serene,
Let idle memory toy
With torment past whose pangs enrich the gust of joy.

II

O peerless Alexander! still
From his kindling words they glow.
Like a straight shaft to a bow

Is their strength unto his will.
He hath done what no man ever dared:
That fierce desert, where great Cyrus lost
All save seven of his unnumbered host,
Where the proud Semiramis despaired,
He hath brought his thousands through.
Vainly, vainly Wind and Fire
Stormed against the way of his desire:
They at last their tamer knew.
O'er mile-broad rivers, like young brooks, he stept,
Walls of unconquered cities overleapt.
And now Earth yields, for storm and strife and heat,
Her greenest valley to his feet.

But lo! the soft Carmanian folk,
Round these warriors gathering nigh,
Down the slopes with murmur shy
The benignant God invoke.
While they stand in wonder and in doubt,
Comes a throng in leaves their heads arraying,
Some on pipes and some on tabors playing,
'Bacchus, Bacchus is our King,' they shout,
'Magic mirth into our blood he pours;
Join us, strangers, in our feast!
All our parching toil hath ceased.
Give us of your fruitful valley's stores!'
Apples they heap on shields in golden domes,
And spear points bear the dripping honeycombs.
'Our Bacchus bids you to his joy,' they sing;
'Lo, where he comes, the King!'

Two massy ivory cars, together bound,
Roll through the parting throng;
A whole uprooted vine enwreathes them round;
Long tendrils over the gold axles trail,
While jubilant pipe and chanted song
The cars' oncoming hail.

By the dark bunches idle helms and greaves
Are hung, and swords that on Hydaspes shone;
Heroic shoulders gleam betwixt the leaves !
There sits reclined on rugs of Susa spread,
Throned amid his Seven of Macedon,
Alexander ! his victorious head
Bound with ivy and pale autumn flowers.
Ah, what a sunny redolence of showers
The wind wafts round him from this promised land !
Over Hephaestion's neck is laid one hand,
Lightly the other holds a spear; but now
No passion fires his eye, nor deep thought knots his brow
Like his own Pella breathes this upland air;
A joy born beauty flushes up his face,
O'ersmoothing old fell rages, to replace
Youth in lost lines most indolently fair.
Remembrance is at peace, desire foregone,
And those winged brows their watchful menace ease
In languor proud as a storm-sailing swan
New lighted on a mere from the wild seas.
Beat, thrilling drums, beat low, and pipes sound on,
While his full soul doth gaze
From this the topmost hour of all his glorious days.

III

The shy Carmanians awed
Gaze on that sun-like head.
'Is it he,' they murmur, 'who led
The mirth of the vineyard abroad?
Surely none else may bear
So regal a beauty; yet why
On us turns not his eye?
We have heard that he loves not care,
But the dance and idle glee
Of the laughing Satyr tribe.
Could toil those brows inscribe?
Is it he? is it surely he?

Are these the revellers of his train?
Yet surely these have passed through fire, through pain!
Can the Gods also suffer throes,
Nor crave to conquer, but repose?'

The King uplifts his bowl.
Peucestas stoops, pours in
From a brown fawn's swelling skin
The ripe grape's rosy soul.
'Pledge us,' he cries, and smiles,
'Lord of Nysa, to-day!
Have we not toiled our way
To a valley of the Blessed Isles?
Drink of a richer boon
Than the water we brought thee to taste
In the fiery Gedrosian waste
When we halted our host at noon,
And thou in the sight of all didst spill
Those longed-for drops on the darkened sand,—O fill,
Remembering how our hearts drank wine
From thy refusing deed divine.'

What hath the King so stirred?
What grief of a great desire
Stung by that spoken word?
Sudden as storm his thoughts tumultuous run
Back into peril, Indus, Issus, Tyre,
And the famed gates of Babylon yet unwon.
Far, far those mighty days in glory tower!
A valley keeps him, while the great peaks call.
O for that supreme exultant hour,
When alone, Achilles-like, he sprang
Mid the astonished Indians o'er the wall,
And a hundred arrows round him rang!
O Alexander, all these thousands own
Thy pleasure, but thy woes were thine alone.
Dulled is the joy that hath no need to dare;
Match thy great self, and breed another heir

To those high deeds, from which thy kindled fame
Runs, as the world's hope runs from youth to youth aflame
Climb, climb again to those lone eagle skies,
Where ocean's unadventured circle bends
And dragon ignorance girdles the world's ends !—
As fire leaps up a tower, that thought leaps to his eyes.
'Off, Maenad mummery,' he cries; his brow
Strips off its garland with indignant hands,
Starts up, and plants his ringing spear; and now,
Soul-flushed through radiant limbs, a man transfigured stands
With joy the marvelling Carmanians bow,
From their long doubting freed:
'It is the God,' they cry, 'the enraptured God indeed!'

FOR THE FALLEN

1914

WITH proud thanksgiving, a mother for her children,
England mourns for her dead across the sea.
Flesh of her flesh they were, spirit of her spirit,
Fallen in the cause of the free.

Solemn the drums thrill: Death august and royal
Sings sorrow up into immortal spheres.
There is music in the midst of desolation
And a glory that shines upon our tears.

They went with songs to the battle, they were young,
Straight of limb, true of eye, steady and aglow.
They were staunch to the end against odds uncounted
They fell with their faces to the foe.

They shall grow not old, as we that are left grow old:
Age shall not weary them, nor the years condemn.
At the going down of the sun and in the morning
We will remember them.

They mingle not with their laughing comrades again;
They sit no more at familiar tables of home;
They have no lot in our labour of the day-time;
They sleep beyond England's foam.

But where our desires are and our hopes profound,
Felt as a well-spring that is hidden from sight,
To the innermost heart of their own land they are known
As the stars are known to the Night;

As the stars that shall be bright when we are dust,
Moving in marches upon the heavenly plain,
As the stars that are starry in the time of our darkness,
To the end, to the end, they remain.

HILAIRE BELLOC

———

THE SOUTH COUNTRY

When I am living in the Midlands
  That are sodden and unkind,
I light my lamp in the evening:
  My work is left behind;
And the great hills of the South Country
  Come back into my mind.

The great hills of the South Country
  They stand along the sea;
And it 's there walking in the high woods
  That I could wish to be,
And the men that were boys when I was a boy
  Walking along with me.

The men that live in North England
  I saw them for a day:
Their hearts are set upon the waste fells,
  Their skies are fast and grey:
From their castle-walls a man may see
  The mountains far away.

The men that live in West England
  They see the Severn strong,
A-rolling on rough water brown
  Light aspen leaves along.
They have the secret of the Rocks,
  And the oldest kind of song.

But the men that live in the South Country
  Are the kindest and most wise,
They get their laughter from the loud surf,
  And the faith in their happy eyes
Comes surely from our Sister the Spring
  When over the sea she flies;
The violets suddenly bloom at her feet,
  She blesses us with surprise.

I never get between the pines
  But I smell the Sussex air;
Nor I never come on a belt of sand
  But my home is there.
And along the sky the line of the Downs
  So noble and so bare.

A lost thing could I never find,
  Nor a broken thing mend:
And I fear I shall be all alone
  When I get towards the end.
Who will there be to comfort me
  Or who will be my friend?

I will gather and carefully make my friends
    Of the men of the Sussex Weald,
They watch the stars from silent folds,
    They stiffly plough the field.
By them and the God of the South Country
    My poor soul shall be heal'd.

If I ever become a rich man,
    Or if ever I grow to be old,
I will build a house with deep thatch
    To shelter me from the cold,
And there shall the Sussex songs be sung
    And the story of Sussex told.

I will hold my house in the high wood
    Within a walk of the sea,
And the men that were boys when I was a boy
    Shall sit and drink with me.

ALFRED DOUGLAS

—

THE CITY OF THE SOUL

I

IN the salt terror of a stormy sea
There are high altitudes the mind forgets;
And undesired days are hunting nets
To snare the souls that fly Eternity.
But we being gods will never bend the knee,
Though sad moons shadow every sun that sets,
And tears of sorrow be like rivulets
To feed the shallows of Humility.

Within my soul are some mean gardens found
Where drooped flowers are, and unsung melodies,
And all companioning of piteous things.

But in the midst is one high terraced ground,
Where level lawns sweep through the stately trees
And the great peacocks walk like painted kings.

II

What shall we do, my soul, to please the King?
Seeing he hath no pleasure in the dance,
And hath condemned the honeyed utterance
Of silver flutes and mouths made round to sing.
Along the wall red roses climb and cling,
And Oh! my prince, lift up thy countenance,
For there be thoughts like roses that entrance
More than the languors of soft lute-playing.

Think how the hidden things that poets see
In amber eves or mornings crystalline,
Hide in the soul their constant quenchless light,
Till, called by some celestial alchemy,
Out of forgotten depths, they rise and shine
Like buried treasure on Midsummer night.

III

The fields of Phantasy are all too wide,
My soul runs through them like an untamed thing.
It leaps the brooks like threads, and skirts the ring
Where fairies danced, and tenderer flowers hide.
The voice of music has become the bride
Of an imprisoned bird with broken wing.
What shall we do, my soul, to please the King,
We that are free, with ample wings untied?

We cannot wander through the empty fields
Till beauty like a hunter hurl the lance.
There are no silver snares and springes set,
Nor any meadow where the plain ground yields.
O let us then with ordered utterance,
Forge the gold chain and twine the silken net.

IV

Each new hour's passage is the acolyte
Of inarticulate song and syllable,
And every passing moment is a bell,
To mourn the death of undiscerned delight.
Where is the sun that made the noon-day bright,
And where the midnight moon?   O let us tell,
In long carved line and painted parable,
How the white road curves down into the night.

Only to build one crystal barrier
Against this sea which beats upon our days;
To ransom one lost moment with a rhyme,
Or, if fate cries and grudging gods demur,
To clutch Life's hair, and thrust one naked phrase
Like a lean knife between the ribs of Time.

THE GREEN RIVER

I KNOW a green grass path that leaves the field,
    And, like a running river, winds along
    Into a leafy wood where is no throng
Of birds at noon-day, and no soft throats yield
Their music to the moon.   The place is seal'd,
    An unclaimed sovereignty of voiceless song,
    And all the unravish'd silences belong
To some sweet singer lost or unreveal'd.

So is my soul become a silent place.
    Oh may I wake from this uneasy night
        To find some voice of music manifold.
Let it be shape of sorrow with wan face,
    Or Love that swoons on sleep, or else delight
        That is as wide-eyed as a marigold.

WILLIAM HENRY DAVIES

TRULY GREAT

My walls outside must have some flowers,
  My walls within must have some books;
A house that 's small; a garden large,
  And in it leafy nooks.

A little gold that 's sure each week;
  That comes not from my living kind,
But from a dead man in his grave,
  Who cannot change his mind:

A lovely wife, and gentle too;
  Contented that no eyes but mine
Can see her many charms, nor voice
  To call her beauty fine:

Where she would in that stone cage live,
  A self-made prisoner with me;
While many a wild bird sang around,
  On gate, on bush, on tree.

And she sometimes to answer them,
  In her far sweeter voice than all;
Till birds, that loved to look on leaves,
  Will doat on a stone wall.

With this small house, this garden large,
  This little gold, this lovely mate,
With health in body, peace at heart—
  Show me a man more great.

THE KINGFISHER

It was the Rainbow gave thee birth,
    And left thee all her lovely hues;
And, as her mother's name was Tears,
    So runs it in thy blood to choose
For haunts the lonely pools, and keep
In company with trees that weep.

Go you and, with such glorious hues,
    Live with proud Peacocks in green parks;
On lawns as smooth as shining glass,
    Let every feather show its mark;
Get thee on boughs and clap thy wings
Before the windows of proud kings.

Nay, lovely Bird, thou art not vain;
    Thou has no proud ambitious mind;
I also love a quiet place
    That's green, away from all mankind;
A lonely pool, and let a tree
Sigh with her bosom over me.

THE MOON

Thy beauty haunts me, heart and soul,
    Oh thou fair Moon, so close and bright;
Thy beauty makes me like the child,
    That cries aloud to own thy light:
The little child that lifts each arm,
To press thee to her bosom warm.

Though there are birds that sing this night
    With thy white beams across their throats,
Let my deep silence speak for me
    More than for them their sweetest notes:
Who worships thee till music fails
Is greater than thy nightingales.

LOVELY DAMES

FEW are my books, but my small few have told
Of many a lovely dame that lived of old;
And they have made me see those fatal charms
Of Helen, which brought Troy so many harms;
And lovely Venus, when she stood so white
Close to her husband's forge in its red light.
I have seen Dian's beauty in my dreams,
When she had trained her looks in all the streams
She crossed to Latmos and Endymion;
And Cleopatra's eyes, that hour they shone
The brighter for a pearl she drank to prove
How poor it was compared to her rich love:
But when I look on thee, love, thou dost give
Substance to those fine ghosts, and make them live.

LEISURE

WHAT is this life if, full of care,
We have no time to stand and stare.

No time to stand beneath the boughs
And stare as long as sheep or cows.

No time to see, when woods we pass,
Where squirrels hide their nuts in grass.

No time to see, in broad daylight,
Streams full of stars, like skies at night.

No time to turn at Beauty's glance,
And watch her feet, how they can dance.

No time to wait till her mouth can
Enrich that smile her eyes began.

A poor life this if, full of care,
We have no time to stand and stare.

SIDNEY ROYSE LYSAGHT

FIRST PATHWAYS

Where were the pathways that your childhood knew?—
  In mountain glens? or by the ocean strands?
  Or where, beyond the ripening harvest lands,
The distant hills were blue?

Where evening sunlight threw a golden haze
  Over a mellow city's walls and towers?
  Or where the fields and lanes were bright with flowers,
In quiet woodland ways?

And whether here or there, or east or west,
  That place you dwelt in first was holy ground;
  Its shelter was the kindest you have found,
Its pathways were the best.

And even in the city's smoke and mire
  I doubt not that a golden light was shed
  On those first paths, and that they also led
To lands of heart's desire.

And where the children in dark alleys penn'd,
  Heard the caged lark sing of the April hills,
  Or where they damm'd the muddy gutter rills,
Or made a dog their friend;

Or where they gather'd, dancing hand in hand,
  About the organ man, for them, too, lay
  Beyond the dismal alley's entrance way,
The gates of wonderland.

For 'tis my faith that Earth's first words are sweet
  To all her children,—never a rebuff;
  And that we only saw, where ways were rough,
The flowers about our feet.

1921

T. STURGE MOORE

THE PANTHER

I

CONSIDER now the panther: Such the beast
On which the naked feet of Circe rest—
Her footstool wherein anger is increased
For ever, yet for ever is suppressed.

Sleek, powerful, and treacherous, and cowed,
With amber eyes like tears that watch a lamp—
A Queen's tears, thwarted by remembrance proud,
Clear cut as gold coins that her mint doth stamp.

How politic is grace in moods morose!
This smooth composure waits but our caress;
'Tis pride put on to beggar love; there glows
Knit with this strength some utter tenderness.

That blunt round paw, and padded glove-like palm!
How strange, if, there, like dulled assassin steel,
Sheathed claws wait ready! Thus in forest calm
That cruel face the ferns' arched fronds conceal.

Then all is glowing, like deep-treasured glee:
E'en butterflies might settle on this coat;
The shy gazelles may snuff full gingerly,—
Rich blossoms drown the odours they should note.

The holy baobab, with grey-blue stems
And aislèd vistas solemn as a church,
Denies this presence, and this life condemns;
Its meek-eyed throngs would wrong it should they search

A bound! a scamper! cry! the sob of death!
And these claws open up the heart that pang
Had filled to bursting with a last gasped breath;
Warm blood is lapped, and fleshed is every fang.

Hereto conspired the beauty of the place,
Whose whole consent seemed given to life's ease.
Thus, by a garden walk, some poppy's grace
Brings down a child sultana to her knees;

Whose tall indifference next prompts her fond hand
To stoop its cup, where drowsy drops of dew
Roll and unite like quick-silver, or stand
In lustrous clots, then self-divide anew:

All, with a kiss, her human heart soon must
Attempt to possess; or quaff, with amorous sip,
Those wilful gems freighted with purple dust,
Where lurks a bee-sting venomed for her lip;

For while large petals closed at shut of eve,
The bee ceased not to gorge—could not burst free—
Fumed through the night, and stingless took his leave.
Thus rage in this beast pent left perfidy.

II

But, lo! they yawn, those wide-hinged python jaws,
Unroof the rose-pink ivory-studded bed,
Where, like a languid flame, the lithe tongue draws
Its moist caress round gums and hollows red.

Dost, cloyed by rich meats spicy as the south,
Expose thy fevered palate to the cool,
Which, like snow melting in an emperor's mouth,
Helps make excess thy life's ironic rule?

Soft-coated, each curved ear seems some weird flower,
Whose gulf with silken lashes gleams replete;
Such yield to let the fond fly, feasting, lower,
But close and stiffen to forbid retreat.

Thus dost thou draw our thought, by subtler hints,
Still further down the vortex of thy spell;
Lace-winged on delicate feet it onward glints—
A trickling tear—a soul hung over hell.

Those cushion brows, with sullen show of thought,
Deceive the eye; so emery, cloaked in state
Of some mock scarlet berry needle-wrought,
Maketh a young child marvel at its weight.

Can they be vacant?   Can thy strong neck raise,
Without the aid of magic, thy full brain?
Of thee our child-thought in the mind delays,
Whence to dislodge it reason toils in vain.

The mystery of evil and its charm
Prevail, like beauty, radiant from thy form;
Thou art an enemy that can disarm
Man's arrogance, which like a swollen storm

Sweeps all creation with the tyrant force
Of his long hunger for congenial dreams;
Though he condemn thee, yet as in remorse
He thy soft pelt a couch for beauty deems—

Spreadeth it for the bride his ecstasy
Crowns Rose of Sharon, Lily of the valleys,—
Voweth it doth become her, likening thee,
Soul of the woods, to her, soul of his palace.

THE GAZELLES

When the sheen on tall summer grass is pale,
Across blue skies white clouds float on
In shoals, or disperse and singly sail,
Till, the sun being set, they all are gone:

Yet, as long as they may shine bright in the sun,
They flock or stray through the daylight bland,
While their stealthy shadows like foxes run
Beneath where the grass is dry and tanned:

And the waste, in hills that swell and fall,
Goes heaving into yet dreamier haze;
And a wonder of silence is over all
Where the eye feeds long like a lover's gaze:

Then, cleaving the grass, gazelles appear
(The gentler dolphins of kindlier waves)
With sensitive heads alert of ear;
Frail crowds that a delicate hearing saves,

That rely on the nostrils' keenest power,
And are governed from trance-like distances
By hopes and fears, and, hour by hour,
Sagacious of safety, snuff the breeze.

They keep together, the timid hearts;
And each one's fear with a panic thrill
Is passed to an hundred; and if one starts
In three seconds all are over the hill.

A Nimrod might watch, in his hall's wan space,
After the feast, on the moonlit floor,
The timorous mice that troop and race,
As tranced o'er those herds the sun doth pour;

Like a wearied tyrant sated with food
Who envies each tiniest thief that steals
Its hour from his abstracted mood,
For it living zest and beauty reveals.

He alone, save the quite dispassionate moon,
Sees them; she stares at the prowling pard
Who surprises their sleep, and, ah! how soon
Is riding the weakest or sleepiest hard!

Let an agony's nightmare course begin,
Four feet with five spurs apiece control,
Like a horse thief reduced to save his skin
Or a devil that rides a human soul!

The race is as long as recorded time,
Yet brief as the flash of assassin's knife;
For 'tis crammed as history is with crime
'Twixt the throbs at taking and losing life;

Then the warm wet clutch on the nape of the neck,
Through which the keen incisors drive;
Then the fleet knees give, down drops the wreck
Of yesterday's pet that was so alive.

Yet the moon is naught concerned, ah no!
She shines as on a drifting plank
Far in some northern sea-stream's flow
From which two numbed hands loosened and sank.

Such thinning their number must suffer; and worse
When hither at times the Shah's children roam,
Their infant listlessness to immerse
In energy's ancient upland home:

For here the shepherd in years of old
Was taught by the stars, and bred a race
That welling forth from these highlands rolled
In tides of conquest o'er earth's face:

On piebald ponies or else milk-white,
Here, with green bridles in silver bound,
A crescent moon on the violet night
Of their saddle cloths, or a sun rayed round,—

With tiny bells on their harness ringing,
And voices that laugh and are shrill by starts,
Prancing, curvetting, and with them bringing
Swift chetahs cooped up in light-wheeled carts,

They come, and their dainty pavilions pitch
In some valley, beside a sinuous pool,
Where a grove of cedars towers in which
Herons have built, where the shade is cool;

Where they tether their ponies to low hung boughs,
Where long through the night their red fires gleam,
Where the morning's stir doth them arouse
To their bath in the lake, as from dreams to a dream.

And thence in an hour their hunt rides forth,
And the chetahs course the shy gazelle
To the east or west or south or north,
And every eve in a distant vale

A hecatomb of the slaughtered beasts
Is piled; tongues loll from breathless throats;
Round large jet eyes the horsefly feasts—
Jet eyes, which now a blue film coats:

Dead there they bleed, and each prince there
Is met by his sister, wife, or bride—
Delicious ladies with long dark hair,
And soft dark eyes, and brows arched wide,

In quilted jacket, embroidered sash,
And tent-like skirts of pleated lawn;
While their silk-lined jewelled slippers flash
Round bare feet bedded like pools at dawn:

So choicefully prepared to please,
Young, female, royal of race and mood,
In indolent compassion these
O'er those dead beauteous creatures brood:

They lean some minutes against their friend,
A lad not slow to praise himself,
Who tells how this one met his end
Out-raced, or trapped by leopard stealth,

And boasts his chetahs fleetest are;
Through his advice the chance occurred,
That leeward vale by which the car
Was well brought round to head the herd.

Seeing him bronzed by sun and wind,
She feels his power and owns him lord,
Then, that his courage may please her mind
With a soft coy hand half draws his sword,

Just shudders to see the cold steel gleam,
And drops it back in the long curved sheath;
She will make his evening meal a dream
And surround his sleep like some rich wreath

Of heavy-lidded flowers bewitched
To speak soft words of ecstasy
To wizard king old, wise, and enriched
With all save youth's and love's sweet glee.

But, while they sleep, the orphaned herd
And wounded stragglers, through the night
Wander in pain, and wail unheard
To the moon and the stars so cruelly bright:

Why are they born? ah! why beget
They in the long November gloom
Heirs of their beauty, their fleetness,—yet
Heirs of their panics, their pangs, their doom?

That to princely spouses children are born
To be daintily bred and taught to please,
Has a fitness like the return of morn:
But why perpetuate lives like these?

Why, with horns that jar and with fiery eyes,
Should the male stags fight for the shuddering does
Through the drear, dark nights, with frequent cries
From tyrant lust or outlawed woes?

Doth the meaningless beauty of their lives
Rave in the spring, when they course afar
Like the shadows of birds, and the young fawn strives
Till its parents no longer the fleetest are?

Like the shadows of flames which the sun's rays throw
On a kiln's blank wall, where glaziers dwell,
Pale shadows as those from glasses they blow,
Yet that lap at the blank wall and rebel,—

Even so to my curious trance-like thought
Those herds move over those pallid hills,
With fever as of a frail life caught
In circumstance o'ercharged with ills;

More like the shadow of lives than life,
Or most like the life that is never born
From baffled purpose and foredoomed strife,
That in each man's heart must be hidden from scorn.

Yet with something of beauty very rare
Unseizable, fugitive, half-discerned;
The trace of intentions that might have been fair
In action, left on a face that yearned

But long has ceased to yearn, alas!
So faint a trace do they leave on the slopes
Of hills as sleek as their coats with grass;
So faint may the trace be of noblest hopes.

Yet why are they born to roam and die?
Can their beauty answer thy query, O soul?
Nay, nor that of hopes which were born to fly,
But whose pinions the common and coarse day stole.

Like that region of grassy hills outspread,
A realm of our thoughts knows days and nights
And summers and winters, and has fed
Ineffectual herds of vanished delights.

* 1921

CHARLOTTE MEW

THE FARMER'S BRIDE

THREE summers since I chose a maid,
Too young maybe—but more 's to do
At harvest-time than bide and woo.
    When us was wed she turned afraid
Of love and me and all things human;
Like the shut of a winter's day.
Her smile went out and 'twasn't a woman—
    More like a little frightened fay.
        One night, in the Fall, she runned away.

'Out 'mong the sheep, her be,' they said,
'Should properly have been abed;
But sure enough she wasn't there
Lying awake with her wide brown stare.
So over seven-acre field and up-along across the down
We chased her, flying like a hare
Before our lanterns.   To Church-Town
    All in a shiver and a scare
We caught her, fetched her home at last
    And turned the key upon her, fast.

She does the work about the house
As well as most, but like a mouse:
    Happy enough to chat and play
    With birds and rabbits and such as they,
    So long as men-folk keep away.

'Not near, not near,' her eyes beseech
When one of us comes within reach.
    The women say that beasts in stall
    Look round like children at her call.
    I 've hardly heard her speak at all.

Shy as a leveret, swift as he,
Straight and slight as a young larch tree,
Sweet as the first wild violets, she,
To her wild self.   But what to me?

The short days shorten and the oaks are brown,
    The blue smoke rises to the low grey sky,
One leaf in the still air falls slowly down,
    A magpie's spotted feathers lie
On the black earth spread white with rime,
The berries redden up to Christmas-time.
    What 's Christmas time without there be
    Some other in the house than we!

She sleeps up in the attic there
    Alone, poor maid.   'Tis but a stair
Betwixt us.   Oh! my God! the down,
The soft young down of her, the brown,
The brown of her—her eyes, her hair, her hair!

JOHN SWINNERTON PHILLIMORE
—

IN A MEADOW

            THIS is the place
Where far from the unholy populace
The daughter of Philosophy and Sleep
        Her court doth keep,
Sweet Contemplation.   To her service bound
        Hover around
The little amiable summer airs,
        Her courtiers.

        The deep black soil
Makes mute her palace-floors with thick trefoil;
The grasses sagely nodding overhead
        Curtain her bed;

And lest the feet of strangers overpass
    Her walls of grass,
Gravely a little river goes his rounds
    To beat the bounds.

    —No bustling flood
To make a tumult in her neighbourhood,
But such a stream as knows to go and come
    Discreetly dumb.
Therein are chambers tapestried with weeds
    And screen'd with reeds;
For roof the waterlily-leaves serene
    Spread tiles of green.

    The sun's large eye
Falls soberly upon me where I lie;
For delicate webs of immaterial haze
    Refine his rays.
The air is full of music none knows what,
    Or half-forgot;
The living echo of dead voices fills
    The unseen hills.

    I hear the song
Of cuckoo answering cuckoo all day long;
And know not if it be my inward sprite
    For my delight
Making remember'd poetry appear
    As sound in the ear:
Like a salt savour poignant in the breeze
    From distant seas.

    Dreams without sleep,
And sleep too clear for dreaming and too deep;
And Quiet very large and manifold
    About me roll'd;

Satiety, that momentary flower,
    Stretch'd to an hour:
These are her gifts which all mankind may use,
    And all refuse.

FORD MADOX HUEFFER
—

TO CHRISTINA AT NIGHTFALL

LITTLE thing, ah! little mouse
Creeping through the twilight house,
To watch within the shadow of my chair
With large blue eyes; the firelight on your hair
    Doth glimmer gold and faint,
    And on your woollen gown
      That folds a-down
From steadfast little face to square-set feet.

Ah, sweet! ah, little one! so like a carven saint,
With your unflinching eyes, unflinching face,
Like a small angel, carved in a high place,
Watching unmoved across a gabled town;
When I am weak and old,
And lose my grip, and crave my small reward
Of tolerance and tenderness and ruth,
The children of your dawning day shall hold
The reins we drop and wield the judge's sword,
And your swift feet shall tread upon my heels,
And I be Ancient Error, you New Truth,
And I be crushed by your advancing wheels. . . .
    Good-night! The fire is burning low,
      Put out the lamp;
    Lay down the weary little head
      Upon the small white bed.
Up from the sea the night winds blow

Across the hill, across the marsh;
   Chill and harsh, harsh and damp,
     The night winds blow.
    But, while the slow hours go,
I, who must fall before you, late shall wait and keep
      Watch and ward,
      Vigil and guard,
      Where you sleep.
Ah, sweet! do you the like where I lie dead.

THE PORTRAIT

She sits upon a tombstone in the shade;
One flake of sunlight, falling thro' the veils
Of quivering poplars, lights upon her hair,
Shot golden, and across her candid brow.
Thus in the pleasant gloom she holds the eye,
Being life amid piled-up remembrances
Of the tranquil dead.
             One hand, dropped lightly down,
Rests on the words of a forgotten name:
Therefore the past makes glad to stay her up.
Closed in, walled off: here's an oblivious place,
Deep, planted in with trees, unvisited:
A still backwater in the tide of life.
Life flows all round; sounds from surrounding streets,
Laughter of unseen children, roll of wheels,
Cries of all vendors.—So she sits and waits.
And she rejoices us who pass her by,
And she rejoices those who here lie still,
And she makes glad the little wandering airs,
And doth make glad the shaken beams of light
That fall upon her forehead: all the world
Moves round her, sitting on forgotten tombs
And lighting in to-morrow. She is Life:
That makes us keep on moving, taking roads,

Hauling great burdens up the unending hills,
Pondering senseless problems, setting sail
For undiscovered anchorages. Here
She waits, she waits, sequestered among tombs,
The sunlight on her hair. She waits, she waits:
The secret music, the resolving note
That sets in tune all this discordant world
And solves the riddles of the Universe.

WALTER DE LA MARE

AN EPITAPH

Here lies a most beautiful lady,
Light of step and heart was she;
I think she was the most beautiful lady
That ever was in the West Country.
But beauty vanishes; beauty passes;
However rare—rare it be;
And when I crumble, who will remember
This lady of the West Country?

ARABIA

Far are the shades of Arabia,
Where the Princes ride at noon,
'Mid the verdurous vales and thickets,
Under the ghost of the moon;
And so dark is that vaulted purple
Flowers in the forest rise
And toss into blossom 'gainst the phantom stars
Pale in the noonday skies.

Sweet is the music of Arabia
  In my heart, when out of dreams
I still in the thin clear mirk of dawn
  Descry her gliding streams;
Hear her strange lutes on the green banks
  Ring loud with the grief and delight
Of the dim-silked, dark-haired Musicians
  In the brooding silence of night.

They haunt me—her lutes and her forests;
  No beauty on earth I see
But shadowed with that dream recalls
  Her loveliness to me:
Still eyes look coldly upon me,
  Cold voices whisper and say—
'He is crazed with the spell of far Arabia,
  They have stolen his wits away.'

THE LISTENERS

'Is there anybody there?' said the Traveller,
  Knocking on the moonlit door;
And his horse in the silence champ'd the grasses
  Of the forest's ferny floor:
And a bird flew up out of the turret,
  Above the Traveller's head:
And he smote upon the door again a second time;
  'Is there anybody there?' he said.
But no one descended to the Traveller;
  No head from the leaf-fringed sill
Lean'd over and look'd into his grey eyes,
  Where he stood perplex'd and still.
But only a host of phantom listeners
  That dwelt in the lone house then
Stood listening in the quiet of the moonlight
  To that voice from the world of men:
Stood thronging the faint moonbeams on the dark stair,

That goes down to the empty hall,
Hearkening in an air stirr'd and shaken
  By the lonely Traveller's call.
And he felt in his heart their strangeness,
  Their stillness answering his cry,
While his horse moved, cropping the dark turf,
  'Neath the starr'd and leafy sky;
For he suddenly smote on the door, even
  Louder, and lifted his head:—
'Tell them I came, and no one answer'd,
  That I kept my word,' he said.
Never the least stir made the listeners,
  Though every word he spake
Fell echoing through the shadowiness of the still house
  From the one man left awake:
Ay, they heard his foot upon the stirrup,
  And the sound of iron on stone,
And how the silence surged softly backward,
  When the plunging hoofs were gone.

FARE WELL

WHEN I lie where shades of darkness
Shall no more assail mine eyes,
Nor the rain make lamentation
  When the wind sighs;
How will fare the world whose wonder
Was the very proof of me?
Memory fades, must the remembered
  Perishing be?

Oh, when this my dust surrenders
Hand, foot, lip, to dust again,
May these loved and loving faces
  Please other men!
May the rusting harvest hedgerow
Still the Traveller's Joy entwine,
And as happy children gather
  Posies once mine.

Look thy last on all things lovely,
Every hour.   Let no night
Seal thy sense in deathly slumber
    Till to delight
Thou have paid thy utmost blessing;
Since that all things thou wouldst praise
Beauty took from those who loved them
    In other days.

GORDON BOTTOMLEY

TO IRONFOUNDERS AND OTHERS

When you destroy a blade of grass
You poison England at her roots:
Remember no man's foot can pass
Where evermore no green life shoots.

You force the birds to wing too high
Where your unnatural vapours creep:
Surely the living rocks shall die
When birds no rightful distance keep.

You have brought down the firmament
And yet no heaven is more near;
You shape huge deeds without event,
And half-made men believe and fear.

Your worship is your furnaces,
Which, like old idols, lost obscenes,
Have molten bowels; your vision is
Machines for making more machines.

O, you are buried in the night,
Preparing destinies of rust;
Iron misused must turn to blight
And dwindle to a tetter'd crust.

The grass, forerunner of life, has gone,
But plants that spring in ruins and shards
Attend until your dream is done:
I have seen hemlock in your yards.

The generations of the worm
Know not your loads piled on their soil;
Their knotted ganglions shall wax firm
Till your strong flagstones heave and toil.

When the old hollow'd earth is crack'd
And when, to grasp more power and feasts,
Its ores are emptied, wasted, lack'd,
The middens of your burning beasts

Shall be raked over till they yield
Last priceless slags for fashionings high,
Ploughs to wake grass in every field,
Chisels men's hands to magnify.

ATLANTIS

WHAT poets sang in Atlantis? Who can tell
The epics of Atlantis or their names?
The sea hath its own murmurs, and sounds not
The secrets of its silences beneath,
And knows not any cadences enfolded
When the last bubbles of Atlantis broke
Among the quieting of its heaving floor.

O, years and tides and leagues and all their billows
Can alter not man's knowledge of men's hearts—
While trees and rocks and clouds include our being
We know the epics of Atlantic still:
A hero gave himself to lesser men,
Who first misunderstood and murdered him,

And then misunderstood and worshipped him;
A woman was lovely and men fought for her,
Towns burnt for her, and men put men in bondage,
But she put lengthier bondage on them all;
A wanderer toiled among all the isles
That fleck this turning star of shifting sea,
Or lonely purgatories of the mind,
In longing for his home or his lost love.

Poetry is founded on the hearts of men:
Though in Nirvana or the Heavenly courts
The principle of beauty shall persist,
Its body of poetry, as the body of man,
Is but a terrene form, a terrene use,
That swifter being will not loiter with;
And, when mankind is dead and the world cold,
Poetry's immortality will pass.

G. K. CHESTERTON

THE DONKEY

When fishes flew and forests walked
 And figs grew upon thorn,
Some moment when the moon was blood
 Then surely I was born;

With monstrous head and sickening cry
 And ears like errant wings,
The devil's walking parody
 On all four-footed things.

The tattered outlaw of the earth,
 Of ancient crooked will;
Starve, scourge, deride me: I am dumb,
 I keep my secret still.

Fools! For I also had my hour;
One far fierce hour and sweet:
There was a shout about my ears,
And palms before my feet.

THE PRAISE OF DUST

'What of vile dust?' the preacher said.
'Methought the whole world woke,
The dead stone lived beneath my foot,
And my whole body spoke.

'You, that play tyrant to the dust,
And stamp its wrinkled face,
This patient star that flings you not
Far into homeless space,

'Come down out of your dusty shrine
The living dust to see,
The flowers that at your sermon's end
Stand blazing silently.

'Rich white and blood-red blossom; stones,
Lichens like fire encrust;
A gleam of blue, a glare of gold,
The vision of the dust.

'Pass them all by; till, as you come
Where, at a city's edge,
Under a tree—I know it well—
Under a lattice ledge,

'The sunshine falls on one brown head.
You, too, O cold of clay,
Eater of stones, may haply hear
The trumpets of that day

'When God to all His paladins
By His own splendour swore
To make a fairer face than heaven,
Of dust and nothing more.'

LEPANTO

WHITE founts falling in the Courts of the sun,
And the Soldan of Byzantium is smiling as they run;
There is laughter like the fountains in that face of all men
    feared,
It stirs the forest darkness, the darkness of his beard,
It curls the blood-red crescent, the crescent of his lips,
For the inmost sea of all the earth is shaken with his ships.
They have dared the white republics up the capes of Italy,
They have dashed the Adriatic round the Lion of the Sea,
And the Pope hast cast his arms abroad for agony and loss,
And called the kings of Christendom for swords about the
    Cross.
The cold Queen of England is looking in the glass;
The shadow of the Valois is yawning at the Mass;
From evening isles fantastical rings faint the Spanish gun,
And the Lord upon the Golden Horn is laughing in the
    sun.

Dim drums throbbing, in the hills half heard,
Where only on a nameless throne a crownless prince has
    stirred,
Where, risen from a doubtful seat and half attainted stall,
The last knight of Europe takes weapons from the wall,
The last and lingering troubadour to whom the bird has
    sung,
That once went singing southward when all the world was
    young.
In that enormous silence, tiny and unafraid,
Comes up along a winding road the noise of the Crusade.
Strong gongs groaning as the guns boom far,
Don John of Austria is going to the war,
Stiff flags straining in the night-blasts cold,
In the gloom black-purple, in the glint old-gold,
Torchlight crimson on the copper kettle-drums,
Then the tuckets, then the trumpets, then the cannon,
    and he comes.

Don John laughing in the brave beard curled,
Spurning of his stirrups like the thrones of all the world,
Holding his head up for a flag of all the free.
Love-light of Spain—hurrah!
Death-light of Africa!
Don John of Austria
Is riding to the sea.

Mahound is in his paradise above the evening star,
(*Don John of Austria is going to the war.*)
He moves a mighty turban on the timeless houri's knees,
His turban that is woven of the sunsets and the seas.
He shakes the peacock gardens as he rises from his ease,
And he strides among the tree-tops and is taller than the
    trees,
And his voice through all the garden is a thunder sent to
    bring
Black Azrael and Ariel and Ammon on the wing.
Giants and the Genii,
Multiplex of wing and eye,
Whose strong obedience broke the sky
When Solomon was king.

They rush in red and purple from the red clouds of the
    morn,
From temples where the yellow gods shut up their eyes in
    scorn;
They rise in green robes roaring from the green hells of the
    sea
Where fallen skies and evil hues and eyeless creatures be;
On them the sea-valves cluster and the grey sea-forests curl,
Splashed with a splendid sickness, the sickness of the
    pearl;
They swell in sapphire smoke out of the blue cracks of the
    ground,—
They gather and they wonder and give worship to Mahound.
And he saith, 'Break up the mountains where the hermit-
    folk can hide,

And sift the red and silver sands lest bone of saint abide,
And chase the Giaours flying night and day, not giving
    rest,
For that which was our trouble comes again out of the
    west.

We have set the seal of Solomon on all things under sun,
Of knowledge and of sorrow and endurance of things done,
But a noise is in the mountains, in the mountains, and I
    know
The voice that shook our palaces—four hundred years ago:
It is he that saith not "Kismet"; it is he that knows not
    Fate;
It is Richard, it is Raymond, it is Godfrey in the gate!
It is he whose loss is laughter when he counts the wager
    worth,
Put down your feet upon him, that our peace be on the
    earth.'
For he heard drums groaning and he heard guns jar
(*Don John of Austria is going to the war*).
Sudden and still—hurrah!
Bolt from Iberia!
Don John of Austria
Is gone by Alcalar.

St. Michael's on his Mountain in the sea-roads of the north,
(*Don John of Austria is girt and going forth.*)
Where the grey seas glitter and the sharp tides shift
And the sea-folk labour and the red sails lift.
He shakes his lance of iron and he claps his wings of stone;
The noise is gone through Normandy; the noise is gone
    alone;
The North is full of tangled things and texts and aching
    eyes
And dead is all the innocence of anger and surprise,
And Christian killeth Christian in a narrow dusty room,
And Christian dreadeth Christ that hath a newer face of
    doom,

And Christian hateth Mary that God kissed in Galilee,
But Don John of Austria is riding to the sea.
Don John calling through the blast and the eclipse,
Crying with the trumpet, with the trumpet of his lips,
Trumpet that sayeth ha!
Domino Gloria!
Don John of Austria
Is shouting to the ships.

King Philip 's in his closet with the Fleece about his neck,
Don John of Austria is armed upon the deck.)
The walls are hung with velvet that is black and soft as
sin,
And little dwarfs creep out of it and little dwarfs creep in.
He holds a crystal phial that has colours like the moon,
He touches, and it tingles, and he trembles very soon,
And his face is as a fungus of a leprous white and grey
Like plants in the high houses that are shuttered from the
day,
And death is in the phial and the end of noble work,
But Don John of Austria has fired upon the Turk.
Don John 's hunting, and his hounds have bayed—
Booms away past Italy the rumour of his raid.
Gun upon gun, ha! ha!
Gun upon gun, hurrah!
Don John of Austria
Has loosed the cannonade.

The Pope was in his chapel before day or battle broke,
Don John of Austria is hidden in the smoke.)
The hidden room in man's house where God sits all the
year,
The secret window whence the world looks small and very
dear.
He sees as in a mirror on the monstrous twilight sea
The crescent of the cruel ships whose name is mystery;
They fling great shadows foe-wards, making Cross and
Castle dark,

They veil the plumèd lions on the galleys of St. Mark;
And above the ships are palaces of brown, black-bearde
    chiefs,
And below the ships are prisons, where with multitudinou
    griefs,
Christian captives sick and sunless, all a labouring race repine
Like a race in sunken cities, like a nation in the mines.
They are lost like slaves that swat, and in the skies of mornin
    hung
The stairways of the tallest gods when tyranny was young.

They are countless, voiceless, hopeless as those fallen c
    fleeing on
Before the high Kings' horses in the granite of Babylon.
And many a one grows witless in his quiet room in hell
Where a yellow face looks inward through the lattice of h
    cell,
And he finds his God forgotten, and he seeks no more
    sign—
But Don John of Austria has burst the battle-line!
Don John pounding from the slaughter-painted poop,
Purpling all the ocean like a bloody pirate's sloop,
Scarlet running over on the silvers and the golds,
Breaking of the hatches up and bursting of the holds,
Thronging of the thousands up that labour under sea,
White for bliss and blind for sun and stunned for liberty.
Vivat Hispania!
Domino Gloria!
Don John of Austria
Has set his people free!

Cervantes on his galley sets the sword back in the sheath,
(*Don John of Austria rides homeward with a wreath.*)
And he sees across a weary land a straggling road in Spai
Up which a lean and foolish knight for ever rides in vain,
And he smiles, but not as Sultans smile, and settles bac
    the blade. . . .
(*But Don John of Austria rides home from the Crusade.*)

THE SECRET PEOPLE

Smile at us, pay us, pass us; but do not quite forget,
For we are the people of England, that never has spoken yet.
There is many a fat farmer that drinks less cheerfully,
There is many a free French peasant who is richer and sadder
     than we.
There are no folk in the whole world so helpless or so wise.
There is hunger in our bellies, there is laughter in our eyes;
You laugh at us and love us, both mugs and eyes are wet:
Only you do not know us.   For we have not spoken yet.

The fine French kings came over in a flutter of flags and dames.
We liked their smiles and battles, but we never could say
     their names.
The blood ran red to Bosworth and the high French lords
     went down;
There was naught but a naked people under a naked crown.
And the eyes of the King's Servants turned terribly every way,
And the gold of the King's Servants rose higher every day.
They burnt the homes of the shaven men, that had been
     quaint and kind,
Till there was no bed in a monk's house, nor food that man
     could find.
The inns of God where no man paid, that were the wall
     of the weak,
The King's Servants ate them all.   And still we did not speak.

And the face of the King's Servants grew greater than the
     King:
He tricked them, and they trapped him, and stood round
     him in a ring.
The new grave lords closed round him, that had eaten the
     abbey's fruits,
And the men of the new religion, with their Bibles in their
     boots,
We saw their shoulders moving, to menace or discuss,

And some were pure and some were vile; but none took
    heed of us.
We saw the King as they killed him, and his face was proud
    and pale;
And a few men talked of freedom, while England talked of
    ale.

A war that we understood not came over the world and
    woke
Americans, Frenchmen, Irish; but we knew not the things
    they spoke.
They talked about rights and nature and peace and the
    people's reign:
And the squires, our masters, bade us fight; and never
    scorned us again.
Weak if we be for ever, could none condemn us then;
Men called us serfs and drudges; men knew that we were
    men.
In foam and flame at Trafalgar, on Albuera plains,
We did and died like lions, to keep ourselves in chains,
We lay in living ruins; firing and fearing not
The strange fierce face of the Frenchmen who knew for
    what they fought,
And the man who seemed to be more than man we strained
    against and broke;
And we broke our own rights with him. And still we never
    spoke.

Our patch of glory ended; we never heard guns again.
But the squire seemed struck in the saddle; he was foolish
    as if in pain
He leaned on a staggering lawyer, he clutched a cringing
    Jew,
He was stricken; it may be, after all, he was stricken at
    Waterloo.
Or perhaps the shades of the shaven men, whose spoil is in
    his house,

Come back in shining shapes at last to spoil his last
  carouse:
We only know the last sad squires ride slowly towards the
  sea,
And a new people takes the land: and still it is not we.

They have given us into the hands of the new unhappy
  lords,
Lords without anger and honour, who dare not carry their
  swords.
They fight by shuffling papers; they have bright dead
  alien eyes;
They look at our labour and laughter as a tired man looks
  at flies.
And the load of their loveless pity is worse than the ancient
  wrongs,
Their doors are shut in the evening; and they know no
  songs.

We hear men speaking for us of new laws strong and sweet,
Yet is there no man speaketh as we speak in the street.
It may be we shall rise the last as Frenchmen rose the first,
Our wrath come after Russia's wrath and our wrath be the
  worst.
It may be we are meant to mark with our riot and our rest
God's scorn for all men governing. It may be beer is best.
But we are the people of England; and we have not spoken
  yet.
Smile at us, pay us, pass us. But do not quite forget.

CHARLES DALMON

THE SONG OF FAVONIUS

THE flagon topped with foaming ale
Invokes the song and faery tale,
And he who sings the sweetest song
To him the flagon shall belong,

The silver flagon richly chased
With hops and barley interlaced;
But he who tells the fairest tale
More than the singer shall prevail,
For he shall win the prize divine,
The fragrant kiss of Proserpine.

The sweetest singer we will lead
In triumph down the river mead,
There lightly brushing with our knees
Through gold and purple irises
Until we reach the spearmint mound,
Where he with bay-leaves shall be crowned.
But he who tells the fairest tale
More than the singer shall prevail,
For he shall win the prize divine,
The fragrant kiss of Proserpine.

A song of love is sweet to hear,
And sweet the song of merry cheer;
So may the muses ever find
True votaries among mankind
In taverns and in maidens' bowers,
In Winter and in Summer hours.
But he who tells the fairest tale
More than the singer shall prevail,
For he shall win the prize divine,
The fragrant kiss of Proserpine.

And he shall be the king, and wear
The muses' circle on his hair,
The magic coronal of old,
The coronal of faery gold;
And triumph over Pluto gain
Where Chaucer, Keats and Morris reign.
The flagon topped with foaming ale
Invokes the song and faery tale.
Now who will win the prize divine,
The fragrant kiss of Proserpine?

MOIRA O'NEILL

CUTTIN' RUSHES

Oh maybe it was yesterday, or fifty years ago!
  Meself was risin' early on a day for cuttin' rushes,
Walkin' up the Brabla' burn, still the sun was low,
  Now I 'd hear the burn run an' then I 'd hear the thrushes.

Young, still young!—an' drenchin' wet the grass,
  Wet the golden honeysuckle hangin' sweetly down;
Here, lad, here! will ye follow where I pass,
  An' find me cuttin' rushes on the mountain.'

Then was it only yesterday, or fifty years or so?
  Rippin' round the bog pools high among the heather,
The hook it made me hand sore, I had to leave it go.
  'Twas he that cut the rushes then for me to bind together.

Come, dear, come!—an' back along the burn,
  See the darlin' honeysuckle hangin' like a crown.
Quick, one kiss,—sure, there 's someone at the turn,
  'Oh, we 're afther cuttin' rushes on the mountain.'

Yesterday, yesterday, or fifty years ago . . .
  I waken out o' dreams when I hear the summer thrushes.
Oh, that 's the Brabla' burn, I can hear it sing an' flow,
  For all that 's fair, I 'd sooner see a bunch o' green rushes.

Run, burn, run! can ye mind when we were young?
  The honeysuckle hangs above, the pool is dark an' brown:
Sing, burn, sing! can ye mind the song ye sung
  The day we cut the rushes on the mountain?

CORRYMEELA

Over here in England I 'm helpin' wi' the hay,
  An' I wisht I was in Ireland the livelong day;
Weary on the English hay, an' sorra take the wheat!
  Och! Corrymeela an' the blue sky over it.

There 's a deep dumb river flowin' by beyont the heavy trees
  This livin' air is moithered wi' the bummin' o' the bees
I wisht I 'd hear the Claddagh burn go runnin' through the hea
  Past Corrymeela, wi' the blue sky over it.

The people that 's in England is richer nor the Jews,
  There not the smallest young gossoon but thravels in hi
    shoes !
I 'd give the pipe between me teeth to see a barefut child,
  Och! Corrymeela an' the low south wind.

Here 's hands so full o' money an' hearts so full o' care,
  By the luck o' love ! I 'd still go light for all I did go bar
'God save ye, *colleen dhas,*' I said: the girl she though
    me wild.
  Far Corrymeela, an' the low south wind.

D' ye mind me now, the song at night is mortial hard t
    raise,
  The girls are heavy goin' here, the boys are ill to plase;
When onest I 'm out this workin' hive, 'tis I 'll be bac
    again—
  Ay, Corrymeela, in the same soft rain.

The puff o' smoke from one ould roof before an Englis
    town !
  For a *shaugh* wid Andy Feelan here I 'd give a silver crow
For a curl o' hair like Mollie's ye 'll ask the like in vain,
  Sweet Corrymeela, an' the same soft rain.

EVA GORE-BOOTH

THE LITTLE WAVES OF BREFFNY

The grand road from the mountain goes shining to the se
  And there is traffic in it, and many a horse and cart,
But the little roads of Cloonagh are dearer far to me,
  And the little roads of Cloonagh go rambling throug
    my heart.

A great storm from the ocean goes shouting o'er the hill,
  And there is glory in it and terror on the wind,
But the haunted air of twilight is very strange and still,
  And the little winds of twilight are dearer to my mind.

The great waves of the Atlantic sweep storming on their
    way,
  Shining green and silver with the hidden herring shoal;
But the Little Waves of Breffny have drenched my heart
    in spray,
  And the Little Waves of Breffny go stumbling through
    my soul.

RE-INCARNATION

THE darkness draws me, kindly angels weep
  Forlorn beyond receding rings of light,
The torrents of the earth's desires sweep
  My soul through twilight downward into light.

Once more the light grows dim, the vision fades,
  Myself seems to myself a distant goal,
I grope among the Body's drowsy shades,
  Once more the Old Illusion rocks my soul.

Once more the Manifold in shadowy streams
  Of falling waters murmurs in my ears,
The One Voice drowns amid the roar of dreams
  That crowd the narrow pathway of the years.

I go to seek the starshine on the waves,
  To count the dewdrops on the grassy hill,
I go to gather flowers that grow on graves,
  The world's wall closes round my prisoned will.

K 921

Yea, for the sake of the wild western wind
   The sphered spirit scorns her flame-built throne,
Because of primroses, time out of mind,
   The Lonely turns away from the Alone.

Who once has loved the cornfields' rustling sheaves,
   Who once has heard the gentle Irish rain
Murmur low music in the growing leaves,
   Though he were god, comes back to earth again.

Oh Earth! green wind-swept Eirinn, I would break
   The tower of my soul's initiate pride
For a grey field and a star-haunted lake,
   And those wet winds that roam the country side.

I who have seen am glad to close my eyes,
   I who have soared am weary of my wings,
I seek no more the secret of the wise,
   Safe among shadowy, unreal human things.

Blind to the gleam of those wild violet rays
   That burn beyond the rainbow's circle dim,
Bound by dark nights and driven by pale days,
   The sightless slave of Time's imperious whim;

Deaf to the flowing tide of dreams divine
   That surge outside the closed gates of birth,
The rhythms of eternity, too fine
   To touch with music the dull ears of earth—

I go to seek with humble care and toil
   The dreams I left undreamed, the deeds undone,
To sow the seed and break the stubborn soil,
   Knowing no brightness whiter than the sun.

Content in winter if the fire burns clear
   And cottage walls keep out the creeping damp,
Hugging the Old Illusion warm and dear,
   The Silence and the Wise Book and the Lamp.

JOHN McCRAE

IN FLANDERS FIELDS

1915

In Flanders fields the poppies blow
Between the crosses, row on row,
　　That mark our place; and in the sky
　　The larks, still bravely singing, fly
Scarce heard amid the guns below.

We are the Dead.　Short days ago
We lived, felt dawn, saw sunset glow,
　　Loved and were loved, and now we lie
　　　　In Flanders fields.

Take up our quarrel with the foe:
To you from failing hands we throw
　　The torch; be yours to hold it high.
　　If ye break faith with us who die
We shall not sleep, though poppies grow
　　　　In Flanders fields.

MAURICE BARING

IN MEMORIAM, A. H.

(AUBERON HERBERT, CAPTAIN LORD LUCAS, R.F.C., KILLED NOVEMBER 3, 1916)

Νωμᾶται δ'ἐν ἀτρυγέτῳ χάει

The wind had blown away the rain
That all day long had soaked the level plain.
Against the horizon's fiery wrack,
The sheds loomed black.
And higher, in their tumultuous concourse met,
The streaming clouds, shot-riddled banners, wet
With the flickering storm,
Drifted and smouldered, warm

With flashes sent
From the lower firmament.
And they concealed—
They only here and there through rifts revealed
A hidden sanctuary of fire and light,
A city of chrysolite.

We looked and laughed and wondered, and I said:
That orange sea, those oriflammes outspread
Were like the fanciful imaginings
That the young painter flings
Upon the canvas bold,
Such as the sage and the old
Make mock at, saying it could never be;
And you assented also, laughingly.
I wondered what they meant,
That flaming firmament,
Those clouds so grey so gold, so wet so warm,
So much of glory and so much of storm,
The end of the world, or the end
Of the war—remoter still to me and you, my friend.

Alas! it meant not this, it meant not that:
It meant that now the last time you and I
Should look at the golden sky,
And the dark fields large and flat,
And smell the evening weather,
And laugh and talk and wonder both together.

The last, last time.　We nevermore should meet
In France or London street,
Or fields of home.　The desolated space
Of life shall nevermore
Be what it was before.
No one shall take your place.
No other face
Can fill that empty frame.
There is no answer when we call your name.

We cannot hear your shout upon the stair.
We turn to speak and find a vacant chair.
Something is broken which we cannot mend.
God has done more than take away a friend
In taking you; for all that we have left
Is bruised and irremediably bereft.
There is none like you.   Yet not that alone
Do we bemoan;
But this; that you were greater than the rest,
And better than the best.

O liberal heart fast-rooted to the soil,
O lover of ancient freedom and proud toil,
Friend of the gipsies and all wandering song,
The forest's nursling and the favoured child
Of woodlands wild—
O brother to the birds and all things free,
Captain of liberty!
Deep in your heart the restless seed was sown;
The vagrant spirit fretted in your feet;
We wondered could you tarry long.
And brook for long the cramping street,
Or would you one day sail for shores unknown,
And shake from you the dust of towns, and spurn
The crowded market-place—and not return?
You found a sterner guide;
You heard the guns.   Then, to their distant fire,
Your dreams were laid aside;
And on that day, you cast your heart's desire
Upon a burning pyre;
You gave your service to the exalted need,
Until at last from bondage freed,
At liberty to serve as you loved best,
You chose the noblest way.   God did the rest.

So when the spring of the world shall shrive our stain,
After the winter of war,
When the poor world awakes to peace once more,

After such night of ravage and of rain,
You shall not come again.

You shall not come to taste the old Spring weather,
To gallop through the soft untrampled heather,
To bathe and bake your body on the grass.
We shall be there, alas!
But not with you.   When Spring shall wake the earth,
And quicken the scarred fields to the new birth,
Our grief shall grow.   For what can Spring renew
More fiercely for us than the need of you?

That night I dreamt they sent for me and said
That you were missing, 'Missing, missing—dead':
I cried when in the morning I awoke,
And all the world seemed shrouded in a cloak;
But when I saw the sun,
And knew another day had just begun,
I brushed the dream away, and quite forgot
The nightmare's ugly blot.
So was the dream forgot.   The dream came true.
Before the night I knew
That you had flown away into the air
For ever.   Then I cheated my despair.
I said
That you were safe—or wounded—but not dead.
Alas!   I knew
Which was the false and true.

And after days of watching, days of lead,
There came the certain news that you were dead.
You had died fighting, fighting against odds,
Such as in war the gods
Aethereal dared when all the world was young;
Such fighting as blind Homer never sung,
Nor Hector nor Achilles ever knew,
High in the empty blue.

High, high, above the clouds, against the setting sun,
The fight was fought, and your great task was done.

Of all your brave adventures this the last
The bravest was and best;
Meet ending to a long embattled past,
This swift, triumphant, fatal quest,
Crowned with the wreath that never perisheth,
And diadem of honourable death;
Swift Death aflame with offering supreme
And mighty sacrifice,
More than all mortal dream;
A soaring death, and near to Heaven's gate;
Beneath the very walls of Paradise.
Surely with soul elate,
You heard the destined bullet as you flew,
And surely your prophetic spirit knew
That you had well deserved that shining fate.

Here is no waste,
No burning Might-have-been,
No bitter aftertaste,
None to censure, none to screen,
Nothing awry, nor anything misspent;
Only content, content beyond content,
Which hath not any room for betterment.

God, who had made you valiant, strong and swift,
And maimed you with a bullet long ago,
And cleft your riotous ardour with a rift,
And checked your youth's tumultuous overflow,
Gave back your youth to you,
And packed in moments rare and few
Achievements manifold
And happiness untold,
And bade you spring to Death as to a bride,
In manhood's ripeness, power and pride,
And on your sandals the strong wings of youth.

He let you leave a name
To shine on the entablatures of truth,
Forever:
To sound forever in answering halls of fame.

For you soared onwards to that world which rags
Of clouds, like tattered flags,
Concealed; you reached the walls of chrysolite,
The mansions white;
And losing all, you gained the civic crown
Of that eternal town,
Wherein you passed a rightful citizen
Of the bright commonwealth ablaze beyond our ken.

Surely you found companions meet for you
In that high place;
You met there face to face
Those you had never known, but whom you knew:
Knights of the Table Round,
And all the very brave, the very true,
With chivalry crowned;
The captains rare,
Courteous and brave beyond our human air;
Those who had loved and suffered overmuch,
Now free from the world's touch.
And with them were the friends of yesterday,
Who went before and pointed you the way;
And in that place of freshness, light and rest,
Where Lancelot and Tristram vigil keep
Over their King's long sleep,
Surely they made a place for you,
Their long-expected guest,
Among the chosen few,
And welcomed you, their brother and their friend,
To that companionship which hath no end.

And in the portals of the sacred hall
You hear the trumpet's call,
At dawn upon the silvery battlement,

Re-echo through the deep
And bid the sons of God to rise from sleep,
And with a shout to hail
The sunrise on the city of the Grail:
The music that proud Lucifer in Hell
Missed more than all the joys that he forwent.
You hear the solemn bell
At vespers, when the oriflammes are furled;
And then you know that somewhere in the world,
That shines far-off beneath you like a gem,
They think of you, and when you think of them
You know that they will wipe away their tears,
And cast aside their fears;
That they will have it so,
And in no otherwise;
That it is well with them because they know,
With faithful eyes,
Fixed forward and turned upwards to the skies,
That it is well with you,
Among the chosen few,
Among the very brave, the very true.

EVELYN UNDERHILL

IMMANENCE

I COME in the little things,
Saith the Lord:
Not borne on morning wings
Of majesty, but I have set My Feet
Amidst the delicate and bladed wheat
That springs triumphant in the furrowed sod.
There do I dwell, in weakness and in power;
Not broken or divided, saith our God!
In your strait garden plot I come to flower:
About your porch My Vine
Meek, fruitful, doth entwine;
Waits, at the threshold, Love's appointed hour.

* K 921

I come in the little things,
Saith the Lord:
Yes! on the glancing wings
Of eager birds, the softly pattering feet
Of furred and gentle beasts, I come to meet
Your hard and wayward heart.   In brown bright eyes
That peep from out the brake, I stand confest.
On every nest
Where feathery Patience is content to brood
And leaves her pleasure for the high emprize
Of motherhood—
There doth My Godhead rest.

I come in the little things,
Saith the Lord:
My starry wings
I do forsake,
Love's highway of humility to take:
Meekly I fit My stature to your need.
In beggar's part
About your gates I shall not cease to plead—
As man, to speak with man—
Till by such art
I shall achieve My Immemorial Plan,
Pass the low lintel of the human heart.

RALPH HODGSON

———

STUPIDITY STREET

I SAW with open eyes
Singing birds sweet
Sold in the shops
For the people to eat,
Sold in the shops of
Stupidity Street.

I saw in vision
The worm in the wheat,
And in the shops nothing
For people to eat;
Nothing for sale in
Stupidity Street.

THE BULL

See an old unhappy bull,
Sick in soul and body both,
Slouching in the undergrowth
Of the forest beautiful,
Banished from the herd he led,
Bulls and cows a thousand head.

Cranes and gaudy parrots go
Up and down the burning sky;
Tree-top cats purr drowsily
In the dim-day green below;
And troops of monkeys, nutting, some,
All disputing, go and come;

And things abominable sit
Picking offal buck or swine,
On the mess and over it
Burnished flies and beetles shine,
And spiders big as bladders lie
Under hemlocks ten foot high;

And a dotted serpent curled
Round and round and round a tree,
Yellowing its greenery,
Keeps a watch on all the world,
All the world and this old bull
In the forest beautiful.

Bravely by his fall he came:
One he led, a bull of blood
Newly come to lustihood,
Fought and put his prince to shame,
Snuffed and pawed the prostrate head
Tameless even when it bled.

There they left him, every one,
Left him there without a lick,
Left him for the birds to pick,
Left him there for carrion,
Vilely from their bosom cast
Wisdom, worth, and love at last.

When the lion left his lair
And roared his beauty through the hills,
And the vultures pecked their quills
And flew into the middle air,
Then this prince no more to reign
Came to life and lived again.

He snuffed the herd in far retreat,
He saw the blood upon the ground,
And snuffed the burning airs around
Still with beevish odours sweet,
While the blood ran down his head
And his mouth ran slaver red.

Pity him, this fallen chief,
All his splendour, all his strength,
All his body's breadth and length
Dwindled down with shame and grief,
Half the bull he was before,
Bones and leather, nothing more.

See him standing dewlap-deep
In the rushes at the lake,
Surly, stupid, half asleep,

Waiting for his heart to break
And the birds to join the flies
Feasting at his bloodshot eyes,—

Standing with his head hung down
In a stupor, dreaming things:
Green savannas, jungles brown,
Battlefields and bellowings,
Bulls undone and lions dead
And vultures flapping overhead.

Dreaming things: of days he spent
With his mother gaunt and lean
In the valley warm and green,
Full of baby wonderment,
Blinking out of silly eyes
At a hundred mysteries;

Dreaming over once again
How he wandered with a throng
Of bulls and cows a thousand strong,
Wandered on from plain to plain,
Up the hill and down the dale,
Always at his mother's tail.

How he lagged behind the herd,
Lagged and tottered, weak of limb,
And she turned and ran to him
Blaring at the loathly bird
Stationed always in the skies,
Waiting for the flesh that dies.

Dreaming maybe of a day
When her drained and drying paps
Turned him to the sweets and saps,
Richer fountains by the way,
And she left the bull she bore
And he looked to her no more;

And his little frame grew stout,
And his little legs grew strong,
And the way was not so long;
And his little horns came out,
And he played at butting trees,
And boulder-stones and tortoises,

Joined a game of knobby skulls
With the youngsters of his year,
And the other little bulls,
Learning both to bruise and bear,
Learning how to stand a shock
Like a little bull of rock.

Dreaming of a day less dim,
Dreaming of a time less far,
When the faint but certain star
Of destiny burned clear for him,
And a fierce and wild unrest
Broke the quiet of his breast,

And the gristles of his youth
Hardened in his comely pow,
And he came to fighting growth,
Beat his bull and won his cow,
And flew his tail and trampled off
Past the tallest, vain enough,

And curved about in splendour full
And curved again and snuffed the airs
As who should say, Come out who dares!
And all beheld a bull, a Bull,
And knew that here was surely one
That backed for no bull, fearing none.

And the leader of the herd
Looked and saw, and beat the ground,
And shook the forest with his sound,
Bellowed at the loathly bird
Stationed always in the skies,
Waiting for the flesh that dies.

Dreaming, this old bull forlorn,
Surely dreaming of the hour
When he came to sultan power,
And they owned him master-horn,
Chiefest bull of all among
Bulls and cows a thousand strong.

And in all the tramping herd
Not a bull that barred his way,
Not a cow that said him nay,
Not a bull or cow that erred
In the furnace of his look
Dared a second, worse rebuke;

Not in all the forest wide,
Jungle, thicket, pasture, fen,
Not another dared him then,
Dared him and again defied;
Not a sovereign buck or boar
Came a second time for more.

Not a serpent that survived
Once the terrors of his hoof
Risked a second time reproof,
Came a second time and lived,
Not a serpent in its skin
Came again for discipline;

Not a leopard bright as flame,
Flashing fingerhooks of steel,
That a wooden tree might feel,
Met his fury once and came
For a second reprimand,
Not a leopard in the land;

Not a lion of them all,
Not a lion of the hills,
Hero of a thousand kills,
Dared a second fight and fall,
Dared that ram terrific twice,
Paid a second time the price. . . .

Pity him, this dupe of dream,
Leader of the herd again
Only in his daft old brain,
Once again the bull supreme
And bull enough to bear the part
Only in his tameless heart.

Pity him that he must wake;
Even now the swarm of flies
Blackening his bloodshot eyes
Bursts and blusters round the lake,
Scattered from the feast half-fed,
By great shadows overhead;

And the dreamer turns away
From his visonary herds
And his splendid yesterday,
Turns to meet the loathly birds
Flocking round him from the skies,
Waiting for the flesh that dies.

JOHN MASEFIELD

BEAUTY

I HAVE seen dawn and sunset on moors and windy hills
Coming in solemn beauty like slow old tunes of Spain:
I have seen the lady April bringing the daffodils,
Bringing the springing grass and the soft warm April rain.
I have heard the song of the blossoms and the old chant of
the sea,
And seen strange lands from under the arched white sails of
ships;
But the loveliest things of beauty God ever has showed to
me,
Are her voice, and her hair, and eyes, and the dear red
curve of her lips.

SEA FEVER

I MUST go down to the seas again, to the lonely sea and the
  sky,
And all I ask is a tall ship, and a star to steer her by;
And the wheel's kick and the wind's song and the white
  sails shaking,
And the grey mist on the sea's face, and a grey dawn
  breaking.

I must go down to the seas again, for the call of the running
  tide
Is a wild call and a clear call that may not be denied;
And all I ask is a windy day with the white clouds flying,
And the flung spray and the blown spume, and the seagulls
  crying.

I must go down to the seas again, to the vagrant gypsy life,
To the gull's way and the whale's way where the wind's like
  a whetted knife;
And all I ask is a merry yarn from a laughing fellow rover,
And quiet sleep and a sweet dream when the long trick's
  over.

C. L. M.

In the dark womb where I began
My mother's life made me a man.
Through all the months of human birth
Her beauty fed my common earth.
I cannot see, nor breathe, nor stir,
But through the death of some of her.

Down in the darkness of the grave
She cannot see the life she gave.
For all her love, she cannot tell
Whether I use it ill or well,
Nor knock at dusty doors to find
Her beauty dusty in the mind.

If the grave's gates could be undone,
She would not know her little son,
I am so grown.   If we should meet
She would pass by me in the street,
Unless my soul's face let her see
My sense of what she did for me.

What have I done to keep in mind
My debt to her and womankind?
What woman's happier life repays
Her for those months of wretched days?
For all my mouthless body leeched
Ere Birth's releasing hell was reached?

What have I done, or tried, or said
In thanks to that dear woman dead?
Men triumph over women still,
Men trample women's rights at will,
And man's lust roves the world untamed.

.   .   .   .   .   .

O grave, keep shut lest I be shamed.

FROM *THE EVERLASTING MERCY*

I DID not think, I did not strive,
The deep peace burnt my me alive;
The bolted door had broken in,
I knew that I had done with sin.
I knew that Christ had given me birth
To brother all the souls on earth,
And every bird and every beast
Should share the crumbs broke at the feast.

O glory of the lighted mind.
How dead I 'd been, how dumb, how blind.
The station brook, to my new eyes,
Was babbling out of Paradise;

The waters rushing from the rain
Were singing Christ has risen again.
I thought all earthly creatures knelt
From rapture of the joy I felt.
The narrow station-wall's brick ledge,
The wild hop withering in the hedge,
The lights in huntsman's upper storey
Were parts of an eternal glory,
Were God's eternal garden flowers.
I stood in bliss at this for hours.

O glory of the lighted soul.
The dawn came up on Bradlow Knoll,
The dawn with glittering on the grasses,
The dawn which pass and never passes.

'It's dawn,' I said, 'and chimney's smoking,
And all the blessed fields are soaking,
It's dawn, and there's an engine shunting;
And hounds, for huntsman's going hunting.
It's dawn, and I must wander north
Along the road Christ led me forth.'

So up the road I wander slow
Past where the snowdrops used to grow
With celandines in early springs,
When rainbows were triumphant things
And dew so bright and flowers so glad,
Eternal joy to lass and lad.
And past the lovely brook I paced,
The brook whose source I never traced,
The brook, the one of two which rise
In my green dream in Paradise,
In wells where heavenly buckets clink
To give God's wandering thirsty drink,
By those clean cots of carven stone
Where the clear water sings alone.

Then down, past that white-blossomed pond,
And past the chestnut trees beyond,
And past the bridge the fishers knew,
Where yellow flag flowers once grew,
Where we'd go gathering cops of clover,
In sunny June times long since over.
O clover-cops half white, half red,
O beauty from beyond the dead.
O blossom, key to earth and heaven,
O souls that Christ has new forgiven.

Then down the hill to gipsies' pitch,
By where the brook clucks in the ditch.
A gipsy's camp was in the copse,
Three felted tents, with beehive tops,
And round black marks where fires had been,
And one old waggon painted green,
And three ribbed horses wrenching grass,
And three wild boys to watch me pass,
And one old woman by the fire
Hulking a rabbit warm from wire.
I loved to see the horses bait.
I felt I walked at Heaven's gate,
That Heaven's gate was opened wide,
Yet still the gipsies camped outside.
The waste souls will prefer the wild,
Long after life is meek and mild.
Perhaps when man has entered in
His perfect city free from sin,
The campers will come past the walls
With old lame horses full of galls,
And waggons hung about with withies,
And burning coke in tinkers' stithies,
And see the golden town, and choose,
And think the wild too good to lose.
And camp outside, as these camped then
With wonder at the entering men.
So past, and past the stone-heap white

That dewberry trailers hid from sight,
And down the field so full of springs,
Where mewing peewits clap their wings,
And past the trap made for the mill
Into the field below the hill.
There was a mist along the stream,
A wet mist, dim, like in a dream;
I heard the heavy breath of cows,
And waterdrops from th' alder boughs;
And eels, and snakes, in dripping grass
Whipping aside to let me pass.
The gate was backed against the ryme
To pass the cows at milking time.
And by the gate as I went out
A moldwarp rooted earth wi's snout.
A few steps up the Callows' Lane
Brought me above the mist again;
The two great fields arose like death
Above the mists of human breath.

All earthly things that blessèd morning
Were everlasting joy and warning.
The gate was Jesus' way made plain,
The mole was Satan foiled again,
Black blinded Satan snouting way
Along the red of Adam's clay;
The mist was error and damnation,
The lane the road unto salvation,
Out of the mist into the light;
O blessed gift of inner sight.
The past was faded like a dream;
There come the jingling of a team,
A ploughman's voice, a clink of chain,
Slow hoofs, and harness under strain.
Up the slow slope a team came bowing,
Old Callow at his autumn ploughing,
Old Callow, stooped above the hales,
Ploughing the stubble into wales;

His grave eyes looking straight ahead,
Shearing a long straight furrow red;
His plough-foot high to give it earth
To bring new food for men to birth.

O wet red swathe of earth laid bare,
O truth, O strength, O gleaming share,
O patient eyes that watch the goal,
O ploughman of the sinner's soul.
O Jesus, drive the coulter deep
To plough my living man from sleep.

Slow up the hill the plough team plod,
Old Callow at the task of God,
Helped by man's wit, helped by the brute
Turning a stubborn clay to fruit,
His eyes for ever on some sign
To help him plough a perfect line.
At top of rise the plough team stopped,
The fore-horse bent his head and cropped,
Then the chains chack, the brasses jingle,
The lean reins gather through the cringle,
The figures move against the sky,
The clay wave breaks as they go by.
I kneeled there in the muddy fallow,
I knew that Christ was there with Callow,
That Christ was standing there with me,
That Christ had taught me what to be,
That I should plough, and as I ploughed
My Saviour Christ would sing aloud,
And as I drove the clods apart
Christ would be ploughing in my heart,
Through rest-harrow and bitter roots,
Through all my bad life's rotten fruits.

O Christ who holds the open gate,
O Christ who drives the furrow straight,
O Christ, the plough, O Christ, the laughter
Of holy white birds flying after,

Lo, all my heart's field red and torn,
And Thou wilt bring the young green corn,
The young green corn divinely springing,
The young green corn for ever singing;
And when the field is fresh and fair,
Thy blessèd feet shall glitter there,
And we will walk the weeded field,
And tell the golden harvest's yield,
The corn that makes the holy bread
By which the soul of man is fed,
Thy holy bread, the food unpriced,
Thy everlasting mercy, Christ.

SONNETS FROM *LOLLINGDON DOWNS*

IX

WHAT is this life which uses living cells
It knows not how nor why, for no known end,
This soul of man upon whose fragile shells
Of blood and brain his very powers depend?
Pour out its little blood or touch its brain,
The thing is helpless, gone, no longer known;
The carrion cells are never man again,
No hand relights the little candle blown.
It comes not from Without, but from the sperm
Fed in the womb; it is a man-made thing
That takes from man its power to live a term,
Served by live cells of which it is the King.
Can it be blood and brain? It is most great.
Through blood and brain alone it wrestles Fate.

XXX

Here in the self is all that man can know
Of Beauty, all the wonder, all the power,
All the unearthly colour, all the glow,
Here in the self which withers like a flower;
Here in the self which fades as hours pass,
And droops and dies and rots and is forgotten
Sooner, by ages, than the mirroring glass

In which it sees its glory still unrotten.
Here in the flesh, within the flesh, behind,
Swift in the blood and throbbing on the bone,
Beauty herself, the universal mind,
Eternal April wandering alone;
The God, the holy Ghost, the atoning Lord,
Here in the flesh, the never yet explored.

XLI

Roses are beauty, but I never see
Those blood drops from the burning heart of June
Glowing like thought upon the living tree
Without a pity that they die so soon,
Die into petals, like those roses old,
Those women, who were summer in men's hearts
Before the smile upon the Sphinx was cold,
Or sand had hid the Syrian and his arts.
O myriad dust of beauty that lies thick
Under our feet that not a single grain
But stirred and moved in beauty and was quick
For one brief moon and died nor lived again;
But when the moon rose lay upon the grass
Pasture to living beauty, life that was.

FRANCES CORNFORD

PRE-EXISTENCE

I LAID me down upon the shore
　　And dreamed a little space;
I heard the great waves break and roar;
　　The sun was on my face.

My idle hands and fingers brown
　　Played with the pebbles grey;
The waves come up, the waves went down,
　　Most thundering and gay.

The pebbles, they were smooth and round
　　And warm upon my hands,
Like little people I had found
　　Sitting among the sands.

The grains of sand so shining-small
　　Soft through my fingers ran;
The sun shone down upon it all,
　　And so my dream began:

How all of this had been before;
　　How ages far away
I lay on some forgotten shore
　　As here I lie to-day.

The waves came shining up the sands,
　　As here to-day they shine;
And in my pre-pelasgian hands
　　The sand was warm and fine.

I have forgotten whence I came,
　　Or what my home might be,—
Or by what strange and savage name
　　I called that thundering sea.

I only know the sun shone down
　　And still it shines to-day,
And in my fingers long and brown
　　The little pebbles lay.

EDWARD THOMAS

LIGHTS OUT

1917

I HAVE come to the borders of sleep,
The unfathomable deep
Forest where all must lose
Their way, however straight,
Or winding, soon or late;
They cannot choose.

Many a road and track
That, since the dawn's first crack,
Up to the forest brink,
Deceived the travellers,
Suddenly now blurs,
And in they sink.

Here love ends,
Despair, ambition ends,
All pleasure and all trouble,
Although most sweet or bitter,
Here ends in sleep that is sweeter
Than tasks most noble.

There is not any book
Or face of dearest look
That I would not turn from now
To go into the unknown
I must enter, and leave, alone,
I know not how.

The tall forest towers;
Its cloudy foliage lowers
Ahead, shelf above shelf;
In silence I hear and obey
That I may lose my way
And myself.

EDWARD JOHN MORETON DRAX PLUNKETT, LORD DUNSANY

A DIRGE OF VICTORY

1918

LIFT not thy trumpet, Victory, to the sky,
  Nor through battalions nor by batteries blow,
  But over hollows full of old wire go,
Where among dregs of war the long-dead lie
With wasted iron that the guns passed by
  When they went eastwards like a tide at flow;
  There blow thy trumpet that the dead may know,
Who waited for thy coming, Victory.

It is not we who have deserved thy wreath,
  They waited there among the towering weeds;
The deep mud burned under the thermite's breath,
  And winter cracked the bones that no man heeds:
Hundreds of nights flamed by: the seasons passed:
And thou hast come to them, at last, at last!

HAROLD MONRO

CHILDREN OF LOVE

THE holy boy
Went from his mother out in the cool of the day
Over the sun-parched fields
And in among the olives shining green and shining grey.

There was no sound,
No smallest voice of any shivering stream.
Poor sinless little boy,
He desired to play and to sing; he could only sigh and dream.

Suddenly came
Running along to him naked, with curly hair,
That rogue of the lovely world,
That other beautiful child whom the virgin Venus bare.

The holy boy
Gazed with those sad blue eyes that all men know.
Impudent Cupid stood
Panting, holding an arrow and pointing his bow.

(Will you not play?
Jesus, run to him, run to him, swift for our joy.
Is he not holy, like you?
Are you afraid of his arrows, O beautiful dreaming boy?)

And now they stand
Watching one another with timid gaze;
Youth has met youth in the wood,
But holiness will not change its melancholy ways.

Cupid at last
Draws his bow and softly lets fly a dart.
Smile for a moment, sad world!—
It has grazed the white skin and drawn blood from the
    sorrowful heart.

Now, for delight,
Cupid tosses his locks and goes wantonly near;
But the child that was born to the cross
Has let fall on his cheek, for the sadness of life, a com
    passionate tear.

Marvellous dream!
Cupid has offered his arrows for Jesus to try;
He has offered his bow for the game.
But Jesus went weeping away, and left him there wondering
    why.

AT A COUNTRY DANCE IN PROVENCE

Comrades, when the air is sweet,
It is fair, in stately measure,
With a sound of gliding feet,
It is fair and very meet
To be join'd in pleasure.
Listen to the rhythmic beat:

Let us mingle, move and sway
Solemnly as at some rite
Of a festive mystic god,
While the sunlight holds the day.
Comrades, is it not delight
To be govern'd by the rod
Of the music, and to go
Moving, moving, moving slow?
Very stately are your ways,
Stately—and the southern glow
Of the sun is in your eyes:
Under lids inclining low
All the light of harvest days,
And the gleam of summer skies
Tenderly reflected lies.
May I not be one of you
Even for this little space?
Humbly I am fain to sue
That our arms may interlace.
I am otherwise I know;
Many books have made me sad:
Yet indeed your stately slow
Motion and its rhythmic flow
Drive me, drive me, drive me mad.
Must I now, as always, gaze
Patiently from far away
At the pageant of the days?—
Only let me live to-day!
For your hair is ebon black,
And your eyes celestial blue;
For your measure is so true,
Slowly forward, slowly back—
I would fain be one of you.
Comrades, comrades! but the sound
Of the music with a start
Ceases, and you pass me by.
Slowly from the dancing ground
To the tavern you depart.

All the earth is silent grown
After so much joy, and I
Suddenly am quite alone
With the beating of my heart.

VIOLET JACOB

TAM I' THE KIRK

O Jean, my Jean, when the bell ca's the congregation
  Owre valley an' hill wi' the ding frae its iron mou',
When a' body's thochts is set on his ain salvation,
  Mine's set on you.

There's a reid rose lies on the Buik o' the Word 'afore ye
  That was growin' braw on its bush at the keek o' day,
But the lad that pu'd yon flower i' the mornin's glory,
  He canna pray.

He canna pray; but there's nane i' the Kirk will heed him
  Whaur he sits sae still his lane at the side of the wa',
For nane but the reid rose kens what my lassie gie'd him,
  It an' us twa.

He canna sing for the sang that his ain he'rt raises,
  He canna see for the mist that's 'afore his een,
And a voice drouns the hale o' the psalms an' the para-
    phrases,
  Cryin' 'Jean, Jean, Jean!'

ALFRED NOYES

SHERWOOD

Sherwood in the twilight, is Robin Hood awake?
Grey and ghostly shadows are gliding through the brake,
Shadows of the dappled deer, dreaming of the morn,
Dreaming of a shadowy man that winds a shadowy horn.

Robin Hood is here again: all his merry thieves
Hear a ghostly bugle-note shivering through the leaves,
Calling as he used to call, faint and far away,
In Sherwood, in Sherwood, about the break of day.

Merry, merry England has kissed the lips of June:
All the wings of fairyland were here beneath the moon,
Like a fleet of rose-leaves fluttering in the mist
Of opal and ruby and pearl and amethyst.

Merry, merry England is waking as of old,
With eyes of blither hazel and hair of brighter gold:
For Robin Hood is here again beneath the bursting spray
In Sherwood, in Sherwood, about the break of day.

Love is in the greenwood building him a house
Of wild rose and hawthorn and honeysuckle boughs:
Love is in the greenwood, dawn is in the skies,
And Marian is waiting with a glory in her eyes.

Hark! The dazzled laverock climbs the golden steep!
Marian is waiting: is Robin Hood asleep?
Round the fairy grass-rings frolic elf and fay,
In Sherwood, in Sherwood, about the break of day.

Oberon, Oberon, rake away the gold,
Rake away the red leaves, roll away the mould,
Rake away the gold leaves, roll away the red,
And wake Will Scarlett from his leafy forest bad.

Friar Tuck and Little John are riding down together
With quarter-staff and drinking-can and grey goose feather.
The dead are coming back again, the years are rolled away
In Sherwood, in Sherwood, about the break of day.

Softly over Sherwood the south wind blows.
All the heart of England hid in every rose
Hears across the greenwood the sunny whisper leap,
Sherwood in the red dawn, is Robin Hood asleep?

Hark, the voice of England wakes him as of old,
And, shattering the silence with a cry of brighter gold,
Bugles in the greenwood echo from the steep,
Sherwood in the red dawn, is Robin Hood asleep?

Where the deer are gliding down the shadowy glen
All across the glades of fern he calls his merry men—
Doublets of the Lincoln green glancing through the May
In Sherwood, in Sherwood, about the break of day—

Calls them and they answer: from aisles of oak and ash
Rings the *Follow! Follow!* and the boughs begin to crash,
The ferns begin to flutter and the flowers begin to fly,
And through the crimson dawning the robber band goes by

Robin! Robin! Robin! All his merry thieves
Answer as the bugle-note shivers through the leaves;
Calling as he used to call, faint and far away,
In Sherwood, in Sherwood, about the break of day.

FOR THE EIGHTIETH BIRTHDAY OF GEORGE MEREDITH

A HEALTH, a ringing health, unto the king
　　Of all our hearts to-day! But what proud song
　　Should follow on the thought, nor do him wrong?
Unless the sea were harp, each mirthful string
The lovely lightning of the nights of Spring,
　　And Dawn the lonely listener, glad and grave
　　With colours of the sea-shell and the wave
In brightening eye and cheek, there is none to sing!

Drink to him, as men upon an Alpine peak
　　Brim one immortal cup of crimson wine,
　　And into it drop one pure cold crust of snow,
Then hold it up, too rapturously to speak,
　　And drink—to the mountains, line on glittering lin
　　Surging away into the sunset glow.

EARTH AND HER BIRDS

BRAVE birds that climb those blue
  Dawn-tinted towers,
With notes like showers of dew
  From elf-tossed flowers,
Shake your mad wings in mirth,
    Betray, betray
    The secret thoughts of May,
That heaven, once more, may marry our wild earth.

Dark gipsy, she would dance
  Unmated still,
Challenging, glance for glance,
  Her lord's high will,
But that her thoughts take wing
    While she lies sleeping;
    And, into glory leaping,
Like birds, at sunrise, to her bridegroom sing.

See how with cheeks aglow
  And lips apart,
While warm winds, murmuring low,
  Lay bare her heart,
She dreams that she can hide
    Its rosy light
    In ferns and flowers this night,
And swim like Dian through this hawthorn-tide.

Then shame her, laverocks, shame her,
  At break of day,
That heaven may trap and tame her
  This mad sweet May.
Let all your feathered choir
    Leave those warm nests
    Between her dawn-flushed breasts,
And soar to heaven, singing her young desire.

ON THE DEATH OF FRANCIS THOMPSON

I

How grandly glow the bays
  Purpureally enwound
With those rich thorns, the brows
  How infinitely crowned
That now thro' Death's dark house
  Have passed with royal gaze:
Purpureally enwound
  How grandly glow the bays.

II

Sweet, sweet and three-fold sweet,
  Pulsing with three-fold pain,
Where the lark fails of flight
  Soared the celestial strain;
Beyond the sapphire height
  Flew the gold-wingéd feet,
Beautiful, pierced with pain,
  Sweet, sweet and three-fold sweet;

III

And where *Is not* and *Is*
  Are wed in one sweet Name,
And the world's rootless vine
  With dew of stars a-flame
Laughs, from those deep divine
  Impossibilities,
Our reason all to shame—
  This cannot be, but is;

IV

Into the Vast, the Deep
  Beyond all mortal sight,
The Nothingness that conceived
  The worlds of day and night,

The Nothingness that heaved
　　Pure sides in virgin sleep,
Brought out of Darkness, light;
　　And man from out the Deep.

V

Into that Mystery
　　Let not thine hand be thrust:
Nothingness is a world
　　Thy science well may trust . . .
But lo, a leaf unfurled,
　　Nay, a cry mocking thee
From the first grain of dust—
　　I am, yet cannot be!

VI

Adventuring un-afraid
　　Into that last deep shrine,
Must not the child-heart see
　　Its deepest symbol shine,
The world's Birth-mystery,
　　Whereto the suns are shade?
Lo, the white breast divine—
　　The Holy Mother-maid!

VII

How miss that sacrifice,
　　That cross of Yea or Nay,
That paradox of heaven
　　Whose palms point either way,
Through each a nail being driven
　　That the arms out-span the skies
And our earth-dust this day
　　Out-sweeten Paradise.

VIII

We part the seamless robe,
　　Our wisdom would divide
The raiment of the King,
　　Our spear is in His side,

Even while the angels sing
  Around our perishing globe,
And Death re-knits in pride
  The seamless purple robe.

.   .   .   .   .   .

IX

How grandly glow the bays
  Purpureally enwound
With those rich thorns, the brows
  How infinitely crowned
That now thro' Death's dark house
  Have passed with royal gaze:
Purpureally enwound
  How grandly glow the bays.

MARGARET SACKVILLE

SYRINX

I AM Syrinx: I am she who when the gold
Sun over the grey mountain burns awake,
Rises and drives the flock from the safe fold;

And all day long hidden in the green brake
Watches; or where the wood's heart grows so still
That the least tremor of small leaves ashake

Seems somehow a foreboding of strange ill.—
And I am she who gleans the scattered wheat,
And prunes the vine on the steep side of the hill.

I follow the white morning on swift feet,
I slumber in the thicket at mid-noon,
The racing wind bears me along with it.

And, for the gods' delight, under the moon
I dance, dance and laugh to feel my hot
Heart leaping frenzied to the wild pipes' tune.

But as for Love, truly I know him not,
I have passionately turned my lips therefrom,
And from that fate the careless gods allot

To woman.   Love who has taken the world by storm,
For all his fury of blind wind and flood,
Has had no power to change me or deform.

For the chill mountain-streams are in my blood,
And pale, phantasmal fires of dawn, twilight,
Shadow and dew are all my maidenhood.

And as the setting sun on the cold, white,
Snow-braided, frozen peak rests his fierce head,
Then goes out in a thin trail of light;

So Love, leaning upon my heart, instead
Of flame finds only snow and falls asleep
Quietly like a child on a soft bed;

And lies there forgetting the broad sweep
At noontide of his sudden, blazing wings,
Which thought my narrow life to overleap;

Not knowing me tameless as the breeze which clings
Round Summer's golden limbs when she moves clad
In music, wonderfully, where the pine-branch swings.

Therefore what thing is this which makes me mad,
So that no laughter of the rose-crowned year
Shall evermore rejoice me or leave glad

My heart which now has a sick core of fear?
I am Syrinx: a strange doom is over me
Like a cloud, hanging about me everywhere:

Yea, listen and marvel how such things may be!
I am bewildered and all overcast
As a spent swimmer struck sideways by the sea.

For once, as through the deep, cool wood I passed
Singing, for it was June, and ah, June goes!
And only song may capture and bind her fast;

I paused: there was no stir among the close
Boughs; for the heat nothing alive might breathe,
And the least wind swooned backwards as it rose.

Outside the sick earth seemed to burn and seethe
Like molten metal in a pot.   I saw
The sun, a wild beast with sharp shining teeth,

Eagerly search the barren land and draw
What of green might still be left therein,
To cool the rage of his insatiate maw.

Yet, through the leaves, his rays on my white skin
Played harmless and I sang, sang till a sound
Fell on my ears and made me reel and spin.

Low laughter welling lightly from the ground
Like water, mocking, sweet, and crystalline
As though up-bubbling from earth's heart profound.

And in it something bestial and divine,
So that my senses hearing it were stirred,
Quickened and overcome, as though with wine;

And motionless I stood as a bird
Beneath a snake's eye; then when life began
To fail within me, once again I heard

The laughter and saw, crouched there before me,—Pan
The very shepherd and godhead of our hills
Whom I have feared more than the Cyprian,

Since his is the sharp secret breath which kills
At nightfall, and he is lord of death and birth,
And the year wanes and waxes as he wills.

Yea, very spirit is he and heart of earth,
And cruel as untempered rain and sun,
In those sick seasons when all falls to dearth.

And there shall none resist him, nay, not one
On whom rest the eyes of his desire:
Wherefore am I too ruined and undone;

For though a little I may escape his fire,
Since he subtle and wise let me depart
That morning, helpless am I though I fly higher

Than the eagle, yea, or press the waves apart,
—The cold, dark, clean, indifferent sea-waves—
Nay, though I shelter in the whirlwind's heart,

Pan, Pan shall have at last the thing he craves,
Me: and my shadowy days must sink to naught,
Falling earthward like shed leaves when the wind raves.

Yet might these weary toils wherein I am caught
Break, break! Would that I might become
A shadow or fast fading flower wrought

From day and night, or sunshine or blown foam
Ere this thing chanced, or a clear drop of rain
New scattered, or music suddenly fallen dumb;

A note of music by its own breath slain,
Blown tenderly from the frail heart of a reed
Whereof the singing shepherd lads are fain,

Who with strong, careless hands from all toil freed,
Pluck joy, pure joy, green-growing from the soil,
And turn and twist and shape it to their need.

If this might be! If some kind god would foil
The inexorable purpose of Pan's lust,
Having pity on my swift youth's recoil;

My frugal, kindly, passionless days which must
Perish, perish like wild wood-berries,
By sharp-hoofed goat-feet trampled all to dust.

If they would sigh towards me, bidding me cease,
Changing into white sap my willing blood,
And granting me the calm of growing trees,

And of the reeds springing in the full flood;
Being myself portion and part of these,
Surely, beyond all longing, it were good!

I am Syrinx: I am afraid: I would have peace.

LASCELLES ABERCROMBIE

HYMN TO LOVE

WE are thine, O Love, being in thee and made of thee,
　　As thóu, Lóve, were the déep thóught
And we the speech of the thought; yea, spoken are we,
　　Thy fires of thought outspoken:

But burn'd not through us thy imagining
　　Like fiérce móod in a sóng cáught,
We were as clamour'd words a fool may fling,
　　Loose words, of meaning broken.

For what more like the brainless speech of a fool,—
　　The lives travelling dark fears,
And as a boy throws pebbles in a pool
　　Thrown down abysmal places?

Hazardous are the stars, yet is our birth
   And our journeying time theirs;
As words of air, life makes of starry earth
   Sweet soul-delighted faces;

As voices are we in the worldly wind;
   The great wind of the world's fate
Is turned, as air to a shapen sound, to mind
   And marvellous desires.

But not in the world as voices storm-shatter'd,
   Not borne down by the wind's weight;
The rushing time rings with our splendid word
   Like darkness filled with fires.

For Love doth use us for a sound of song,
   And Love's meaning our life wields,
Making our souls like syllables to throng
   His tunes of exultation.

Down the blind speed of a fatal world we fly,
   As rain blown along earth's fields;
Yet are we god-desiring liturgy,
   Sung joys of adoration;

Yea, made of chance and all a labouring strife,
   We go charged with a strong flame;
For as a language Love hath seized on life
   His burning heart to story.

Yea, Love, we are thine, the liturgy of thee,
   Thy thought's golden and glad name,
The mortal conscience of immortal glee,
   Love's zeal in Love's own glory.

MARRIAGE SONG

I

COME up, dear chosen morning, come,
Blessing the air with light,
And bid the sky repent of being dark:
Let all the spaces round the world be white,
And give the earth her green again.
Into new hours of beautiful delight,
Out of the shadow where she has lain,
Bring the earth awake for glee,
Shining with dews as fresh and clear
As my beloved's voice upon the air.
For now, O morning chosen of all days, on thee
A wondrous duty lies:
There was an evening that did loveliness foretell;
Thence upon thee, O chosen morn, it fell
To fashion into perfect destiny
The radiant prophecy.
For in an evening of young moon, that went
Filling the moist air with a rosy fire,
I and my beloved knew our love;
And knew that thou, O morning, wouldst arise
To give us knowledge of achieved desire.
For, standing stricken with astonishment,
Half terrified in the delight,
Even as the moon did into clear air move
And made a golden light,
Lo there, croucht up against it, a dark hill,
A monstrous back of earth, a spine
Of hunchèd rock, furred with great growth of pine,
Lay like a beast, snout in its paws, asleep;
Yet in its sleeping seemed it miserable,
As though strong fear must always keep
Hold of its heart, and drive its blood in dream.
Yea, for to our new love, did it not seem,
That dark and quiet length of hill,

The sleeping grief of the world?—Out of it we
Had like imaginations stept to be
Beauty and golden wonder; and for the lovely fear
Of coming perfect joy, had changed
The terror that dreamt there!
And now the golden moon had turned
To shining white, white as our souls that burned
With vision of our prophecy assured:
Suddenly white was the moon; but she
At once did on a woven modesty
Of cloud, and soon went in obscured:
And we were dark, and vanisht that strange hill.
But yet it was not long before
There opened in the sky a narrow door,
Made with pearl lintel and pearl sill;
And the earth's night seem'd pressing there,—
All as a beggar on some festival would peer,—
To gaze into a room of light beyond,
The hidden silver splendour of the moon.
Yea, and we also, we
Long gazed wistfully
Toward thee, O morning, come at last,
And towards the light that thou wilt pour upon us soon!

II

O soul who still art strange to sense,
Who often against beauty wouldst complain,
Doubting between joy and pain:
If like the startling touch of something keen
Against thee, it hath been
To follow from an upland height
The swift sun hunting rain
Across the April meadows of a plain,
Until the fields would flash into the air
Their joyous green, like emeralds alight;
Or when in the blue of night's mid-noon
The burning naked moon

Draws to a brink of cloudy weather near,
A breadth of snow, firm and soft as a wing,
Stretcht out over a wind that gently goes,—
Through the white sleep of snowy cloud there grows
An azure-border'd shining ring,
The gleaming dream of the approaching joy of her;—
What now wilt thou do, Soul? What now,
If with such things as these troubled thou wert?
How wilt thou now endure, or how
Not now be strangely hurt?—
When utter beauty must come closer to thee
Than even anger or fear could be;
When thou, like metal in a kiln, must lie
Seized by beauty's mightily able flame;
Enjoyed by beauty, as by the ruthless glee
Of an unescapable power;
Obeying beauty as air obeys a cry;
Yea, one thing made of beauty and thee,
As steel and a white heat are made the same!
—Ah! but I know how this infirmity
Will fail and be not, no, not memory,
When I begin the marvellous hour.
This only is my heart's strain'd eagerness,
Long waiting for its bliss.—
But from those other fears, from those
That keep to Love so close,
From fears that are the shadow of delight,
Hide me, O joys; make them unknown to-night!

III

Thou bright God that in dream camest to me last night,
Thou with the flesh made of a golden light,
Knew I not thee, thee and thy heart,
Know I not well, God, who thou wert?
Yea, and my soul divinely understood
The light that was beneath thee a ground,
The golden light that cover'd thee round,

Turning my sleep to a fiery morn,
Was as a heavenly oath there sworn
Promising me an immortal good:
Well I knew thee, God of Marriages, thee and thy flame!
Ah! but wherefore beside thee came
That fearful sight of another mood?
Why, in thy light, to thy hand chained,
Towards me its bondage terribly strained,
Why came with thee that dreadful hound,
The wild hound Fear, black, ravenous, and gaunt?
Why him with thee should thy dear light surround?
Why brightest thou that beast to haunt
The blissful footsteps of my golden dream?—
All shadowy black the body dread,
All frenzied fire the head,—
The hunger of its mouth a hollow crimson flame,
The hatred in its eyes a blaze
Fierce and green, stabbing the ruddy glaze,
And sharp white jetting fire the teeth snarl'd at me,
And while the dribbling rage of froth,—
A throat that gaped to bay and paws working violently,
Yet soundless all as a winging moth;
Tugging towards me, famishing for my heart;—
Even while thou, O golden God, wert still
Looking the beautiful kindness of thy will
Into my soul, even then must I be,
With thy bright promise looking at me,
Then bitterly of that hound afraid?—
Darkness, I know, attendeth bright,
And light comes not but shadow comes:
And heart must know, if it know thy light,
Thy wild hound Fear, the shadow of love's delight.
Yea, is it thus? Are we so made
Of death and darkness, that even thou
O golden God of the joys of love,
Thy mind to us canst only prove,
The glorious devices of thy mind,
By so revealing how thy journeying here

Through this mortality, doth closely bind
Thy brightness to the shadow of dreadful Fear?—
Ah no, it shall not be! Thy joyous light
Shall hide me from the hunger of fear to-night.

IV

For wonderfully to live I now begin:
So that the darkness which accompanies
Our being here, is fasten'd up within
The power of light that holdeth me;
And from these shining chains, to see
My joy with bold misliking eyes,
The shrouded figure will not dare arise.
For henceforth, from to-night,
I am wholly gone into the bright
Safety of the beauty of love:
Not only all my waking vigours plied
Under the searching glory of love,
But knowing myself with love all satisfied
Even when my life is hidden in sleep;
As high clouds, to themselves that keep
The moon's white company, are all possest
Silverly with the presence of their guest;
Or as a darken'd room
That hath within it roses, whence the air
And quietness are taken everywhere
Deliciously by sweet perfume.

CEREMONIAL ODE INTENDED FOR A UNIVERSITY

When from Eternity were separate
  The curdled element
And gathered forces, and the world began,—
The Spirit that was shut and darkly blent
Within this being, did the whole distress
With its blind hanker after spaciousness.

Into its wrestle, strictly tied up in Fate
And closely natured, came like an open'd grate
   At last the Mind of Man,
Letting the sky in, and a faculty
To light the cell with lost Eternity.

So commerce with the Infinite was regain'd:
   For upward grew Man's ken
And trod with founded footsteps the grievous fen
Where other life festering and prone remain'd.
With knowledge painfully quarried and hewn fair,
Platforms of lore, and many a hanging stair
Of strong imagination Man has raised
His Wisdom like the watch-towers of a town;
   That he, though fasten'd down
In law, be with its cruelty not amazed,
But be of outer vastness greatly aware.

This, then, is yours: to build exultingly
   High, and yet more high,
The knowledgeable towers above base wars
And sinful surges reaching up to lay
Dishonouring hands upon your work, and drag
From their uprightness your desires to lag
Among low places with a common gait.
That so Man's mind, not conquer'd by his clay,
   May sit above his fate,
Inhabiting the purpose of the stars,
And trade with his Eternity.

PADRAIC COLUM

THE PLOUGHER

SUNSET and silence! A man: around him earth savage,
    earth broken;
Beside him two horses—a plough!

Earth savage, earth broken, the brutes, the dawn man there
    in the sunset,
And the Plough that is twin to the Sword, that is founder
    of cities!

'Brute-tamer, plough-maker, earth-breaker! Can'st hear?
    There are ages between us.
Is it praying you are as you stand there alone in the sunset?

'Surely as sky-born gods can be naught to you, earth child
    and earth master?
Surely your thoughts are of Pan, or of Wotan, or Dana?

'Yet, why give thought to the gods? Has Pan led your
    brutes where they stumble?
Has Dana numbed pain of the child-bed, or Wotan put hands
    to your plough?

'What matter your foolish reply? O, man, standing alone
    and bowed earthward,
Your task is a day near its close. Give thanks to the night-
    giving God.'

.   .   .   .   .   .

Slowly the darkness falls, the broken lands blend with the
    savage;
The brute-tamer stands by the brutes, a head's-breadth only
    above them.

A head's-breadth? Ay, but therein is hell's depth, and the
    height up to heaven,
And the thrones of the gods and their halls, their chariots,
    purples, and splendours.

AN OLD WOMAN OF THE ROADS

O, to have a little house!
To own the hearth and stool and all!
The heaped up sods upon the fire,
The pile of turf against the wall!

To have a clock with weights and chains
And pendulum swinging up and down!
A dresser filled with shining delph,
Speckled and white and blue and brown!

I could be busy all the day
Clearing and sweeping hearth and floor,
And fixing on their shelf again
My white and blue and speckled store!

I could be quiet there at night
Beside the fire and by myself,
Sure of a bed, and loth to leave
The ticking clock and the shining delph!

Och! but I 'm weary of mist and dark,
And roads where there 's never a house nor bush,
And tired I am of bog and road
And the crying wind and the lonesome hush!

And I am praying to God on high,
And I am praying Him night and day,
For a little house—a house of my own—
Out of the wind's and the rain's way.

W. M. LETTS

A SOFT DAY

A soft day, thank God!
A wind from the south
With a honeyed mouth;
A scent of drenching leaves,
Briar and beech and lime,
White elder-flower and thyme,

And the soaking grass smells sweet,
Crushed by my two bare feet,
  While the rain drips,
Drips, drips, drips from the leaves.

A soft day, thank God!
The hills wear a shroud
Of silver cloud;
The web the spider weaves
Is a glittering net;
The woodland path is wet,

And the soaking earth smells sweet,
Under my two bare feet,
  And the rain drips,
Drips, drips, drips from the leaves.

ROSE MACAULAY

NEW YEAR

1918

Whatever the year brings, he brings nothing new,
For time, caught on the ancient wheel of change,
Spins round, and round, and round, and nothing is strange,
    Or shall amaze
Mankind, in whom the heritage of all days
Stirs suddenly, as dreams half remembered do.
Whatever the year brings, he brings nothing new.

Pale, pale he stands,
Carrying world-old gifts in his cold hands—
Winds, and the sky's keen blue,
Woods, and the wild cuckoo,
Lovers, and loveliness, and death, and life.
Does he hold Peace, the derelict babe of strife
And of wan penury?
Will she ride in on the wash of the storming sea,
Be dropped at last by its ebb on the trampled sands,
To lie there helplessly?
War's orphan, she,
And ungrown mother of wars yet to be,
She smiles and croons for a space between those two.
Whatever the year brings, he brings nothing new.

Dreams and desires and hopes does the year hold.
Bad and good, tinsel and gold,
Lying and true,
One and all they are old, so old,
They were dreamt and desired and told
By the first men swinging in trees by strong tails.
Not till the last man fails
And the sun's fire pales,
Shall the embers of these flaming dreams be cold.
Whatever the year brings, he brings nothing new.

Turn, turn the page!
It turns, and we, and the squirrel in his cage,
And the sun, and the moon, and the moon's salt tide;
And the earth turns too.
As flies on the rim of a wheel we ride
From age round to age,
And the dreams and the toys which make our pride
Are an old heritage,
Worn properties from some primeval stage
All curtained now from view . . .
Whatever the year brings, he brings nothing new.

Go through the door.
You shall find nothing that has not been before,
Nothing so bitter it will not be once more.
All this our sad estate was known of yore,
    In old worlds red with pain,
Borne by hearts sullen and sick as ours, through
Desperate, forgotten other winters, when
        Tears fell, and hopes, and men,
And crowns and cities, and blood, on a trampled plain,
And nations, and honour, and God, and always rain . . .
And honour, and hope, and God rose up again,
        And like trees nations grew . . .
Whatever the year brings, he brings nothing new.

Should some year suddenly bring something new,
We should grope as lost children, without a clue,
We should drift all amazed through such a queer
        And unimagined year,
Riding uncharted seas; a derelict crew,
Whistling in vain for the old winds that blew
From the old skies, we should seek far and near
        Some mark by which to steer,
And some known port, that we might sail thereto.
        Black nightmare and blind fear
        Shall seize and hold him who
In some year suddenly finds something new.

RICHARD MIDDLETON

———

PAGAN EPITAPH

SERVANT of the eternal Must
    I lie here, here let me lie,
In the ashes and the dust,
    Dreaming, dreaming pleasantly.

When I lived I sought no wings,
　Schemed no heaven, planned no hell,
But, content with little things,
　Made an earth, and it was well.

Song and laughter, food and wine,
　Roses, roses red and white,
And a star or two to shine
　On my dewy world at night.
Lord, what more could I desire?
　With my little heart of clay
I have lit no eternal fire
　To burn my dreams on Judgment Day!

Well I loved, but they who knew
　What my laughing heart could be,
What my singing lips could do,
　Lie a-dreaming here with me.

I can feel their finger-tips
　Stroke the darkness from my face,
And the music of their lips
　Fills my pleasant resting-place
In the ashes and the dust,
　Where I wonder as I lie,
Servant of the eternal Must,
　Dreaming, dreaming pleasantly.

JOHN DRINKWATER

BIRTHRIGHT

Lord Rameses of Egypt sighed
　Because a summer evening passed;
And little Ariadne cried
　That summer fancy fell at last
To dust; and young Verona died
　When beauty's hour was overcast.

Theirs was the bitterness we know
   Because the clouds of hawthorn keep
So short a state, and kisses go
   To tombs unfathomably deep,
While Rameses and Romeo
   And little Ariadne sleep.

JUNE DANCE

THE chestnut cones were in the lanes,
Blushing, and eyed with ebony,
And young oak-apples lovingly
Clung to their stems with rosy veins
Threading their glossy amber; still
As wind may be, among the bloom
Of lilac and the burning broom
The dear wind moved deliciously,
And stayed upon the fragrant hill
And lighted on the sea;
And brushed the nettles nodding through
The budding globes of cloudy may,
And wavelike flowed upon the blue
Flowers of the wood.
                It was a day
When pearled blossom of peach and pear
Of blossoming season made an end,
Drifting along the sunlight, rare
Of beauty as thoughts between friend and friend
That have no cunning, but merely know
The way of truth for the heart is so.

It was such a time at the birth of June,
When the day was hushed at the hour of noon,
And whispering leaves gave out a tune
Ghostly as moves the bodiless moon
High in the full-day skies of June,

That they passed, a throng
Of toilers whose eyes
Were dull with toiling, passed along
By a path that lies
Between the city of mean emprise
And a forest set in mellow lands,
Far out from the city of broken hands.

Meanly clad, with bodies worn,
They came upon the forest hour,
From open fields of springing corn
To cloistered shades
They passed, from June light to June bower,
Tall men, and maids
Deep-bosomed, apt for any seed
That life should passionately sow,
Yet pale and troubled of a creed
Cried out by men who nothing know
Of joy's diviner excellence.
Along the silent glades they stept,
Till, flowing in each drowsy sense,
June came upon them, and they slept.

Beneath cool clustered branch and bloom,
Littered with stars of amethyst,
Sun-arrows glancing through the gloom,
They slept; the lush bracken kissed
The tired forms.   Ah, well-away,
Within so wide a peace to see
Fellows who measure every day
Merely the roads of misery.
Tall men, deep-bosomed maids were they,
As who should face the world and run
Fleet-footed down the laughing way,
With brows set fearless to the sun,
But slackened were the rippling thews
And all clear moods of courage dead,
Defeated by ignoble use
And sullen dread.

So in the sweet June-tide they slept,
Nor any dream of healing deep
Came over them; heart-sick they kept
A troubled sleep;
Companions of calamity,
Their sleep was but remembered pain,
And all their hunger but to be
Poor pilgrims in oblivion's train.

    The stems each had a little shadow
    In the early afternoon,
    When the toilers first were lured
    By a music long immured
    In the central forest ways
    Where no human footfall strays,
    To the dreaming dance of June.

One by one they woke, their faces
Still with some new wonder,
As when in quiet shadowy places
Wandering hands may move asunder
Secret foliage, and intrude
On the ancestral solitude
Of some untutored forest thing—
Neither doubt nor fear they bring,
But just a strange new wonder.

So now the toilers woke.　No thought
Of the old-time trouble came
Over them; the cares deep-wrought,
Furrowing, by years of shame,
Lightened, as upon their ears
Fell a music very low,
Sweet with moving of the years,
Burdened with the beat and flow
Of a garnered ecstasy
Gathered from the deeps of pain,
Music vaster than the sea,
Softer than the rain.

Then they rose,—the music played
But a little way ahead.
And with never question made
They were well to follow.   Red
And gold and opal flashed the noon
On lichened trunk.   Their raiment mean
Grew heavy in the dance of June,
And man and maid among the green
Unburdened them, and stood revealed
In clean unblushing loveliness,
Clean glowing limbs, all supple, steeled
And shining; many a streaming tress
Slipped beautiful to breast and knee,
They proved a world where was no sin,
Exultant, pure in passion, free,
Young captives bidden to begin
New being.   Sweet the music called,
Promising immortal boon,
Swift they set their feet, enthralled,
To the dreaming dance of June.

They passed into the forest's heart,
Where the shadows thickened,
Soul and trembling body thrilled
With a joy new-quickened.
It was as though from early days
Their familiars
Had been the words of worship of the lonely woodland
     ways
And the articulate voices of the stars.

   Keeping perfect measure
   To the music's chime,
   Reaping all the treasure
   Of the summer time,

Noiselessly along the glades,
Lithe white limbs all glancing,
Comely men and comely maids
Drifted in their dancing.

When chestnut cones were in the lanes,
Blushing, and eyed with ebony,
And young oak-apples lovingly
Clung to their stems with rosy veins
Threading their glossy amber—then
They took them to faring, maids and men,
Whose eyes were dull with toiling, far
From their toil in the time of a perfect noon,
To where the quiet shadows are,
And joined the dreaming dance of June.

THE MIDLANDS

BLACK in the summer night my Cotswold hill
    Aslant my window sleeps, beneath a sky
Deep as the bedded violets that fill
    March woods with dusky passion.   As I lie
Abed between cool walls I watch the host
    Of the slow stars lit over Gloucester plain,
And drowsily the habit of these most
    Beloved of English lands moves in my brain,
While silence holds dominion of the dark,
Save when the foxes from the spinneys bark.

I see the valleys in their morning mist
    Wreathed under limpid hills in moving light,
Happy with many a yeoman melodist;
    I see the little roads of twinkling white
Busy with fieldward teams and market gear
    Of rosy men, cloth-gaitered, who can tell
The many-minded changes of the year,
    Who know why crops and kine fare ill or well;
I see the sun persuade the mist away,
Till town and stead are shining to the day.

I see the wagons move along the rows
　Of ripe and summer-breathing clover-flower,
I see the lissom husbandman who knows
　Deep in his heart the beauty of his power,
As, lithely pitched, the full-heaped fork bids on
　The harvest home.　I hear the rickyard fill
With gossip as in generations gone,
　While wagon follows wagon from the hill.
I think how, when our seasons are all sealed,
Shall come the unchanging harvest from the field.

I see the barns and comely manors planned
　By men who somehow moved in comely thought,
Who, with a simple shippon to their hand,
　As men upon some godlike business wrought;
I see the little cottages that keep
　Their beauty still where since Plantagenet
Have come the shepherds happily to sleep,
　Finding the loaves and cups of cider set;
I see the twisted shepherds, brown and old,
Driving at dusk their glimmering sheep to fold.

And now the valleys that upon the sun
　Broke from their opal veils are veiled again,
And the last light upon the wolds is done,
　And silence falls on flocks and fields and men;
And black upon the night I watch my hill,
　And the stars shine, and there an owly wing
Brushes the night, and all again is still,
　And, from this land of worship that I sing,
I turn to sleep, content that from my sires
I draw the blood of England's midmost shires.

JAMES STEPHENS

IN THE COOL OF THE EVENING

I THOUGHT I heard Him calling.   Did you hear
A sound, a little sound?   My curious ear
Is dinned with flying noises, and the tree
Goes—whisper, whisper, whisper silently
Till all its whispers spread into the sound
Of a dull roar.   Lie closer to the ground,
The shade is deep and He may pass us by,
We are so very small, and His great eye,
Customed to starry majesties, may gaze
Too wide to spy us hiding in the maze:
Ah, misery ! the sun has not yet gone
And we are naked: He may look upon
Our crouching shame, may make us stand upright
Burning in terror—O that it were night !
He may not come. . . . What? listen, listen, now—
He is here ! lie closer. . . . *Adam, where art thou?*

DEIRDRE

Do not let any woman read this verse;
It is for men, and after them their sons
And their sons' sons.

The time comes when our hearts sink utterly;
When we remember Deirdre and her tale,
And that her lips are dust.

Once she did tread the earth: men took her hand;
They looked into her eyes and said their say,
And she replied to them.

More than a thousand years it is since she
Was beautiful: she trod the waving grass;
She saw the clouds.

A thousand years! The grass is still the same,
The clouds as lovely as they were that time
When Deirdre was alive.

But there has never been a woman born
Who was so beautiful, not one so beautiful
Of all the women born.

Let all men go apart and mourn together;
No man can ever love her; not a man
Can ever be her lover.

No man can bend before her: no man say—
What could one say to her? There are no words
That one could say to her!

Now she is but a story that is told
Beside the fire! No man can ever be
The friend of that poor queen.

JOHN FREEMAN

———

MUSIC COMES

Music comes
Sweetly from the trembling string
When wizard fingers sweep
Dreamily, half asleep;
When through remembering reeds
Ancient airs and murmurs creep,
Oboe oboe following,
Flute answering clear high flute,
Voices, voices—falling mute,
And the jarring drums.

At night I heard
First a waking bird
Out of the quiet darkness sing . . .
Music comes
Strangely to the brain asleep!
And I heard
Soft, wizard fingers sweep
Music from the trembling string,
And through remembering reeds
Ancient airs and murmurs creep;
Oboe, oboe following,
Flute calling clear high flute,
Voices faint, falling mute,
And low jarring drums;
Then all those airs
Sweetly jangled—newly strange,
Rich with change . . .
Was it the wind in the reeds?
Did the wind range
Over the trembling string;
Into flute and oboe pouring
Solemn music; sinking, soaring
Low to high,
Up and down the sky?
Was it the wind jarring
Drowsy far-off drums?

Strangely to the brain asleep
Music comes.

NOVEMBER SKIES

THAN these November skies
Is no sky lovelier.   The clouds are deep;
Into their grey the subtle spies
Of colour creep,

Changing that high austerity to delight.
Till ev'n the leaden interfolds are bright
And, where the cloud breaks, faint far azure peers
Ere a thin flushing cloud again
Shuts up that loveliness, or shares.
The huge great clouds move slowly, gently, as
Reluctant the quick sun should shine in vain,
Holding in bright caprice their rain.
      And when of colours none,
Nor rose, nor amber, nor the scarce late green,
Is truly seen,—
In all the myriad grey,
In silver height and dusky deep, remain
The loveliest,
Faint purple flushes of the unvanquished sun.

JAMES ELROY FLECKER

RIOUPÉROUX

High and solemn mountains guard Rioupéroux,
—Small untidy village where the river drives a mill:
Frail as wood anemones, white and frail were you,
And drooping a little, like the slender daffodil.

Oh, I will go to France again, and tramp the valley through,
And I will change these gentle clothes for clog and corduroy,
And work with the mill-hands of black Rioupéroux,
And walk with you, and talk with you, like any other boy.

TO A POET A THOUSAND YEARS HENCE

I who am dead a thousand years,
    And wrote this sweet archaic song,
Send you my words for messengers
    The way I shall not pass along.

I care not if you bridge the seas,
　　Or ride secure the cruel sky,
Or build consummate palaces
　　Of metal or of masonry.

But have you wine and music still,
　　And statues and a bright-eyed love,
And foolish thoughts of good and ill,
　　And prayers to them who sit above?

How shall we conquer?　Like a wind
　　That falls at eve our fancies blow,
And old Maeonides the blind
　　Said it three thousand years ago.

O friend unseen, unborn, unknown,
　　Student of our sweet English tongue,
Read out my words at night, alone:
　　I was a poet, I was young.

Since I can never see your face,
　　And never shake you by the hand,
I send my soul through time and space
　　To greet you.　You will understand.

THE OLD SHIPS

I HAVE seen old ships sail like swans asleep
Beyond the village which men still call Tyre,
With leaden age o'ercargoed, dipping deep
For Famagusta and the hidden sun
That rings black Cyprus with a lake of fire;
And all those ships were certainly so old
Who knows how oft with squat and noisy gun,
Questing brown slaves or Syrian oranges,
The pirate Genoese

Hell-raked them till they rolled
Blood, water, fruit and corpses up the hold.
But now through friendly seas they softly run,
Painted the mid-sea blue or shore-sea green,
Still patterned with the vine and grapes in gold.

But I have seen,
Pointing her shapely shadows from the dawn
And image tumbled on a rose-swept bay,
A drowsy ship of some yet older day;
And, wonder's breath indrawn,
Thought I—who knows—who knows—but in that same
(Fished up beyond Aeaea, patched up new
—Stern painted brighter blue—)
That talkative, bald-headed seaman came
(Twelve patient comrades sweating at the oar)
From Troy's doom-crimson shore,
And with great lies about his wooden horse
Set the crew laughing, and forgot his course.

It was so old a ship—who knows, who knows?
—And yet so beautiful, I watched in vain
To see the mast burst open with a rose,
And the whole deck put on its leaves again.

GATES OF DAMASCUS

FOUR great gates has the city of Damascus,
 And four Grand Wardens, on their spears reclining,
All day long stand like tall stone men
 And sleep on the towers when the moon is shining.

This is the song of the East Gate Warden
When he locks the great gate and smokes in his garden.

ostern of Fate, the Desert Gate, Disaster's Cavern, Fort
 of Fear,
he Portal of Bagdad am I, the Doorway of Diarbekir.

The Persian Dawn with new desires may net the flushin
    mountain spires,
But my gaunt buttress still rejects the suppliance of thos
    mellow fires.

Pass not beneath, O Caravan, or pass not singing. Have yo
    heard
That silence where the birds are dead yet something pipet
    like a bird?

Pass not beneath! Men say there blows in stony deser
    still a rose
But with no scarlet to her leaf—and from whose heart n
    perfume flows.

Wilt thou bloom red where she buds pale, thy sister ros
    Wilt thou not fail
When noonday flashes like a flail? Leave, nightinga
    the Caravan!

Pass then, pass all! 'Bagdad!' ye cry, and down t
    billows of blue sky
Ye beat the bell that beats to hell, and who shall thrust
    back? Not I.

The Sun who flashes through the head and paints the shado
    green and red—
The Sun shall eat thy fleshless dead, O Caravan, O Carava

And one who licks his lips for thirst with fevered eyes sh
    face in fear
The palms that wave, the streams that burst, his last mira
    O Caravan!

And one—the bird-voiced Singing-man—shall fall behi
    thee, Caravan!
And God shall meet him in the night, and he shall sing
    best he can.

nd one the Bedouin shall slay, and one, sand-stricken on
 the way,
o dark and blind; and one shall say—'How lonely is
 the Caravan!'

ass out beneath, O Caravan, Doom's Caravan, Death's
 Caravan!
had not told ye, fools, so much, save that I heard your
 Singing-man.

> *This was sung by the West Gate's keeper*
> *When heaven's hollow dome grew deeper.*

am the gate toward the sea: O sailor men, pass out from
 me!
hear you high on Lebanon, singing the marvels of the sea.

he dragon-tree, the luminous, the dark, the serpent-
 haunted sea,
he snow-besprinkled wine of earth, the white-and-blue-
 flower foaming sea.

eyond the sea are towns with towers, carved with lions
 and lily flowers,
nd not a soul in all those lonely streets to while away
 the hours.

eyond the towns, an isle where, bound, a naked giant bites
 the ground:
he shadow of a monstrous wing looms on his back: and
 still no sound.

eyond the isle a rock that screams like madmen shouting
 in their dreams,
om whose dark issues night and day blood crashes in a
 thousand streams.

eyond the rock is Restful Bay, where no wind breathes or
 ripple stirs,
nd there on Roman ships, they say, stand rows of metal
 mariners.

Beyond the bay in utmost West old Solomon the Jewish
    King
Sits with his beard upon his breast, and grips and guards
    his magic ring;

And when that ring is stolen, he will rise in outraged
    majesty,
And take the World upon his back, and fling the World
    beyond the sea.

> *This is the song of the North Gate's master,*
> *Who singeth fast, but drinketh faster.*

I am the gay Aleppo Gate: a dawn, a dawn and thou art
    there:
Eat not thy heart with fear and care, O brother of the beast
    we hate!

Thou hast not many miles to tread, nor other foes than fleas
    to dread;
Homs shall behold thy morning meal, and Hama see thee
    safe in bed.

Take to Aleppo filigrane, and take them paste of apricots,
And coffee tables botched with pearl, and little beaten
    brassware pots:

And thou shalt sell thy wares for thrice the Damascene
    retailers' price,
And buy a fat Armenian slave who smelleth odorous and
    nice.

Some men of noble stock were made: some glory in the
    murder-blade:
Some praise a Science or an Art, but I like honourable
    Trade!

Sell them the rotten, buy the ripe! Their heads are weak;
    their pockets burn.
Aleppo men are mighty fools. Salaam Aleikum! Safe
    return!

This is the song of the South Gate Holder,
A silver man, but his song is older.

I am the Gate that fears no fall: the Mihrab of Damascus
    wall,
The bridge of booming Sinai: the Arch of Allah all in all.

O spiritual pilgrim, rise: the night has grown her single
    horn:
The voices of the souls unborn are half adream with
    Paradise.

To Meccah thou hast turned in prayer with aching heart
    and eyes that burn:
Ah, Hajji, whither wilt thou turn when thou art there,
    when thou art there?

God be thy guide from camp to camp: God be thy shade
    from well to well;
God grant beneath the desert stars thou hear the Prophet's
    camel bell.

And God shall make thy body pure, and give thee knowledge
    to endure
This ghost-life's piercing phantom-pain, and bring thee
    out to Life again.

And God shall make thy soul a Glass where eighteen thousand
    Aeons pass,
And thou shalt see the gleaming Worlds as men see dew upon
    the grass.

And son of Islam, it may be that thou shalt learn at journey's
    end
Who walks thy garden eve on eve, and bows his head, and
    calls thee Friend.

D. H. LAWRENCE

SICILIAN CYCLAMENS

When he pushed his brush of black hair off his brow:
When she lifted her mop from her eyes, and screwed it in
    knob behind
        —O act of fearful temerity!
When they felt their foreheads bare, naked to heaven, the
    eyes revealed:
When they felt the light of heaven brandished like a knif
    at their defenceless eyes,
And the sea like a blade at their face,
Mediterranean savages:
When they came out, face-revealed, under heaven, from th
    shaggy undergrowth of their own hair
For the first time,
They saw tiny rose cyclamens between their toes, growin
Where the slow toads sat brooding on the past.

Slow toads, and cyclamen leaves
Stickily glistening with eternal shadow
Keeping to earth.
Cyclamen leaves
Toad-filmy, earth-iridescent
Beautiful
Frost-filigreed
Spumed with mud
Snail-nacreous
Low down.

The shaking aspect of the sea
And man's defenceless bare face
And cyclamens putting their ears back.
Long, pensive, slim-muzzled greyhound buds
Dreamy, not yet present,
Drawn out of earth
At his toes.
Dawn-rose
Sub-delighted, stone-engendered

Cyclamens, young cyclamens
Arching
Waking, pricking their ears
Like delicate, very-young greyhound bitches
Half-yawning at the open, inexperienced
Vista of day,
Folding back their soundless petalled ears.

Greyhound bitches
Bending their rosy muzzles pensive down,
And breathing soft, unwilling to wake to the new day
Yet sub-delighted.

Ah Mediterranean morning, when our world began !
Far-off Mediterranean mornings,
Pelasgic faces uncovered,
And budding cyclamens.

The hare suddenly goes uphill
Laying back her long ears with unwinking bliss.

And up the pallid, sea-blenched Mediterranean stone slopes
Rose cyclamen, ecstatic fore-runner !
Cyclamens, ruddy-muzzled cyclamens
In little bunches like bunches of wild hares
Muzzled together, ears-aprick,
Whispering witchcraft
Like women at a well, the dawn-fountain.

Greece, and the world's morning
Where all the Parthenon marbles still fostered the roofs of
    the cyclamen.

Violets
Pagan, rosy-muzzled violets
Autumnal,
Dawn-pink,
Dawn-pale
Among squat toad-leaves sprinkling the unborn
Erechtheion marbles.

ROBERT GRAVES

IN THE WILDERNESS

CHRIST of his gentleness
Thirsting and hungering,
Walked in the wilderness;
Soft words of grace He spoke
Unto lost desert-folk
That listened wondering.
He heard the bitterns call
From ruined palace-wall,
Answered them brotherly.
He held communion
With the she-pelican
Of lonely piety.
Basilisk, cockatrice,
Flocked to His homilies,
With mail of dread device,
With monstrous barbèd stings,
With eager dragon-eyes;
Great bats on leather wings
And poor blind broken things,
Foul in their miseries.
And ever with Him went,
Of all His wanderings
Comrade, with ragged coat,
Gaunt ribs—poor innocent—
Bleeding foot, burning throat,
The guileless old scape-goat;
For forty nights and days
Followed in Jesus' ways,
Sure guard behind Him kept,
Tears like a lover wept.

FREDEGOND SHOVE

THE NEW GHOST

'And he, casting away his garment, rose and came to Jesus.'

And he cast it down, down, on the green grass,
Over the young crocuses, where the dew was—
He cast the garment of his flesh that was full of death,
And like a sword his spirit showed out of the cold sheath.

He went a pace or two, he went to meet his Lord,
And, as I said, his spirit looked like a clean sword,
And seeing him the naked trees began shivering,
And all the birds cried out aloud as it were late spring.

And the Lord came on, He came down, and saw
That a soul was waiting there for Him, one without flaw,
And they embraced in the churchyard where the robins
    play,
And the daffodils hang down their heads, as they burn
    away.

The Lord held his head fast, and you could see
That he kissed the unsheathed ghost that was gone free—
As a hot sun, on a March day, kisses the cold ground;
And the spirit answered, for he knew well that his peace
    was found.

The spirit trembled, and sprang up at the Lord's word—
As on a wild, April day, springs a small bird—
So the ghost's feet lifting him up, he kissed the Lord's
    cheek,
And for the greatness of their love neither of them could
    speak.

But the Lord went then, to show him the way,
Over the young crocuses, under the green may
That was not quite in flower yet—to a far-distant land;
And the ghost followed, like a naked cloud holding the
    sun's hand.

* M 921

ROBERT NICHOLS

THE TOWER

It was deep night, and over Jerusalem's low roofs
The moon floated, drifting through high vaporous woofs.
The moonlight crept and glistened silent, solemn, sweet,
Over dome and column, up empty, endless street;
In the closed, scented gardens the rose loosed from th
  stem
Her white showery petals; none regarded them;
The starry thicket breathed odours to the sentinel palm;
Silence possessed the city like a soul possessed by calm.

Not a spark in the warren under the giant night,
Save where in a turret's lantern beamed a grave, still light:
There in the topmost chamber a gold-eyed lamp was lit—
Marvellous lamp in darkness, informing, redeeming it!
For, set in that tiny chamber, Jesus, the blessed and
  doomed,
Spoke to the lone apostles as light to men entombed;
And spreading His hands in blessing, as one soon to be dead
He put soft enchantment into spare wine and bread.

The hearts of the disciples were broken and full of tears,
Because their Lord, the spearless, was hedgèd about with
  spears;
And in His face the sickness of departure had spread a gloom
At leaving His young friends friendless.
                                  They could not forget the tomb
He smiled subduedly, telling, in tones soft as voice of th
  dove,
The endlessness of sorrow, the eternal solace of love;
And lifting the earthly tokens, wine and sorrowful bread,
He bade them sup and remember One who lived and w
  dead.
And they could not restrain their weeping.

But one rose up to depart,
Having weakness and hate of weakness raging within his
heart,
And bowed to the robed assembly whose eyes gleamed wet
in the light.
Judas arose and departed: night went out to the night.

Then Jesus lifted His voice like a fountain in an ocean of
tears,
And comforted His disciples and calmed and allayed their
fears.
But Judas wound down the turret, creeping from floor to
floor,
And would fly; but one leaning, weeping, barred him
beside the door.
And he knew her by her ruddy garment and two yet-
watching men:
Mary of Seven Evils, Mary Magdalen.
And he was frighted at her. She sighed: 'I dreamed
him dead.
We sell the body for silver . . .'
Then Judas cried out and fled
Forth into the night! . . . The moon had begun to set:
A drear, deft wind went sifting, setting the dust afret;
Into the heart of the city Judas ran on and prayed
To stern Jehovah lest his deed make him afraid.

But in the tiny lantern, hanging as if on air,
The disciples sat unspeaking. Amaze and peace were there.
For *His* voice, more lovely than song of all earthly birds,
In accents humble and happy spoke slow, consoling words.

Thus Jesus discoursed, and was silent, sitting upright, and
soon
Past the casement behind Him slanted the sinking moon;
And, rising for Olivet, all stared, between love and
dread,
Seeing the torrid moon a ruddy halo behind His head.

J. C. SQUIRE

THERE WAS AN INDIAN

THERE was an Indian, who had known no change,
  Who strayed content along a sunlit beach
Gathering shells.   He heard a sudden strange
  Commingled noise: looked up; and gasped for speech.

For in the bay, where nothing was before,
  Moved on the sea, by magic, huge canoes,
With bellying cloths on poles, and not one oar,
  And fluttering coloured signs and clambering crews.

And he, in fear, this naked man alone,
  His fallen hands forgetting all their shells,
His lips gone pale, knelt low behind a stone,
  And stared, and saw, and did not understand,
Columbus's doom-burdened caravels
  Slant to the shore, and all their seamen land.

THE LILY OF MALUD

THE lily of Malud is born in secret mud.
It is breathed like a word in a little dark ravine
Where no bird was ever heard and no beast was ever seen,
And the leaves are never stirred by the panther's velvet
    sheen.

It blooms once a year in summer moonlight,
In a valley of dark fear full of pale moonlight:
It blooms once a year, and dies in a night,
And its petals disappear with the dawn's first light;
And when that night has come, black small-breasted maids,
With ecstatic terror dumb, steal fawn-like through the shades
To watch, hour by hour, the unfolding of the flower.

When the world is full of night, and the moon reigns alone
And drowns in silver light the known and the unknown,
When each hut is a mound, half blue-silver and half black,
And casts upon the ground the hard shadow of its back,
When the winds are out of hearing and the tree-tops never
  shake,
When the grass in the clearing is silent but awake
Neath a moon-paven sky: all the village is asleep
And the babes that nightly cry dream deep:
                    From the doors the maidens creep,
Tiptoe over dreaming curs, soft, so soft, that no one stirs,
And stand curved and a-quiver, like bathers by a river,
Looking at the forest wall, groups of slender naked girls,
Whose black bodies shine like pearls where the moonbeams
  fall.

They have waked, they know not why, at a summons from
  the night,
They have stolen fearfully from the dark to the light,
Stepping over sleeping men, who have moved and slept
  again:
And they know not why they go to the forest, but they
  know,
As their moth-feet pass to the shore of the grass
And the forest's dreadful brink, that their tender spirits
  shrink:
They would flee, but cannot turn, for their eyelids burn
With still frenzy, and each maid, ere she leaves the moonlit
  space,
If she sees another's face is thrilled and afraid.

Now like little phantom fawns they thread the outer lawns
Where the boles of giant trees stand about in twos and
  threes,
Till the forest grows more dense and the darkness more
  intense,

And they only sometimes see in a lone moon-ray
A dead and spongy trunk in the earth half-sunk,
Or the roots of a tree with fungus grey,
Or a drift of muddy leaves, or a banded snake that heaves

And the towering unseen roof grows more intricate, an
soon
It is featureless and proof to the lost forgotten moon.
But they could not look above as with blind-drawn fee
they move
Onwards on the scarce-felt path, with quick and desperat
breath,
For their circling fingers dread to caress some slimy head,
Or to touch the icy shape of a hunched and hairy ape,
And at every step they fear in their very midst to hear
A lion's rending roar or a tiger's snore . . .
And when things swish or fall, they shiver but dare not cal

O what is it leads the way that they do not stray?
What unimagined arm keeps their bodies from harm?
What presence concealed lifts their little feet that yield
Over dry ground and wet till their straining eyes are met
With a thinning of the darkness?

And the foremost faintly cries in awed surprise:
And they one by one emerge from the gloom to the verge
Of a small sunken vale full of moonlight pale.
And they hang along the bank, clinging to the branches dank
A shadowy festoon out of sight of the moon;
And they see in front of them, rising from the mud,
A single straight stem and a single pallid bud
In that little lake of light from the moon's calm height.

A stem, a ghostly bud, on the moon-swept mud
That shimmers like a pond; and over there beyond
The guardian forest high, menacing and strange,
Invades the empty sky with its wild black range.

And they watch hour by hour that small lonely flower
In that deep forest place that hunter never found.

It shines without sound, as a star without space.

And the silence all around that solitary place
Is like silence in a dream; till a sudden flashing gleam
Down their dark faces flies; and their lips fall apart
And their glimmering great eyes with excitement dart
And their fingers, clutching the branches they were
    touching,
Shake and arouse hissing leaves on the boughs.
And they whisper aswoon: Did it move in the moon?

O it moved as it grew!
It is moving, opening, with calm and gradual will
And their bodies where they cling are shadowed and still,
And with marvel they mark that the mud now is dark,
For the unfolding flower, like a goddess in her power,
Challenges the moon with a light of her own,
That lovelily grows as the petals unclose,
Wider, more wide with an awful inward pride
Till the heart of it breaks and stilled is their breath,
For the radiance it makes is as wonderful as death.

The morning's crimson stain tinges their ashen brows
As they part the last boughs and slowly step again
On to the village grass, and chill and languid pass
Into the huts to sleep.
                Brief slumber, yet so deep
That, when they wake to day, darkness and splendour seem
Broken and far away, a faint miraculous dream;
And when those maidens rise they are as they ever were
Save only for a rare shade of trouble in their eyes.
And the surly thick-lipped men, as they sit about their huts
Making drums out of guts, grunting gruffly now and then,
Carving sticks of ivory, stretching shields of wrinkled skin,
Smoothing sinister and thin squatting gods of ebony,
Chip and grunt and do not see.

But each mother, silently,
Longer than her wont stays shut in the dimness of her hut,
For she feels a brooding cloud of memory in the air,
A lingering thing there that makes her sit bowed
With hollow shining eyes, as the night-fire dies,
And stare softly at the ember, and try to remember,
Something sorrowful and far, something sweet and vaguely
   seen
Like an early evening star when the sky is pale green:
A quiet silver tower that climbed in an hour,
Or a ghost like a flower, or a flower like a queen:
Something holy in the past that came and did not last . .
But she knows not what it was.

RIVERS

RIVERS I have seen which were beautiful,
Slow rivers winding in the flat fens,
With bands of reed like thronged green swords
   Guarding the mirrored sky;
And streams down-tumbling from the chalk hills
To valleys of meadows and watercress-beds,
And bridges whereunder, dark weed-coloured shadows
   Trout flit or lie.

I know those rivers that peacefully glide
Past old towers and shaven gardens,
Where mottled walls rise from the water
   And mills all streaked with flour;
And rivers with wharves and rusty shipping,
That flow with a stately tidal motion
Towards their destined estuaries
   Full of the pride of power;

Noble great rivers, Thames and Severn,
Tweed with his gateway of many grey arches,
Clyde, dying at sunset westward
   In a sea as red as blood;

Rhine and his hills in close procession,
Placid Elbe, Seine slaty and swirling,
And Isar, son of the Alpine snows,
    A furious turquoise flood.

All these I have known, and with slow eyes
I have walked on their shores and watched them,
And softened to their beauty and loved them
    Wherever my feet have been;
And a hundred others also
Whose names long since grew into me,
That, dreaming in light or darkness,
    I have seen, though I have not seen.

Those rivers of thought: cold Ebro
And blue racing Guadiana,
Passing white houses, high-balconied,
    That ache in a sun-baked land,
Congo, and Nile, and Colorado,
Niger, Indus, Zambesi,
And the Yellow River, and the Oxus,
    And the river that dies in sand.

What splendours are theirs, what continents,
What tribes of men, what basking plains,
Forests and lion-hided deserts,
    Marshes, ravines, and falls:
All hues and shapes and tempers
Wandering they take as they wander
From those far springs that endlessly
    The far sea calls.

O in reverie I know the Volga
That turns his back upon Europe,
And the two great cities on his banks,
    Novgorod and Astrakhan;
Where the world is a few soft colours,
And under the dove-like evening
The boatmen chant ancient songs,
    The tenderest known to man.

And the holy river Ganges,
His fretted cities veiled in moonlight,
Arches and buttresses silver-shadowy
    In the high moon,
And palms grouped in the moonlight
And fanes girdled with cypresses,
Their domes of marble softly shining
    To the high silver moon.

And that aged Brahmapootra
Who beyond the white Himalayas
Passes many a lamassery
    On rocks forlorn and frore,
A block of gaunt grey stone walls
With rows of little barred windows,
Where shrivelled young monks in yellow silk
    Are hidden for evermore. . . .

But O that great river, the Amazon,
I have sailed up its gulf with eyelids closed,
And the yellow waters tumbled round,
    And all was rimmed with sky,
Till the banks drew in, and the trees' heads,
And the lines of green grew higher
And I breathed deep, and there above me
    The forest wall stood high.

Those forest walls of the Amazon
Are level under the blazing blue,
And yield no sound but the whistles and shrieks
    Of the swarming bright macaws;
And under their lowest drooping boughs
Mud-banks torpidly bubble,
And the water drifts, and logs in the water
    Drift and twist and pause.

And everywhere, tacitly joining,
Float noiseless tributaries,
Tall avenues paved with water:
    And as I silent fly

The vegetation like a painted scene,
Spars and spikes and monstrous fans
And ferns from hairy sheaths up-springing,
　Evenly passes by.

And stealthier stagnant channels
Under low niches of drooping leaves
Coil into deep recesses:
　And there have I entered, there
To heavy, hot, dense, dim places
Where creepers climb and sweat and climb,
And the drip and splash of oozing water
　Loads the stifling air.

Rotting scrofulous steaming trunks,
Great horned emerald beetles crawling,
Ants and huge slow butterflies
　That had strayed and lost the sun;
Ah, sick I have swooned as the air thickened
To a pallid brown ecliptic glow,
And on the forest, fallen with languor,
　Thunder has begun.

Thunder in the dun dusk, thunder
Rolling and battering and cracking,
The caverns shudder with a terrible glare
　Again and again and again,
Till the land bows in the darkness,
Utterly lost and defenceless,
Smitten and blinded and overwhelmed
　By the crashing rods of rain.

And then in the forests of the Amazon,
When the rain has ended, and silence come,
What dark luxuriance unfolds
　From behind the night's drawn bars:

The wreathing odours of a thousand trees
And the flowers' faint gleaming presences,
And over the clearings and the still waters
   Soft indigo and hanging stars.

    .   .   .   .   .

O many and many are rivers,
And beautiful are all rivers,
And lovely is water everywhere
   That leaps or glides or stays;
Yet by starlight, moonlight, or sunlight,
Long, long though they look, these wandering eyes
Even on the fairest waters of dream,
   Never untroubled gaze.

For whatever stream I stand by,
And whatever river I dream of,
There is something still in the back of my mind
   From very far away;
There is something I saw and see not,
A country full of rivers
That stirs in my heart and speaks to me
   More sure, more dear than they.

And always I ask and wonder
   (Though often I do not know it):
Why does this water not smell like water?
   Where is the moss that grew
Wet and dry on the slabs of granite
And the round stones in clear brown water?
—And a pale film rises before them
   Of the rivers that first I knew.

Though famous are the rivers of the great world,
Though my heart from those alien waters drinks
Delight however pure from their loveliness,
   And awe however deep,

Would I wish for a moment the miracle,
That those waters should come to Chagford,
Or gather and swell in Tavy Cleave
    Where the stones cling to the steep?

No, even were they Ganges and Amazon
In all their great might and majesty,
League upon league of wonders,
    I would lose them all, and more,
For a light chiming of small bells,
A twisting flash in the granite,
The tiny thread of a pixie waterfall
    That lives by Vixen Tor.

Those rivers in that lost country,
They were brown as a clear brown bead is,
Or red with the earth that rain washed down,
    Or white with china-clay;
And some tossed foaming over boulders,
And some curved mild and tranquil,
In wooded vales securely set
    Under the fond warm day.

Okement and Erme and Avon,
Exe and his ruffled shallows,
I could cry as I think of those rivers
    That knew my morning dreams;
The weir by Tavistock at evening
When the circling woods were purple,
And the Lowman in spring with the lent-lilies,
    And the little moorland streams.

For many a hillside streamlet
There falls with a broken tinkle,
Falling and dying, falling and dying,
    In little cascades and pools,
Where the world is furze and heather
And flashing plovers and fixed larks,
And an empty sky, whitish blue,
    That small world rules.

There, there, where the high waste bog-lands
And the drooping slopes and the spreading valleys,
The orchards and the cattle-sprinkled pastures
    Those travelling musics fill,
There is my lost Abana,
And there is my nameless Pharphar
That mixed with my heart when I was a boy,
    And time stood still.

And I say I will go there and die there:
But I do not go there, and sometimes
I think that the train could not carry me there,
    And it's possible, maybe,
That it's farther than Asia or Africa,
Or any voyager's harbour,
Farther, farther, beyond recall . . .
    O even in memory!

FRANCIS BRETT YOUNG

PROTHALAMION

When the evening came my love said to me:
    Let us go into the garden now that the sky is cool;
The garden of black hellebore and rosemary,
    Where wild woodruff spills in a milky pool.

Low we passed in the twilight, for the wavering heat
    Of day had waned; and round that shaded plot
Of secret beauty the thickets clustered sweet:
    Here is heaven, our hearts whispered, but our lips spake
    not.

Between that old garden and the seas of lazy foam
    Gloomy and beautiful alleys of trees arise
With spire of cypress and dreamy beechen dome,
    So dark that our enchanted sight knew nothing but the
    skies:

Veiled with a soft air, drench'd in the roses' musk
  Or the dusky, dark carnation's breath of clove:
No stars burned in their deeps, but through the dusk
  I saw my love's eyes, and they were brimmed with love.

No star their secret ravished, no wasting moon
  Mocked the sad transience of those eternal hours:
Only the soft, unseeing heaven of June,
  The ghosts of great trees, and the sleeping flowers.

For doves that crooned in the leafy noonday now
  Were silent; the night-jar sought his secret covers,
Nor even a mild sea-whisper moved a creaking bough—
  Was ever a silence deeper made for lovers?

Was ever a moment meeter made for love?
  Beautiful are your close lips beneath my kiss;
And all your yielding sweetness beautiful—
  Oh, never in all the world was such a night as this!

GERALD GOULD

THE EARTH CHILD

Out of the veins of the world comes the blood of me;
The heart that beats in my side is the heart of the sea;
The hills have known me of old, and they do not forget;
Long ago was I friends with the wind; I am friends with it yet.

The hills are grey, they are strange; they breed desire
Of a tune that the feet may march to and not tire;
For always up in the distance the thin roads wind,
And passing out of sight, they pass not out of mind.

I am glad when morning and evening alter the skies;
There speaks no voice of the stars but my voice replies;
When wave on wave all night cries out in its need,
I listen, I understand; my heart takes heed.

Out of the red-brown earth, out of the grey-brown streams,
Came this perilous body, cage of perilous dreams;

To the ends of all waters and lands they are tossed, they are
        whirled,
For my dreams are one with my body, yea, one with the
        world.

SONNET

THE creeping hours have caught us unawares,
    And while we yet stand breathless from the thrill
    Of the warm noon, the twilight wide and chill
Has stol'n the colour from the golden airs:
The dead and equal light of evening bares
    The world of shade ere shade shall have its fill;
    And the vague gleams on river, fold, and hill
Are lost and lonely as unanswered prayers.

Draw closer to me, dear: the greater need
    Must breed the greater solace.   All about
    The moods and marvels of the day go out
Like candles blown upon: the heat, the speed,
Are sped: but all things bring their own redress,
And love that's weary is not love the less.

SHANE LESLIE

FLEET STREET

I NEVER see the newsboys run
    Amid the whirling street,
    With swift untiring feet,
To cry the latest venture done,
But I expect one day to hear
    Them cry the crack of doom
    And risings from the tomb,
With great Archangel Michael near;
And see them running from the Fleet
    As messengers of God,
    With Heaven's tidings shod
About their brave unwearied feet.

EZRA POUND

NIGHT LITANY

O Dieu, purifiez nos cœurs !
   Purifiez nos cœurs !

Yea, the lines hast thou laid unto me
   in pleasant places,
And the beauty of this thy Venice
   hast thou shown unto me
Until its loveliness became unto me
   a thing of tears.

O God, what great kindness
   have we done in times past
   and forgotten it,
That thou givest this wonder unto us,
   O God of waters?

O God of the night,
   What great sorrow
Cometh unto us,
   That thou thus repayest us
Before the time of its coming?

O God of silence,
   Purifiez nos cœurs,
   Purifiez nos cœurs,
For we have seen
The glory of the shadow of the
   likeness of thine handmaid,

Yea, the glory of the shadow
   of thy Beauty hath walked
Upon the shadow of the waters
In this thy Venice,

And before the holiness
Of the shadow of thy handmaid
   Have I hidden mine eyes,
      O God of waters.

O God of silence,
   Purifiez nos cœurs,
   Purifiez nos cœurs,
O God of waters,
   make clean our hearts within us,
   For I have seen the
Shadow of this thy Venice
Floating upon the waters,
   And thy stars.

Have seen this thing, out of their far courses
Have they seen this thing,
   O God of waters,
Even as are thy stars
Silent unto us in their far-coursing,
Even so is mine heart
   become silent within me.

   Purifiez nos cœurs,
O God of the silence.
   Purifiez nos cœurs,
O God of the waters.

BALLAD OF THE GOODLY FERE [1]

*Simon Zelotes speaketh it somewhile after
the Crucifixion.*

Ha' we lost the goodliest fere o' all
For the priests and the gallows tree?
Aye lover he was of brawny men
O' ships and the open sea.

---

[1] Fere = mate, companion.

When they came wi' a host to take Our Man
His smile was good to see,
'First let these go!' quo' our Goodly Fere,
'Or I 'll see ye damned,' says he.

Aye he sent us out through the crossed high spears
And the scorn of his laugh rang free,
'Why took ye not me when I walked about
Alone in the town?' says he.

Oh we drank his 'Hale' in the good red wine
When we last made company,
No capon priest was the Goodly Fere,
But a man o' men was he.

I ha' seen him drive a hundred men
Wi' a bundle o' cords swung free,
That they took the high and holy house
For their pawn and treasury.

They 'll no' get him a' in a book I think
Though they write it cunningly;
No mouse of the scrolls was the Goodly Fere
But aye loved the open sea.

If they think they ha' snared our Goodly Fere
They are fools to the last degree.
'I 'll go to the feast,' quo' our Goodly Fere,
'Though I go to the gallows tree.'

'Ye ha' seen me heal the lame and blind,
And wake the dead,' says he,
'Ye shall see one thing to master all:
'Tis how a brave man dies on the tree.'

A Son of God was the Goodly Fere
That bade us his brothers be.
I ha' seen him cow a thousand men.
I have seen him upon the tree.

He cried no cry when they drave the nails
And the blood gushed hot and free,
The hounds of the crimson sky gave tongue
But never a cry cried he.

I ha' seen him cow a thousand men
On the hills o' Galilee,
They whined as he walked out calm between,
Wi' his eyes like the grey o' the sea.

Like the sea that brooks no voyaging
With the winds unleashed and free,
Like the sea that He cowed at Geneseret
Wi' twey words spoke suddenly.

PRAISE OF YSOLT

In vain I have striven,
   to teach my heart to bow;
In vain have I said to him
 'There be many singers greater than thou.'

But his answer cometh, as winds and as lutany,
As a vague crying upon the night
That leaveth me no rest, saying ever,
    'Song, a song.'

Their echoes play upon each other in the twilight
Seeking ever a song.
Lo, I am worn with travail
And the wandering of many roads hath made my eyes
As dark red circles filled with dust.

Yet there is a trembling upon me in the twilight,
    And little red elf words crying 'A song,'
    Little grey elf words crying for a song,
    Little brown leaf words crying 'A song,'
    Little green leaf words crying for a song.
The words are as leaves, old brown leaves in the spring
    time
Blowing they know not whither, seeking a song.

White words as snow flakes but they are cold,
Moss words, lip words, words of slow streams.

In vain I have striven
        to teach my soul to bow,
In vain have I pled with him:
    'There be greater souls than thou.'

For in the morn of my years there came a woman
As moonlight calling,
As the moon calleth the tides,
                'Song, a song.'
Wherefore I made her a song, and she went from me
As the moon doth from the sea,
But still came the leaf words, little brown elf words
Saying, 'The soul sendeth us.'
                'A song, a song!'
And in vain I cried unto them, 'I have no song,
For she I sang of hath gone from me.'

But my soul sent a woman, a woman of the wonder folk,
A woman as fire upon the pine woods
        crying, 'Song, a song.'
As the flame crieth unto the sap.
My song was ablaze with her, and she went from me
As flame leaveth the embers so went she unto new
        forests
And the woods were with me
        crying ever 'Song, a song.'

And I, 'I have no song,'
Till my soul sent a woman as the sun:
Yea as the sun calleth to the seed,
As the spring upon the bough
So is she that cometh the mother of songs,
She that holdeth the wonder words within her eyes
The words, little elf words
    that call ever unto me,
                    'Song, a song.'

ENVOI

In vain have I striven with my soul
        to teach my soul to bow.
What soul boweth
        while in his heart art thou?

HERBERT E. PALMER

IN AUTUMN: AN ODE

In Autumn the last fruits turn mellow,
And many flowers flaunt yellow,
And brown and russet-yellow are the hill-places
That the winds haunt.

And as dripping nights daunt the sun's lights
The famished leaves flutter yellow
Round the trees growing gaunt.

Autumn is a brown and yellow time
Soon after life's prime,
The time of a knell
Of everything man loved too well,—
When from some dim belfry of starshine
The gold and brassy bells of Change
Utter mournful ding-dongs
To the changing sing-songs
Crying, sighing where the grasses shone,
'It is all all over,

The leaping of life is over,
The cherry and the clover are gone.'

Very strangely the music flows,
And the woof across the warp dims and glows,—
Brown and yellow with a glint of rose.
But the soul of man grieves;
And thick as whirled leaves,
While tired Time weaves
This third of his mysteries,
The birds crowd in the aching trees
And where late stood the corn-sheaves.

How the birds twitter and complain!
How they complain to the creeping grey rain!

And yet near the heart of the weeping there is mirth;
For many days laugh with the joy of the Sun
And the hued brightness of Earth
That recks not Death's whiteness.

And bridal seem the stubble field-ways,
When crowned with a coronal of tinted weeds
And blackberry beads,
Decay pipes sweetly on her Pan-reeds;

Or dances full of amaze,
Heavy garlanded with the red berries
(Redder than the farm cherries)
From the hedge that the bright sun bleeds
And the Night slays
With her blanket of haze.

Then, though man scarce heeds,
Out of the West a finger beckons,
Westward beckons,—
Some strange allure
That throbs in the heart of all Change.

Very strange and pure are the days
When the bright sun through a silver haze
Steals slowly into a zenith of blue.
And you and I, I and you,
Stand as if on the brink of Spring
Listening,
Wondering.

For strange lovers walk softly in the field-ways
As the sky falters and the wind sways.

And the ageing man turns a flushed face to the green girl,
Saying in a low tone that shudders to the wind's moan,
'Look! how lovely there where the tossed leaves whirl.
Is it not good that something is lost?'

And yet it is only Death that cometh
With his sickle of frost
And his diadem of snow-pearl.

W. J. TURNER

THE CAVES OF AUVERGNE

He carved the red deer and the bull
    Upon the smooth cave rock,
Returned from war with belly full,
    And scarred with many a knock,
He carved the red deer and the bull
    Upon the smooth cave rock.

The stars flew by the cave's wide door,
    The clouds wild trumpets blew,
Trees rose in wild dreams from the floor,
    Flowers with dream faces grew
Up to the sky, and softly hung
    Golden and white and blue.

The woman ground her heap of corn,
    Her heart a guarded fire;
The wind played in his trembling soul
    Like a hand upon a lyre,
The wind drew faintly on the stone
    Symbols of his desire:

The red deer of the forest dark,
    Whose antlers cut the sky,
That vanishes into the mirk
    And like a dream flits by,
And by an arrow slain at last
    Is but the wind's dark body.

The bull that stands in marshy lakes
    As motionless and still
As a dark rock jutting from a plain
    Without a tree or hill;
The bull that is the sign of life,
    Its sombre, phallic will.

And from the dead, white eyes of them
    The wind springs up anew,
It blows upon the trembling heart,
    And bull and deer renew
Their flitting life in the dim past
    When the dead Hunter drew.

I sit beside him in the night,
    And, fingering his red stone,
I chase through endless forests dark
    Seeking that thing unknown,
That which is not red deer or bull,
    By which by them was shown:

By those stiff shapes in which he drew
    His soul's exalted cry,
When flying down the forest dark
    He slew and knew not why,
When he was filled with song, and strength
    Flowed to him from the sky.

The wind blows from red deer and bull,
  The clouds wild trumpets blare,
Trees rise in wild dreams from the earth,
  Flowers with dream faces stare,
O Hunter, your own shadow stands
  Within your forest lair!

SIEGFRIED SASSOON

EVERYONE SANG

1917

Everyone suddenly burst out singing;
And I was filled with such delight
As prisoned birds must find in freedom,
Winging wildly across the white
Orchards and dark green fields; on—on—and out of sight.

Everyone's voice was suddenly lifted,
And beauty came like the setting sun.
My heart was shaken with tears, and horror
Drifted away . . . O, but Everyone
Was a bird; and the song was wordless; the singing wi
  never be done.

THE DEATH-BED

1917

He drowsed and was aware of silence heaped
Round him, unshaken as the steadfast walls;
Aqueous-like floating rays of amber light,
Soaring and quivering in the wings of sleep,—
Silence and safety; and his mortal shore
Lipped by the inward, moonless waves of death.

Someone was holding water to his mouth.
He swallowed, unresisting; moaned and dropped
Through crimson gloom to darkness; and forgot
The opiate throb and ache that was his wound.

Water—calm, sliding green above the weir;
Water—a sky-lit alley for his boat,
Bird-voiced, and bordered with reflected flowers
And shaken hues of summer: drifting down,
He dipped contented oars, and sighed, and slept.

Night, with a gust of wind, was in the ward,
Blowing the curtain to a glimmering curve.
Night. He was blind; he could not see the stars
Glinting among the wraiths of wandering cloud;
Queer blots of colour, purple, scarlet, green,
Flickered and faded in his drowning eyes.

Rain; he could hear it rustling through the dark
Fragrance and passionless music woven as one;
Warm rain on drooping roses; pattering showers
That soak the woods; not the harsh rain that sweeps
Behind the thunder, but a trickling peace
Gently and slowly washing life away.

.   .   .   .   .   .

He stirred; shifting his body; then the pain
Leaped like a prowling beast, and gripped and tore
His groping dreams with grinding claws and fangs.
But someone was beside him; soon he lay
Shuddering because that evil thing had passed.
And Death, who'd stepped toward him, paused and
      stared.

Light many lamps and gather round his bed.
Lend him your eyes, warm blood, and will to live.
Speak to him; rouse him; you may save him yet.
He's young; he hated war; how should he die
When cruel old campaigners win safe through?

But Death replied: 'I choose him.' So he went,
And there was silence in the summer night;
Silence and safety; and the veils of sleep.
Then, far away, the thudding of the guns.

RUPERT BROOKE

———

THE FISH

In a cool curving world he lies
And ripples with dark ecstasies.
The kind luxurious lapse and steal
Shapes all his universe to feel
And know and be; the clinging stream
Closes his memory, glooms his dream,
Who lips the roots o' the shore, and glides
Superb on unreturning tides.
Those silent waters weave for him
A fluctuant mutable world and dim,
Where wavering masses bulge and gape
Mysterious, and shape to shape
Dies momently through whorl and hollow,
And form and line and solid follow
Solid and line and form to dream
Fantastic down the eternal stream;
An obscure world, a shifting world,
Bulbous, or pulled to thin, or curled,
Or serpentine, or driving arrows,
Or serene slidings, or March narrows.
There slipping wave and shore are one,
And weed and mud.   No ray of sun,
But glow to glow fades down the deep
(As dream to unknown dream in sleep);
Shaken translucency illumes
The hyaline of drifting glooms;
The strange soft-handed depth subdues
Drowned colour there, but black to hues,
As death to living, decomposes—
Red darkness of the heart of roses,
Blue brilliant from dead starless skies,
And gold that lies behind the eyes,

The unknown unnameable sightless white
That is the essential flame of night,
Lustreless purple, hooded green,
The myriad hues that lie between
Darkness and darkness! . . .

                    And all 's one,
Gentle, embracing, quiet, dun,
The world he rests in, world he knows,
Perpetual curving.   Only—grows
An eddy in that ordered falling,
A knowledge from the gloom, a calling
Weed in the wave, gleam in the mud—
The dark fire leaps along his blood;
Dateless and deathless, blind and still,
The intricate impulse works its will;
His woven world drops back; and he,
Sans providence, sans memory,
Unconscious and directly driven,
Fades to some dank sufficient heaven.

O world of lips, O world of laughter,
Where hope is fleet and thought flies after,
Of lights in the clear night, of cries
That drift along the wave and rise
Thin to the glittering stars above,
You know the hands, the eyes of love!
The strife of limbs, the sightless clinging,
The infinite distance, and the singing
Blown by the wind, a flame of sound,
The gleam, the flowers, and vast around
The horizon, and the heights above—
You know the sigh, the song of love!

But there the night is close, and there
Darkness is cold and strange and bare;
And the secret deeps are whisperless;
And rhythm is all deliciousness;

And joy is in the throbbing tide,
Whose intricate fingers beat and glide
In felt bewildering harmonies
Of trembling touch; and music is
The exquisite knocking of the blood.
Space is no more, under the mud;
His bliss is older than the sun.
Silent and straight the waters run.
The lights, the cries, the willows dim,
And the dark tide are one with him.

THE HILL

BREATHLESS, we flung us on the windy hill,
  Laughed in the sun, and kissed the lovely grass.
  You said, 'Through glory and ecstasy we pass;
Wind, sun, and earth remain, the birds sing still,
When we are old, are old. . . .'   'And when we die
  All's over that is ours; and life burns on
Through other lovers, other lips,' said I,
  'Heart of my heart, our heaven is now, is won!'

'We are Earth's best, that learnt her lesson here.
  Life is our cry.   We have kept the faith!' we said;
  'We shall go down with unreluctant tread
Rose-crowned into the darkness!' . . . Proud we were,
And laughed, that had such brave true things to say.
—And then you suddenly cried, and turned away.

CLOUDS

DOWN the blue night the unending columns press
  In noiseless tumult, break and wave and flow,
  Now tread the far South, or lift rounds of snow
Up to the white moon's hidden loveliness.

Some pause in their grave wandering comradeless,
   And turn with profound gesture vague and slow,
   As who would pray good for the world, but know
Their benediction empty as they bless.

They say that the Dead die not, but remain
   Near to the rich heirs of their grief and mirth.
     I think they ride the calm mid-heaven, as these,
In wise majestic melancholy train,
   And watch the moon, and the still-raging seas,
And men, coming and going on the earth.

THE OLD VICARAGE, GRANTCHESTER

(*Café des Westens, Berlin, May* 1912)

Just now the lilac is in bloom,
All before my little room;
And in my flower-beds, I think,
Smile the carnation and the pink;
And down the borders, well I know,
The poppy and the pansy blow. . . .
Oh! there the chestnuts, summer through,
Beside the river make for you
A tunnel of green gloom, and sleep
Deeply above; and green and deep
The stream mysterious glides beneath,
Green as a dream and deep as death.
—Oh, damn! I know it! and I know
How the May fields all golden show,
And when the day is young and sweet,
Gild gloriously the bare feet

That run to bathe. . . .

                Du lieber Gott!

Here I am, sweating, sick, and hot,

And there the shadowed waters fresh
Lean up to embrace the naked flesh.
Temperamentvoll German Jews
Drink beer around;—and *there* the dews
Are soft beneath a morn of gold.
Here tulips bloom as they are told;
Unkempt about those hedges blows
An English unofficial rose;
And there the unregulated sun
Slopes down to rest when day is done,
And wakes a vague unpunctual star,
A slippered Hesper; and there are
Meads towards Haslingfield and Coton
Where *das Betreten*'s not *verboten*.

εἴθε γενοίμην . . . would I were
In Grantchester, in Grantchester!—
Some, it may be, can get in touch
With Nature there, or Earth, or such.
And clever modern men have seen
A Faun a-peeping through the green,
And felt the Classics were not dead,
To glimpse a Naiad's reedy head,
Or hear the Goat-foot piping low: . . .
But these are things I do not know.
I only know that you may lie
Day long and watch the Cambridge sky,
And, flower-lulled in sleepy grass,
Hear the cool lapse of hours pass,
Until the centuries blend and blur
In Grantchester, in Grantchester. . . .
Still in the dawnlit waters cool
His ghostly Lordship swims his pool,
And tries the strokes, essays the tricks,
Long learnt on Hellespont, or Styx.
Dan Chaucer hears his river still
Chatter beneath a phantom mill.

Tennyson notes, with studious eye,
How Cambridge waters hurry by . . .
And in that garden, black and white,
Creep whispers through the grass all night;
And spectral dance, before the dawn,
A hundred Vicars down the lawn;
Curates, long dust, will come and go
On lissom, clerical, printless toe;
And oft between the boughs is seen
The sly shade of a Rural Dean . . .
Till, at a shiver in the skies,
Vanishing with Satanic cries,
The prim ecclesiastic rout
Leaves but a startled sleeper-out,
Grey heavens, the first bird's drowsy calls,
The falling house that never falls.

God! I will pack, and take a train,
And get me to England once again!
For England's the one land, I know,
Where men with Splendid Hearts may go;
And Cambridgeshire, of all England,
The shire for Men who Understand;
And of *that* district I prefer
The lovely hamlet Grantchester.
For Cambridge people rarely smile,
Being urban, squat, and packed with guile;
And Royston men in the far South
Are black and fierce and strange of mouth;
At Over they fling oaths at one,
And worse than oaths at Trumpington,
And Ditton girls are mean and dirty,
And there's none in Harston under thirty,
And folks in Shelford and those parts
Have twisted lips and twisted hearts,
And Barton men make Cockney rhymes,
And Coton's full of nameless crimes,

And things are done you 'd not believe
At Madingley, on Christmas Eve.
Strong men have run for miles and miles,
When one from Cherry Hinton smiles;
Strong men have blanched, and shot their wives,
Rather than send them to St. Ives;
Strong men have cried like babes, bydam,
To hear what happened at Babraham.
But Grantchester! ah, Grantchester!
There 's peace and holy quiet there,
Great clouds along pacific skies,
And men and women with straight eyes,
Lithe children lovelier than a dream,
A bosky wood, a slumbrous stream,
And little kindly winds that creep
Round twilight corners, half asleep.
In Grantchester their sins are white;
They bathe by day, they bathe by night;
The women there do all they ought;
The men observe the Rules of Thought.
They love the Good; they worship Truth;
They laugh uproariously in youth;
(And when they get to feeling old,
They up and shoot themselves, I 'm told).

Ah, God! to see the branches stir
Across the moon at Grantchester!
To smell the thrilling-sweet and rotten
Unforgettable, unforgotten
River-smell, and hear the breeze
Sobbing in the little trees.
Say, do the elm-clumps greatly stand
Still guardians of that holy land?
The chestnuts shade, in reverend dream,
The yet unacademic stream?
Is dawn a secret shy and cold
Anadyomene, silver-gold?

And sunset still a golden sea
From Haslingfield to Madingley?
And after, ere the night is born,
Do hares come out about the corn?
Oh, is the water sweet and cool,
Gentle and brown, above the pool?
And laughs the immortal river still
Under the mill, under the mill?
Say, is there Beauty yet to find?
And Certainty? and Quiet kind?
Deep meadows yet, for to forget
The lies, and truths, and pain? . . . oh! yet
Stands the Church clock at ten to three?
And is there honey still for tea?

THE DEAD

1914

BLOW out, you bugles, over the rich Dead!
  There's none of these so lonely and poor of old,
  But, dying, has made us rarer gifts than gold.
These laid the world away; poured out the red
Sweet wine of youth; gave up the years to be
  Of work and joy, and that unhoped serene,
  That men call age; and those who would have been,
Their sons, they gave, their immortality.

Blow, bugles, blow! They brought us, for our dearth,
  Holiness, lacked so long, and Love, and Pain.
Honour has come back, as a king, to earth,
  And paid his subjects with a royal wage;
And Nobleness walks in our ways again;
  And we have come into our heritage.

THE SOLDIER

1914

IF I should die, think only this of me:
That there 's some corner of a foreign field
That is for ever England.   There shall be
In that rich earth a richer dust concealed;
A dust whom England bore, shaped, made aware,
Gave, once, her flowers to love, her ways to roam,
A body of England's, breathing English air,
Washed by the rivers, blest by sons of home.

And think, this heart, all evil shed away,
A pulse in the eternal mind, no less
Gives somewhere back the thoughts by England given;
Her sights and sounds; dreams happy as her day;
And laughter, learnt of friends; and gentleness,
In hearts at peace, under an English heaven.

JULIAN GRENFELL

INTO BATTLE

1915

THE naked earth is warm with Spring,
And with green grass and bursting trees
Leans to the sun's gaze glorying,
And quivers in the sunny breeze;
And life is Colour and Warmth and Light,
And a striving evermore for these;
And he is dead who will not fight,
And who dies fighting has increase.

The fighting man shall from the sun
Take warmth, and life from the glowing earth;
Speed with the light-foot winds to run,
And with the trees to newer birth;
And find, when fighting shall be done,
Great rest, and fullness after dearth.

All the bright company of Heaven
  Hold him in their high comradeship,
The Dog-star, and the Sisters Seven,
  Orion's Belt and sworded hip.

The woodland trees that stand together,
  They stand to him each one a friend;
They gently speak in the windy weather;
  They guide to valley and ridge's end.

The kestrel hovering by day,
  And the little owls that call by night,
Bid him be swift and keen as they,
  As keen of ear, as swift of sight.

The blackbird sings to him, 'Brother, brother,
  If this be the last song you shall sing
Sing well, for you may not sing another;
  Brother, sing.'

In dreary doubtful waiting hours,
  Before the brazen frenzy starts,
The horses show him nobler powers;—
  O patient eyes, courageous hearts!

And when the burning moment breaks,
  And all things else are out of mind,
And only Joy of Battle takes
  Him by the throat and makes him blind,

Through joy and blindness he shall know,
  Not caring much to know, that still
Nor lead nor steel shall reach him, so
  That it be not the Destined Will.

The thundering line of battle stands,
  And in the air Death moans and sings;
Byt Day shall clasp him with strong hands,
  And Night shall fold him in soft wings.

WILFRED OWEN

STRANGE MEETING

1918

It seemed that out of the battle I escaped
Down some profound dull tunnel long since scooped
Through granites which Titanic wars had groined.
Yet also there encumbered sleepers groaned,
Too fast in thought or death to be bestirred.
Then, as I probed them, one sprang up, and stared
With piteous recognition in fixed eyes,
Lifting distressful hands as if to bless;
And by his smile, I knew that sullen hall.
With a thousand fears that vision's face was grained;
Yet no blood reached there from the upper ground,
And no guns thumped, or down the flues made moan.
'Strange, friend,' I said, 'Here is no cause to mourn,'
'None,' said the other, 'Save the undone years,
The hopelessness.   Whatever hope is yours,
Was my life also; I went hunting wild
After the wildest beauty in the world,
Which lies not calm in eyes, or braided hair,
But mocks the steady running of the hour,
And if it grieves, grieves richlier than here.
For by my glee might many men have laughed,
And of my weeping something has been left
Which must die now.   I mean the truth untold,
The pity of war, the pity war distilled.
Now men will go content with what we spoiled,
Or, discontent, boil bloody, and be spilled.
They will be swift with swiftness of the tigress,
None will break ranks, though nations trek from progress.
Courage was mine, and I had mystery,
Wisdom was mine, and I had mastery;
To miss the march of this retreating world
Into vain citadels that are not walled.

Then, when much blood had clogged their chariot-wheels
I would go up and wash them from sweet wells,
Even with truths that be too deep for taint.
I would have poured my spirit without stint
But not through wounds; not on the cess of war.
Foreheads of men have bled where no wounds were.
I am the enemy you killed, my friend.
I knew you in this death: for so you frowned
Yesterday through me as you jabbed and killed.
I parried; but my hands were loath and cold.
Let us sleep now. . . .'

ANTHEM FOR DOOMED YOUTH

1918

WHAT passing-bells for those who die as cattle?
　　Only the monstrous anger of the guns.
　　Only the stuttering rifles' rapid rattle
Can patter out their hasty orisons.
　　No mockeries for them; no prayer nor bells,
　　Nor any voice of mourning save the choirs,—
　　The shrill, demented choirs of wailing shells;
And bugles calling for them from sad shires.

What candle may be held to speed them all?
　　Not in the hands of boys, but in their eyes
Shall shine the holy glimmer of good-byes.
　　The pallor of girls' brows shall be their pall;
Their flowers the tenderness of patient minds,
And each slow dusk a drawing-down of blinds.

THE SHOW

'We have fallen in the dreams the ever-living
Breathe on the tarnished mirror of the world,
And then smooth out with ivory hands and sigh.'
                                    W. B. YEATS.

My soul looked down from a vague height with Death,
As unremembering how I rose or why,
And saw a sad land, weak with sweats of dearth,
Grey, cratered like the moon with hollow woe,
And pitted with great pocks and scabs of plagues.

Across its beard, that horror of harsh wire,
There moved thin caterpillars, slowly uncoiled.
It seemed they pushed themselves to be as plugs
Of ditches, where they writhed and shrivelled, killed.

By them had slimy paths been trailed and scraped
Round myriad warts that might be little hills.

From gloom's last dregs these long-strung creatures crept,
And vanished out of dawn down hidden holes.

(And smells came up from those foul openings
As out of mouths, or deep wounds deepening.)

On dithering feet upgathered, more and more,
Brown strings, towards strings of grey, with bristling spines,
All migrants from green fields, intent on mire.

Those that were grey, of more abundant spawns,
Ramped on the rest and ate them and were eaten.

I saw their bitten backs curve, loop, and straighten,
I watched those agonies curl, lift, and flatten.

Whereat, in terror what the sight might mean,
I reeled and shivered earthward like a feather.

And Death fell with me, like a deepening moan.
And He, picking a manner of worm, which half had hid
Its bruises in the earth, but crawled no further,
Showed me its feet, the feet of many men,
And the fresh-severed head of it, my head.

HERBERT READ

THE END OF A WAR: MEDITATION OF THE DYING GERMAN OFFICER

GOD dies in this dying light.   The mists receive
my spent spirit: there is no one to hear
my last wish.   Already my thoughts
rebound in a tenement whose doors
are shut: strange muscles clench my jaws
these limbs are numb.   I cannot lift
a finger to my will.   But the mind
rises like a crystal sphere above the rigid wreck
is poised there, perhaps to fall into the void
still dreaming of an Empire of the West.
And so still feels no fear!   Mind triumphs over flesh
ordering the body's action in direst danger.
Courage is not born in men, but born of love.
love of life and love of giving, love
of this hour of death, which all love seeks.
I die, but death was destined.   My life was given
my death ordained when first my hand
held naked weapons in this war.   The rest
has been a waiting for this final hour.
In such a glory I could not always live.

My brow falls like a shutter of lead, clashes
on the clenched jaw.   The curtain of flesh
is wreathed about these rigid lines
in folds that have the easy notion of a smile.
So let them kiss earth and acid corruption:
extinction of the clod.   The bubble is free
to expand to the world's confines or to break
against the pricking stars.   The last lights shine
across its perfect crystal: rare ethereal glimmer
of mind's own intensity.   Above the clod
all things are clear, and what is left
is petulant scorn, implanted passions,
everything not tensely ideal.   Blind emotions
wreck the image with their blundering wings.
Mind must define before the heart intrigues.

Last light above the world, wavering in the darkest
void of Nothing   how still and tenuous
no music of the spheres   and so break with a sigh
against the ultimate
shores of the world
so finite
so small
Nichts

RICHARD CHURCH

——

THEN AND NOW

I HEAR the gate catch and latch, but now
It is an echo thirty years ago.
Here where I sleep in life, the droning planes,
The traffic of minted gold, the fevered gains
In time and pace, I join a later race,
Men not as men were then, but slower and dark;
Yes, moving it seems—but this may be my dream's
Illusion; through sleep the scene is murk,

The sun slowed, the moon tarnished, the stars
But muted candles mirrored in the streams
Sliding between the mountains and the firs.

All that I see and hear is mirror-scenes,
Mirror-sounds; no straight glance, no sun-shaft
Falling direct upon a blazing flower:
Nothing so bright or candid; eyes averted
And even a laugh—if any could have laughed—
Withdrawn and shoulder-hidden, a shade lower
Than present life.   Thirty years have parted
That mirth from this my hearing.   There is left
A meagre percolation through opaque
Time.   I do not wonder these things make
But faint seeming of what they were, or are,
Since having crept from then to now, they break
The laws of Time, the invisible tyrant, shake
His dynasty founded on forgetfulness.

To remember, to see as I see now, the star
Diminished in the pool, the moon tarnished,
The sun dimmed, even so is a conquest,
Capturing vanished kings and their dead pride,
And taking to my present humble breast
The poisoned Cleopatra for a bride,
And setting the crowns again upon the towers
Of Ilium; yes, and garnishing a feast
Of Eden fruits in the morning of mankind:
And of my own frail thirty years not least,
Gathering with dew on them the book-pressed flowers
Whose odour faded long before the love
That now is faded, too.
                              Such are the powers
Of memory, king of kings, Death's treasurer.
And yet some say man is no measurer
Of eternity, which lacking time and space,
Never converges into now, yet passes hence
Into life vanished, where the moon is tarnished,

The sun dimmed, the stars veiled in grace,
Where opposites have found a trysting-place,
Sorrow with joy, light with dark, age with youth,
To share at last the ripened fruit of truth
And overturn false destiny and fate.

This is our triumph, we who dwell with pain,
That by the dream-borne latching of a gate
We spin the drying universe again.

T. S. ELIOT

PORTRAIT OF A LADY

'Thou hast committed—
Fornication : but that was in another country,
And besides, the wench is dead.'

The Jew of Malta.

I

AMONG the smoke and fog of a December afternoon
You have the scene arrange itself—as it will seem to do—
With 'I have saved this afternoon for you';
And four wax candles in the darkened room,
Four rings of light upon the ceiling overhead,
An atmosphere of Juliet's tomb
Prepared for all the things to be said, or left unsaid.
We have been, let us say, to hear the latest Pole
Transmit the Preludes, through his hair and fingertips.
'So intimate, this Chopin, that I think his soul
Should be resurrected only among friends
Some two or three, who will not touch the bloom
That is rubbed and questioned in the concert room.'
—And so the conversation slips
Among velleities and carefully caught regrets
Through attenuated tones of violins
Mingled with remote cornets
And begins.

'You do not know how much they mean to me, my friends,
And how, how rare and strange it is, to find
In a life composed so much, so much of odds and ends,
(For indeed I do not love it . . . you knew? you are not
   blind !
How keen you are !)
To find a friend who has these qualities,
Who has, and gives
Those qualities upon which friendship lives.
How much it means that I say this to you—
Without these friendships—life, what *cauchemar* !'
Among the windings of the violins
And the ariettes
Of cracked cornets
Inside my brain a dull tom-tom begins
Absurdly hammering a prelude of its own,
Capricious monotone
That is at least one definite 'false note.'
—Let us take the air, in a tobacco trance,
Admire the monuments,
Discuss the late events,
Correct our watches by the public clocks.
Then sit for half an hour and drink our bocks.

II

Now that lilacs are in bloom
She has a bowl of lilacs in her room
And twists one in her fingers while she talks.
'Ah, my friend, you do not know, you do not know
What life is, you should hold it in your hands';
(Slowly twisting the lilac stalks)
'You let it flow from you, you let it flow,
And youth is cruel, and has no remorse
And smiles at situations which it cannot see.'
I smile, of course,
And go on drinking tea.

'Yet with these April sunsets, that somehow recall
My buried life, and Paris in the Spring,
I feel immeasurably at peace, and find the world
To be wonderful and youthful, after all.'

The voice returns like the insistent out-of-tune
Of a broken violin on an August afternoon:
'I am always sure that you understand
My feelings, always sure that you feel,
Sure that across the gulf you reach your hand.

You are invulnerable, you have no Achilles' heel.
You will go on, and when you have prevailed
You can say: at this point many a one has failed.
But what have I, but what have I, my friend,
To give you, what can you receive from me?
Only the friendship and the sympathy
Of one about to reach her journey's end.

I shall sit here, serving tea to friends. . . .'

I take my hat: how can I make a cowardly amends
For what she has said to me?
You will see me any morning in the park
Reading the comics and the sporting page.
Particularly I remark
An English countess goes upon the stage.
A Greek was murdered at a Polish dance,
Another bank defaulter has confessed.
I keep my countenance,
I remain self-possessed
Except when a street piano, mechanical and tired
Reiterates some worn-out common song
With the smell of hyacinths across the garden
Recalling things that other people have desired.
Are these ideas right or wrong?

III

The October night comes down; returning as before
Except for a slight sensation of being ill at ease
I mount the stairs and turn the handle of the door
And feel as if I had mounted on my hands and knees.
'And so you are going abroad; and when do you return?
But that's a useless question.
You hardly know when you are coming back,
You will find so much to learn.'
My smile falls heavily among the bric-à-brac.

'Perhaps you can write to me.'
My self-possession flares up for a second;
This is as I had reckoned.

'I have been wondering frequently of late
(But our beginnings never know our ends!)
Why we have not developed into friends.'
I feel like one who smiles, and turning shall remark
Suddenly, his expression in a glass.
My self-possession gutters; we are really in the dark.

'For everybody said so, all our friends,
They all were sure our feelings would relate
So closely!   I myself can hardly understand.
We must leave it now to fate.
You will write, at any rate.
Perhaps it is not too late.
I shall sit here, serving tea to friends.'

And I must borrow every changing shape
To find expression . . . dance, dance
Like a dancing bear,
Cry like a parrot, chatter like an ape.
Let us take the air, in a tobacco trance—
Well! and what if she should die some afternoon,
Afternoon grey and smoky, evening yellow and rose;

Should die and leave me sitting pen in hand
With the smoke coming down above the housetops;
Doubtful, for a while
Not knowing what to feel or if I understand
Or whether wise or foolish, tardy or too soon . . .
Would she not have the advantage, after all?
This music is successful with a 'dying fall'
Now that we talk of dying—
And should I have the right to smile?

THE JOURNEY OF THE MAGI

'A COLD coming we had of it,
Just the worst time of the year
For a journey, and such a long journey:
The ways deep and the weather sharp,
The very dead of winter.'
And the camels galled, sore-footed, refractory,
Lying down in the melting snow.
There were times we regretted
The summer palaces on slopes, the terraces,
And the silken girls bringing sherbet.
Then the camel men cursing and grumbling
And running away, and wanting their liquor and women,
And the night-fires going out, and the lack of shelters,
And the cities hostile and the towns unfriendly
And the villages dirty and charging high prices:
A hard time we had of it.

At the end we preferred to travel all night,
Sleeping in snatches,
With the voices singing in our ears, saying
That this was all folly.
Then at dawn we came down to a temperate valley,
Wet, below the snow line, smelling of vegetation;
With a running stream and a water-mill beating the darkness
And three trees on the low sky,
And an old white horse galloped away in the meadow.

Then we came to a tavern with vine-leaves over the lintel,
Six hands at an open door dicing for pieces of silver,
And feet kicking the empty wine-skins.
But there was no information, and so we continued
And arrived at evening, not a moment too soon
Finding the place; it was (you may say) satisfactory.

All this was a long time ago, I remember,
And I would do it again, but set down
This set down
This: were we led all that way for
Birth or Death? There was a Birth, certainly,
We had evidence and no doubt. I had seen birth and
  death,
But had thought they were different; this Birth was
Hard and bitter agony for us, like Death, our death.
We returned to our places, these Kingdoms,
But no longer at ease here, in the old dispensation,
With an alien people clutching their gods.
I should be glad of another death.

JOHN MIDDLETON MURRY

TOLSTOY

*He is like a God, not a Sabaoth or an Olympian, but the kind of
Russian god who ' sits on a maple throne under a golden limetree,' not
very majestic, but perhaps more cunning than all the other gods.*—
MAXIM GORKY, *Recollections of Tolstoy.*

WHAT secret knowledge, old and cunning god,
Purses your eyes in their inhuman leer?
What grim disdain lurks in your hateful nod,
What arrogance, and what more awful fear
Of things we cannot see,
Strong spirit of the tree,
Who knows wherein the roots are set of all mortality?

Whence camest thou, a mortal man in seeming,
Speaking our tongue, supreme in all our skill,
To spurn them both aside for thy dread dreaming
Of the ungovernable, mighty Will
That sent thee to deride
The triumphs of our pride
And pierce our hearts with terror of thine own eyes
    terrified?

What centaur-king at battle with the beasts
Begat thee in the flush of victory
Upon what fierce-eyed queen?   What drunken feasts
Within the matted walls once drowned the cry
Of the swift ravishment
Of her whose pride was bent
To hide the seed that bore thee in the darkness of his tent?

The wild-maned horses neighed thee to thy rest;
The jackals howled their hunger round the horde
While thy fierce mother clutched thee to her breast,
Suckling a chieftain worthy of her lord
Whose bloody hand had led
Her captive to his bed,
Bidding her raise up new kinsmen in the men she bore and
    bred.

Through what unnumbered ages hast thou sped,
Thou mighty horseman, o'er the Asian plain?
What teeming tribes of nomads hast thou led
To battle and to plunder and to pain?
Slant-eyed watcher of the nights,
Master of creeping fights,
To what god what victims gav'st thou in thy sacrificia
    rites?

He was thy sire who would not to the tomb,
At whose dark terrors his grim spirit quailed,
Go comfortless; but took to share his doom
A thousand warriors on their steeds impaled,

Who girded him around
In the darkness of his mound
To be his guard against the fang of death's grey, ghostly
    hound.

Not of thy kin was he who dreamed to hear
The spinning stars make heavenly harmony,
Obedient in sweet celestial fear
To love that lasts to all eternity;
To thine the stars gave light
To aid them in the fight,
And guide their fearful courses through the menace of the
    night.

And when the unending journey came to rest
Thou slumbered still, still shaped within thy sleep,
In the proud loins of men who to the West
Turned scornful eyes to mark where they might reap
A harvest from the mind
Their wandering as a wind
Had suffered them not pause to sow with dreams of human-
    kind.

As men who rush into a new-found land,
They stormed the gates of dreaming and desire;
Within the grasp of their all-daring hand
Believed the shadows of the magic fire,
Urging their journey on
Till earthly hosts had won
To peaks lit by the farthest ray of thought's unearthly sun.

In this dim realm they wandered once again,
Passing beyond the smooth and charted ways
Into a wilderness unknown of men
Where hearts grew faint with hunger and the maze
Of their imaginings,
Visions of shadowy things
Confounded by the ghostly breath of immaterial wings.

The God they sought came not, but thou wert born;
In thy proud nostrils was the earth's strong breath;
Thou laughedst their baffled wisdom into scorn;
Thine eyes glanced backward at the hound of death;
And things they could not see
Struck anguish into thee,
Remembering where the roots are set of all mortality.

After a little space of urgent days,
Wherein thou wert supreme in all our skill,
The memory of the waste, ancestral ways,
The might of an ungovernable Will
Locked the once eager tongue
That in thy youth had rung
O'er Europe like a mighty bell in a high belfry hung;

Till at last thou wandered forth alone
To meet thy death where only stars might see,
On the dim plain that echoes with the moan
Of the impenetrable mystery
To which no man has trod,
Nor old and cunning god
Who leers and fears and frights men with the blindness of his
    nod.

EDMUND BLUNDEN

ALMSWOMEN

AT Quincey's moat the squandering village ends,
And there in the almshouse dwell the dearest friends
Of all the village, two old dames that cling
As close as any true-loves in the spring.
Long, long ago they passed threescore-and-ten,
And in this doll's house lived together then;

All things they have in common, being so poor,
And their one fear, Death's shadow at the door.
Each sundown makes them mournful, each sunrise
Brings back the brightness in their failing eyes.
How happy go the rich fair-weather days
When on the roadside folk stare in amaze
At such a honeycomb of fruit and flowers
As mellows round their threshold; what long hours
They gloat upon their steepling hollyhocks,
Bee's balsams, feathery southernwood, and stocks,
Fiery dragons'-mouths, great mallow leaves
For salves, and lemon-plants in bushy sheaves,
Shagged Esau's-hands with fine green finger-tips.
Such old sweet names are ever on their lips.
As pleased as little children where these grow
In cobbled pattens and worn gowns they go,
Proud of their wisdom when on gooseberry shoots
They stuck eggshells to fright from coming fruits
The brisk-billed rascals; pausing still to see
Their neighbour owls saunter from tree to tree,
Or in the hushing half-light mouse the lane
Long-winged and lordly.
                              But when those hours wane
Indoors they ponder, scared by the harsh storm
Whose pelting saracens on the window swarm,
And listen for the mail to clatter past
And church clock's deep bay withering on the blast;
They feed the fire that flings a freakish light
On pictured kings and queens grotesquely bright,
Platters and pitchers, faded calendars
And graceful hour-glass trim with lavenders.

Many a time they kiss and cry, and pray
That both be summoned on the selfsame day,
And wiseman linnet tinkling in his cage
End too with them the friendship of old age,
And all together leave their treasured room
Some bell-like evening when the May's in bloom.

ROY CAMPBELL

TRISTAN DA CUNHA

SNORE in the foam: the night is vast and blind,
The blanket of the mist around your shoulders,
Sleep your old sleep of rock, snore in the wind,
Snore in the spray!   The storm your slumber lulls,
His wings are folded on your nest of boulders
As on their eggs the grey wings of your gulls.

No more as when, ten thousand years ago,
You hissed a giant cinder from the ocean—
Around your rocks you furl the shawling snow,
Half sunk in your own darkness, vast and grim,
And round you on the deep with surly motion
Pivot your league-long shadow as you swim.

Why should you haunt me thus but that I know
My surly heart is in your own displayed,
Round whom such wastes in endless circuit flow,
Whose hours in such a gloomy compass run—
A dial with its league-long arm of shade
Slowly revolving to the moon and sun.

My heart has sunk, like your grey fissured crags,
By its own strength o'ertoppled and betrayed:
I too have burned the wind with fiery flags,
Who now am but a roost for empty words—
An island of the sea whose only trade
Is in the voyages of its wandering birds.

Did you not, when your strength became your pyre,
Deposed and tumbled from your flaming tower,
Awake in gloom from whence you sank in fire
To find Antaeus-like, more vastly grown,
A throne in your own darkness, and a power
Sheathed in the very coldness of your stone?

Your strength is that you have no hope or fear,
You march before the world without a crown:
The nations call you back, you do not hear:
The cities of the earth grow grey behind you,
You will be there when their great flames go down
And still the morning in the van will find you.

You march before the continents: you scout
In front of all the earth: alone you scale
The masthead of the world, a lorn look-out,
Waving the snowy flutter of your spray
And gazing back in infinite farewell
To suns that sink, and shores that fade away.

From your grey tower what long regrets you fling
To where, along the low horizon burning,
The great swan-breasted seraphs soar and sing,
And suns go down, and trailing splendours dwindle,
And sails on lonely errands unreturning,
Glow with a gold no sunrise can rekindle.

Turn to the Night, these flames are not for you
Whose steeple for the thunder swings its bells:
Grey Memnon, to the tempest only true,
Turn to the night, turn to the shadowing foam,
And let your voice, the saddest of farewells,
With sullen curfew toll the grey wings home.

The wind your mournful syren haunts the gloom:
The rocks, spray-clouded, are your signal-guns
Whose stony nitre, puffed with flying spume,
Rolls forth in grim salute your broadside hollow,
Over the gorgeous burials of suns,
To sound the tocsin of the storms that follow.

Plunge forward; like a ship to battle hurled,
Slip the long cables of the failing light,
The level rays that moor you to the world:

Sheathed in your armour of eternal frost,
Plunge forward, in the thunder of the fight
To lose yourself as I would fain be lost.

Exiled, like you, and severed from my race
By the cold ocean of my own disdain,
Do I not freeze in such a wintry space,
Do I not travel through a storm as vast
And rise at times, victorious from the main,
To fly the sunrise at my shattered mast?

Your path is but a desert where you reap
Only the bitter knowledge of your soul,
You fish with nets of seaweed in the deep
As fruitlessly as I with nets of rhyme,
Yet forth you stride: yourself the way, the goal,
The surges are your strides, your path is time.

Hurled by what aim to what tremendous range!
A missile from the great sling of the past
Your passage leaves its track of death and change
And ruin on the world: you fly beyond,
Leaping the current of the ages vast
As lightly as a pebble skims a pond.

The years are undulations in your flight
Whose awful motion we can only guess:
Too swift for sense, too terrible for sight,
We only know how fast behind you darken
Our days like lonely beacons of distress:
We know that you stride on and will not harken.

Now in the eastern sky the fairest planet
Pierces the dying wave with dangled spear,
And in the whirring hollows of your granite
That vaster Sea, to which you are a shell,
Sighs with a ghostly rumour like the drear
Moan of the nightwind in a hollow cell.

We shall not meet again: over the wave
Our ways divide, and yours is straight and endless—
But mine is short and crooked to the grave:
Yet what of these dark crowds, amid whose flow
I battle like a rock, aloof and friendless—
Are not their generations, vague and endless,
The waves, the strides, the feet on which I go?

RICHARD ALDINGTON

BROMIOS

(A Frieze in the Vatican)

THE withered bonds are broken.
The waxed reeds and the double pipe
Clamour about me;
The hot wind swirls
Through the red pine trunks.
Io! The fauns and the satyrs.
The touch of their shagged curled fur
And blunt horns.

They have wine in heavy craters
Painted black and red;
Wine to splash on her white body.
Io!
She shrinks from the cold shower—
Afraid, afraid!

Let the Maenads break through the myrtles
And the boughs of the rhododaphnai.
Let them tear the quick deer's flesh.
Ah, the cruel exquisite fingers.
Io!
I have brought you the brown clusters,
The ivy-boughs and pine-cones.
Your breasts are cold sea-ripples,
But they smell of the warm grasses.

Throw wide the chiton and the peplum,
Maidens of the dew,
Beautiful are your bodies, O Maenads,
Beautiful the sudden folds,
The vanishing curves of the white linen
About you.

Io !
Hear the rich laughter of the forest,
The cymbals,
The trampling of the panisks and the centaurs.

MARTIN ARMSTRONG

THE BUZZARDS

When evening came and the warm glow grew deeper,
And every tree that bordered the green meadows,
And in the yellow cornfields every reaper
And every corn-shock stood above their shadows
Flung eastward from their feet in longer measure,
Serenely far there swam in the sunny height
A buzzard and his mate who took their pleasure
Swirling and poising idly in golden light.

On great pied motionless moth-wings borne along,
So effortless and so strong,
Cutting each other's paths together they glided,
Then wheeled asunder till they soared divided
Two valleys' width (as though it were delight
To part like this, being sure they could unite
So swiftly in their empty, free dominion),
Curved headlong downward, towered up the sunny steep,
Then, with a sudden lift of the one great pinion,
Swung proudly to a curve, and from its height
Took half a mile of sunlight in one long sweep.

And we, so small on the swift immense hillside,
Stood tranced, until our souls arose uplifted
On those far-sweeping, wide,
Strong curves of flight—swayed up and hugely drifted,
Were washed, made strong and beautiful in the tide
Of sun-bathed air.   But far beneath, beholden
Through shining deeps of air, the fields were golden
And rosy burned the heather where cornfields ended.

And still those buzzards whirled, while light withdrew
Out of the vales and to surging slopes ascended,
Till the loftiest flaming summit died to blue.

EDGELL RICKWORD

ASSUAGEMENT

In Covent Garden Market, early

WHAT messages are these the morning brings
my angry city from kind-bosomed fields?
The cool, soft words of vegetable things
placating her whose rumour never yields
to the far-blown persuasion of quiet grass;
whose wrinkled fever dew-fall never cools;
now for a moment stilled, as wagons pass,
to faint remembrance of her ancient pools.

The streets of pain and theatres of despair,
the heart's metropolis, this peace dispute,
matching solidity against permanence;
only the moon wears a consistent air,
watching the clouds answer the winds' thin flute
in azure meadows' poor inheritance.

FRANK KENDON

THE HAUNTED CUCKOO CALLING

I THOUGHT the trees were passionate trees;
    Because the wind that rocked them,
That tossed and swayed them as it crossed them,
Although it moved in the deep air about them,
    Moved the air unseen,
And eyes beheld the passion, only in the trees.

They stood in lines and waved their arms,
Their whole bodies northward yearning;
They tossed their heads; then, peace shortly returning,
They lifted all boughs together
    And drooped them with a sigh;
But it was not love that woke their wild alarms,
It was only a south-west wind blowing swiftly by.

    Over the trees the hills stood clear;
      Sun poured his hot virtue down;
Out of the thick and misty atmosphere
From three miles off a white house in its woods
Plainly shone; and an early buttercup
Near at hand looked up into day's face.
Starlings flew down to peck about the grass;
   A swallow stooped from heaven,
Making a playground of the sky and earth,
And in an arc of genius, down and across,
And up again, he shot into the light,
But kissed a daisy headlong in his fall.
    And hither and thither in useless flight
    A fragile butterfly was blown,
    Blown across the happy grasses.
    Homeless he was, and without desire;
      Unable to fix his choice
      Among so many joys;
A soul weary, on wings that would never tire.

I, too, had been a creature of this land,
As bird and butterfly and tree of longing:
I was a child so long, and summer, then,
   Was beauty easily borne;
     For I was part of all.
   But that there is a wood, I know,
   Hiding behind the visible trees !
Hark, now hark !   The spring has found her voice,
The haunted cuckoo calls,
Chiming unearthly hours—
The haunted cuckoo !   And the hollow air
   Sustains her level notes . . .
   Now far and far from me
This dream I catch at slips beyond my keeping.

Deep down through time and space their senses stretch
Their filaments, and still I see and hear—
I see and hear, and cannot understand.
But, by the forms and lives and living songs,
I swear my spirit had the kiss of a god !
Could death at once now snap the threads of sense,
   Taking the green and light,
   Stopping the cuckoo's call,
I should not know the moment, or the change !

HUGH MACDIARMID

STONY LIMITS

(In Memoriam : Charles Doughty, 1843–1927)

UNDER no hanging heaven-rooted tree,
Though full of mammuks' nests,
Bone of old Britain we bury thee
But heeding your unspoken hests
Naught not coeval with the Earth
And indispensable till its end

With what whom you despised may seem the death
Of your last resting-place dare blend.
Where nature is content with little so are you
So be it the little to which all else is due.

Nor in vain mimicry of the powers
That lifted up the mountains shall we raise
A stone less of nature's shaping than of ours
   To mark the unfrequented place.
You were not filial to all else
Save to the Dust, the mother of all men,
And where you lie no other sign needs tells
(Unless a gaunt shape resembled you again
In some momentary effect of light on rock)
But your family likeness to all her stock.

Flowers may be strewn upon your grave
   Of easy come easy go.
Fitly only some earthquake or tidal wave
O'er you its red rose or its white may throw
But naught else smaller than darkness and light
   —Both here, though of no man's bringing!—
And as any past time had been in your sight
Were you now from your bed upspringing,
Now or a billion years hence, you would see
Scant difference, eyed like eternity.

How should we have anything to give you
   In death who had nothing in life
Attempting in our sand-riddles to sieve you
Who were with nothing but the sheer elements rife?
Anchor of truth, facile as granite you lie,
A plug suspended in England's false dreams.
Your worth will be seen by and by,
Like God's purpose in what men deem their schemes,
Nothing ephemeral can seek what lies in this ground
Since nothing can be sought but the found.

The poem that would praise you must be
Like the glass of some rock, sleek brown, crowded
With dark incipient crystal growths, we see;
Or a glimpse of Petavius may have endowed it
With the tubular and dumb-bell-shaped inclusions surrounded
  By the broad reaction rims it needs.
I have seen it in dreams and know how it abounded
—Ah! would I could find it in me like seeds!—
As the north-easterly garden in the lunation grows,
A spectacle not one man in a million knows.

I belong to a different country than yours
And none of my travels have been in the same lands
Save where Arzaihel or Langrenus allures
Such spirits as ours, and the Straight Wall stands,
But crossing sheer planes extruded in long lines of ridges,
Torsion cylinders, crater rings, and circular seas
And ultra-basic xenoliths that make men like midges
Belong to my quarter as well, and with ease
I too can work in bright green and all the curious inter-
  ference
Colours that under crossed nicols have a mottled appearance.

Let my first offering be these few pyroxenes twined
On the orthopinacoid and hour-glass scheme,
Fine striae, microline cross-hatchings, and this wind
Blowing plumes of vapour forever it would seem
From cone after cone diminishing sterile and grey
In the distance; dun sands in ever-changing squalls;
Crush breccias and overthrusts; and such little array
Of Geology's favourite fal-de-lals
And demolitions and entrenchments of weather
As any turn of my eyes brings together.

I know how on turning to the noble hills
And stark deserts happily still preserved
For men whom no gregariousness fills
With the loneliness for which they are nerved

—The lonely at-one-ment with all worth while—
I can feel as if the vastest contours lie
And share the gladness and peace you knew,
—The supreme human serenity that was you!

I have seen Silence lift his head
And Song, like his double, lift yours,
And know, while nearly all that seems living is dead,
You were always consubstantial with all that endures.
Would it were on Earth! Not since Ezekiel has that faw
    sun ringed
A worthier head; red as Adam you stood
In the desert, the horizon with vultures black-winged,
And sang and died in this still greater solitude
Where I sit by your skull whose emptiness is worth
The sum of almost all the full heads now on Earth
—By your roomy skull where most men might well spend
Longer than you did in Arabia, friend!

V. SACKVILLE-WEST

—

SAILING SHIPS

LYING on Downs above the wrinkling bay
I with the kestrels shared the cleanly day,
The candid day; wind-shaven, brindled turf;
Tail cliffs; and long sea-line of marbled surf
From Cornish Lizard to the Kentish Nore
Lapping the bulwarks of the English shore,
While many a lovely ship below sailed by
On unknown errand, kempt and leisurely;
And after each, oh, after each, my heart
Fled forth, as, watching from the Downs apart,
I shared with ships good joys and fortunes wide
That might befall their beauty and their pride;

Shared first with them the blessèd void repose
Of oily days at sea, when only rose

The porpoise's slow wheel to break the sheen
Of satin water indolently green,
When for'ard the crew, caps tilted over eyes,
Lay heaped on deck; slept; murmured; smoked;
      threw dice;
The sleepy summer days; the summer nights
(The coast pricked out with rings of harbour-lights);
The motionless nights, the vaulted nights of June
When high in the cordage drifts the entangled moon,
And blocks go knocking, and the sheets go slapping,
And lazy swells against the sides come lapping;
And summer mornings off red Devon rocks,
Faint inland bells at dawn and crowing cocks.

Shared swifter days, when headlands into ken
Trod grandly; threatened; and were lost again,
Old fangs along the battlemented coast;
And followed still my ship, when winds were most
Night-purified, and, lying steeply over,
She fled the wind as flees a girl her lover,
Quickened by that pursuit for which she fretted,
Her temper by the contest proved and whetted;
Wild stars swept overhead; her lofty spars
Reared to a ragged heaven sown with stars
As leaping out from narrow English ease
She faced the roll of long Atlantic seas.

Her captain then was I, I was her crew,
The mind that laid her course, the wake she drew,
The waves that rose against her bows, the gales,—
Nay; I was more: I was her very sails
Rounded before the wind, her eager keel,
Her straining mast-heads, her responsive wheel,
Her pennon stiffened like a swallow's wing;
Yes, I was all her slope and speed and swing,
Whether by yellow lemons and blue sea
She dawdled through the isles off Thessaly,

Or saw the palms like sheaves of scimitars
On desert's verge below the sunset bars,
Or passed the girdle of the planet where
The Southern Cross looks over to the Bear,
And strayed, cool Northerner beneath strange skies,
Flouting the lure of tropic estuaries,
Down that long coast, and saw Magellan's Clouds arise.

And some that beat up Channel homeward-bound
I watched, and wondered what they might have found,
What alien ports enriched their teeming hold
With crates of fruit or bars of unwrought gold?
And thought how London clerks with paper-clips
Had filed the bills of lading of those ships,
Clerks that had never seen the embattled sea,
But wrote down jettison and barratry,
Perils, Adventures, and the Act of God,
Having no vision of such wrath flung broad;
Wrote down with weary and accustomed pen
The classic dangers of seafaring men;
And wrote 'Restraint of Princes,' and 'the acts
Of the King's Enemies,' as vacant facts,
Blind to the ambushed seas, the encircling roar
Of angry nations foaming into war.

W. W. GIBSON

——

FLANNAN ISLE

'THOUGH three men dwell on Flannan Isle
To keep the lamp alight,
As we steer'd under the lee, we caught
No glimmer through the night.'

A passing ship at dawn had brought
The news; and quickly we set sail,
To find out what strange thing might ail
The keepers of the deep-sea light.

The winter day broke blue and bright,
With glancing sun and glancing spray,
As o'er the swell our boat made way,
As gallant as a gull in flight.

But, as we near'd the lonely Isle;
And look'd up at the naked height;
And saw the lighthouse towering white,
With blinded lantern, that all night
Had never shot a spark
Of comfort through the dark,
So ghostly in the cold sunlight
It seem'd, that we were struck the while
With wonder all too dread for words.

And, as into the tiny creek
We stole beneath the hanging crag,
We saw three queer, black, ugly birds—
Too big, by far, in my belief,
For guillemot or shag [1]—
Like seamen sitting bolt-upright
Upon a half-tide reef:
But, as we near'd, they plunged from sight,
Without a sound, or spurt of white.

And still too 'mazed to speak,
We landed; and made fast the boat;
And climb'd the track in single file,
Each wishing he was safe afloat,
On any sea, however far,
So it be far from Flannan Isle:
And still we seem'd to climb, and climb,
As though we 'd lost all count of time,
And so must climb for evermore.
Yet, all too soon, we reached the door—
The black, sun-blister'd lighthouse-door,
That gaped for us ajar.

[1] The crested cormorant.

As, on the threshold, for a spell,
We paused, we seem'd to breathe the smell
Of limewash and of tar,
Familiar as our daily breath,
As though 'twere some strange scent of death:
And so, yet wondering, side by side,
We stood a moment, still tongue-tied:
And each with black foreboding eyed
The door, ere we should fling it wide,
To leave the sunlight for the gloom:
Till, plucking courage up, at last,
Hard on each other's heels we pass'd
Into the living-room.

Yet, as we crowded through the door,
We only saw a table, spread
For dinner, meat and cheese and bread;
But all untouch'd; and no one there:
As though, when they sat down to eat,
Ere they could even taste,
Alarm had come; and they in haste
Had risen and left the bread and meat:
For at the table-head a chair
Lay tumbled on the floor.

We listen'd; but we only heard
The feeble cheeping of a bird
That starved upon its perch:
And, listening still, without a word,
We set about our hopeless search.
We hunted high, we hunted low;
And soon ransack'd the empty house;
Then o'er the Island, to and fro,
We ranged, to listen and to look
In every cranny, cleft or nook
That might have hid a bird or mouse:
But, though we search'd from shore to shore,
We found no sign in any place:

And soon again stood face to face
Before the gaping door:
And stole into the room once more
As frighten'd children steal.

Aye: though we hunted high and low,
And hunted everywhere,
Of the three men's fate we found no trace
Of any kind in any place,
But a door ajar, and an untouch'd meal,
And an overtoppled chair.
And, as we listen'd in the gloom
Of that forsaken living-room—
A chill clutch on our breath—
We thought how ill-chance came to all
Who kept the Flannan Light:
And how the rock had been the death
Of many a likely lad:
How six had come to a sudden end,
And three had gone stark mad:
And one whom we'd all known as friend
Had leapt from the lantern one still night,
And fallen dead by the lighthouse wall:
And long we thought
On the three we sought,
And of what might yet befall.

Like curs, a glance has brought to heel,
We listen'd, flinching there:
And look'd, and look'd, on the untouched meal,
And the overtoppled chair.
We seem'd to stand for an endless while,
Though still no word was said,
Three men alive on Flannan Isle,
Who thought on three men dead.

ALDOUS HUXLEY

THE CICADAS

SIGHTLESS, I breathe and touch; this night of pines
Is needly, resinous and rough with bark.
Through every crevice in the tangible dark
The moonlessness above it all but shines.

Limp hangs the leafy sky; never a breeze
Stirs, nor a foot in all this sleeping ground;
And there is silence underneath the trees—
The living silence of continuous sound.

For like inveterate remorse, like shrill
Delirium throbbing in the fevered brain,
An unseen people of cicadas fill
Night with their one harsh note, again, again.

Again, again, with what insensate zest!
What fury of persistence, hour by hour!
Filled with what demon that denies them rest,
Drunk with what source of pleasure and of power!

Life is their madness, life that all night long
Bids them to sing and sing, they know not why;
Mad cause and senseless burden of their song;
For life commands and 'life!' is all their cry.

I hear them sing, who in the double night
Of clouds and branches fancied that I went
Through my own spirit's dark discouragement,
Deprived of inward as of outward sight;

Who, seeking, even as here in the wild wood,
A lamp to beckon through my tangled fate,
Found only darkness and, disconsolate,
Mourned the lost purpose and the vanished good,

Now in my empty heart the crickets' shout
Re-echoing denies and still denies
With stubborn folly all my learned doubt,
In madness more than I in reason wise.

Life, life! The word is magical. They sing,
And in my darkened soul the great sun shines;
My fancy blossoms with remembered spring,
And all my autumns ripen on the vines.

Life! and each knuckle of the fig-tree's pale
Dead skeleton breaks out with emerald fire.
Life! and the tulips blow, the nightingale
Calls back the rose, calls back the old desire.

And old desire that is for ever new,
Desire, life's earliest and latest birth,
Life's instrument to suffer and to do,
Springs with the roses from the teeming earth.

Desire that from the world's bright body strips
Deforming time and makes each kiss the first;
That gives to hearts, to satiated lips
The endless bounty of to-morrow's thirst.

Time passes and the watery moonrise peers
Between the tree-trunks. But no outer light
Tempers the chances of our groping years,
No moon beyond our labyrinthine night.

Clueless we go; but I have heard thy voice,
Divine unreason! harping in the leaves,
And grieve no more; for wisdom never grieves,
And thou hast taught me wisdom; I rejoice.

HUMBERT WOLFE

—

RESIGNATION

COME ! let us draw the curtains,
    heap up the fire and sit,
hunched by the flame together,
    and make a friend of it.

Listen ! the wind is rising,
    and the air is wild with leaves,
we have had our summer evenings:
    now for October eves !

The great beech-trees lean forward,
    and strip like a diver.   We
had better turn to the fire,
    and shut our minds to the sea,

where the ships of youth are running
    close-hauled on the edge of the wind,
with all adventure before them,
    and only the old behind.

Love and youth and the seabirds
    meet in the stormy weather,
and with one bright flash of laughter
    clap into the dark together.

Come ! let us draw the curtains,
    and talk of other things,
and presently all will be quiet—
    love, youth, and the sound of wings.

MOUNTAIN FLOWERS

Tread softly! For I think the gentian
  is blue enamel on the smooth green grass,
painted long since by some Italian
  or Dutch artificer in coloured glass;
and still more softly when you reach the Pass!
  For, though these are narcissus, the same man
used them for tapers, lighting at High Mass
  the blue-green windows of a Vatican.
Take off your shoes! Tread very soft and slowly!
  For, though we can no longer walk beside him,
  the mountain-path is still the way love goes,
and, where his feet have been, the ground is holy,
  and those small bushes, though all else denied him,
  burn with the torches of his Alpine rose.

F. C. BODEN

THE LIGHT

I am the voice of the people,
  I was born in the night.
I am the voice of the people,
  Of love and love's might.
I am the voice of the people
  Demanding the Light.

Behold, I was born of a slave
  And none made rejoice,
Nay, none but the two that begot me,
  Having no choice.
And I, that was got in the grave,
  I am the voice.

I cried thro' the suffering land
   And none heard me cry.
All the doors were bolted and barred
   As I came by.
But behold, the time is at hand,
   The hour is nigh.

Open the miserable doors,
   O children of night;
Open the miserable doors,
   O heavy of sight.
I say to you, Open the doors,
   For I am the Light.

IN NORMANDY

In Normandy, at the eventide,
Lovers go wandering, side by side,
Down a lane 'neath an orchard wall,
And dusk steals after them, hiding all.
Long is the lane and long they bide,
In Normandy, at the evenfall.

In Normandy, by that orchard-plot,
A thousand and three lie there and rot.
The Normandy youths go overhead
Each with the lass he hopes to wed.
Softly they go and murmur not,
Scarcely a sound, so soft they tread.

A thousand and three fair loves I had,
And every one was a lovely lad.
Every one was brave and tall,
And true as a lad could be, withal.
Every one with a dream was clad,
And there were stars in the eyes of all.

Every one had a crown to wear,
A queen to get and a purse to share.
Every one had a staff and pack,
But never a guide to show the track.
Never a guide nor a torch was there;
And so of my loves not one came back.

In Normandy, 'neath the apple-trees,
They lie so quiet and take their ease.
Normandy lovers go softly by,
Softly under the evening sky.
And the apple-blossom stirs in the breeze,
In Normandy, where my lovers lie.

PHILIP HENDERSON

HOW CAN WE LIVE?

WHY should we live on in this sick uncertainty,
Fearing the continuance of our lives, or fearing
The advent of a state that will harry solitude
And stamp down all sensitive vision in the common mud?

Is it that life runs at a more metallic speed
Than heretofore, elements of glory dimmed now
With a general mechanistic counterfeit
For earth, for air, for light and the living personality?

Is it that now we live in ever recurrent dread
Of horrible extinction falling from the skies,
Unimaginable death and useless agony
We shall be driven to grapple with and deal to others,
That those among us poor and hungry and without a home
Shall never again want food or house or money—
Blown to air, or one with the slow-crumbling earth?

How can we live, how, being citizens, collective ants
Feverishly undermining our own content,
Daily perverted by malicious print,
Blindly diverted with amusements that no longer amuse,
Smoke-confused, din-deafened, speed-blunted,
How can we, citizens, assert our right to live—
Offal of a system that must destroy us or decay?

STEPHEN SPENDER

THE LANDSCAPE NEAR AN AERODROME

MORE beautiful and soft than any moth
With burring furred antennae feeling its huge path
Through dusk, the air-liner with shut-off engines
Glides over suburbs and the sleeves set trailing tall
To point the wind.   Gently, broadly, she falls
Scarcely disturbing charted currents of air.

Lulled by descent, the travellers across sea
And across feminine land indulging its easy limbs
In miles of softness, now let their eyes trained by watching
Penetrate through dusk the outskirts of this town
Here where industry shows a fraying edge.
Here they may see what is being done.

Beyond the winking masthead light
And the landing-ground, they observe the outposts
Of work: chimneys like lank black fingers
Or figures frightening and mad: the squat buildings
With their strange air behind trees, like women's faces
Shattered by grief.   Here where a few houses
Moan with faint light behind their blinds
They remark the unhomely sense of complaint, like a dog
Shut out and shivering at the foreign moon.

In the last sweep of love, they pass over fields
Behind the aerodrome, where boys play all day
Hacking dead grass: whose cries, like wild birds,
Settle upon the nearest roofs
But soon are hid under the loud city.

Then, as they land, they hear the tolling bell
Reaching across the landscape of hysteria
To where, larger than all the charcoaled batteries
And imagined towers against that dying sky,
Religion stands, the Church blocking the sun.

C. DAY LEWIS

IN THESE OUR WINTER DAYS

IN these our winter days
Death's iron tongue is glib
Numbing with fear all flesh upon
A fiery-hearted globe.

An age once green is buried,
Numbered the hours of light;
Blood-red across the snow our sun
Still trails his faint retreat.

Spring through death's iron guard
Her million blades shall thrust;
Love that was sleeping, not extinct,
Throw off the nightmare crust.

Eyes, though not ours, shall see
Sky-high a signal flame,
The sun returned to power above
A world, but not the same.

WHAT DO WE ASK FOR, THEN?

(For Francis Warner)

WHAT do we ask for, then?
Not for pity's pence nor pursy affluence,
Only to set up house again:
Neither a coward's heaven, cessation of pain,
Nor a new world of sense,
But that we may be given the chance to be men.
For what, then, do we hope?
Not longer sight at once but enlarged scope;
Miraculous no seed or growth of soul, but soil
Cleared of weed, prepared for good:
We shall expect no birth-hour without blood
No fire without recoil.

Publish the vision, broadcast and screen it,
Of a world where the will of all shall be raised to highest
    power,
Village or factory shall form the unit.
Control shall be from the centres, quick brain, warm heart,
And the bearings bathed in a pure
Fluid of sympathy.   There possessions no more shall be part
Of the man, where riches and sacrifice
Are of flesh and blood, sex, muscles, limbs, and eyes,
Each shall give of his best.   It shall seem proper
For all to share what all produced.
Men shall be glad of company, love shall be more than a
    guest
And the bond no more of paper.

Open your eyes, for vision
Is here of a world that has ceased to be bought and sold
With traitor silver and fairy gold;
But the diamond endurance, the wrought-iron of passion
Is all their currency.

As the body that knows through action they are splendid,
Feeling head and heart agree;
Young men proud of their output, women no longer stale
With deferred crisis; the old, a full day ended,
Able to stand down and sit still.
Only the exploiter, the public nuisance, the quitter
Receive no quarter.

Here they do not need
To flee the birthplace. There 's room for growing and
    working.
Bright of eye, champions for speed,
They sing their own songs, they are active, they play not
    watch:
Happy at night talking
Of the demon bowler, cracked over the elm trees,
The reverse pass that won the match.
At festivals knowing themselves normal and well-born
They remember the ancestors that gave them ease,
Harris who fought the bully at Melbourne,
What Wainwright wrote with his blood, Rosa in prison—
All who sucked out the poison.

INDEX OF FIRST LINES

417